Routledge Revivals

Local Authorities and New Technologies

First published in 1988, *Local Authorities and New Technologies* seeks to address some of the key issues facing local government in the related areas of economic rejuvenation, new technology and European Community support. It considers what local authorities can learn from experience of technology promotion elsewhere in Western Europe, it considers which developments at European Community level are more relevant to technology promotion at the local level and discusses the role of European Community funding in the development of local initiatives in Britain. This book will be of interest to students of political science, European studies and geography.

Local Authorities and New Technologies

The European Dimension

Edited by Kenneth Dyson

Routledge
Taylor & Francis Group
ROUTLEDGE REVIVALS

First published in 1988
By Croom Helm Ltd.

This edition first published in 2023 by Routledge
4 Park Square, Milton Park, Abingdon, Oxon, OX14 4RN
and by Routledge
605 Third Avenue, New York, NY 10017

Routledge is an imprint of the Taylor & Francis Group, an informa business

Publisher's Note

The publisher has gone to great lengths to ensure the quality of this reprint but points out that some imperfections in the original copies may be apparent.

Disclaimer

The publisher has made every effort to trace copyright holders and welcomes correspondence from those they have been unable to contact.

A Library of Congress record exists under ISBN: 0709945701

ISBN: 978-1-032-64044-0 (hbk)
ISBN: 978-1-032-64050-1 (ebk)
ISBN: 978-1-032-64047-1 (pbk)

Book DOI 10.4324/9781032640501

LOCAL AUTHORITIES AND NEW TECHNOLOGIES

THE EUROPEAN DIMENSION

Edited by
KENNETH DYSON

CROOM HELM
London • New York • Sydney

Croom Helm Ltd, Provident House, Burrell Row,
Beckenham, Kent, BR3 1AT

Croom Helm Australia, 44-50 Waterloo Road,
North Ryde, 2113, New South Wales

Published in the USA by
Croom Helm
in association with Methuen, Inc.
29 West 35th Street
New York, NY 10001

British Library Cataloguing in Publication Data

Local authorities and new technologies: the
European dimension.
1. Local government — European Economic
Community countries. 2. Technological
innovations — European Economic Community
countries
I. Dyson, Kenneth
352.94 JS3000

ISBN 0-7099-4570-1

Library of Congress Cataloging-in-Publication Data

ISBN 0-7099-4570-1

Printed and bound in Great Britain by Mackays of Chatham Ltd, Kent

CONTENTS

LIST OF CONTRIBUTORS

Peter Aitken is Research Officer with The Planning Exchange in Glasgow.

John Blackburn is Head of the Strategy Section in the Chief Executive's Department of Calderdale Metropolitan District Council.

David Charles is Research Officer with the Centre for Urban and Regional Development Studies of the University of Newcastle.

Serge Dormard is Professor at the University of Lille, France.

Kenneth Dyson is Professor of European Studies at the University of Bradford.

Jeremy Howells is Research Officer with the Centre for Urban and Regional Development Studies of the University of Newcastle.

Tony Jowitt is Lecturer in Adult Education at the University of Leeds.

David Kennedy is Head of the Unemployment Unit in Bradford Metropolitan District Council.

Jack Malan is an official of the European Business and Innovation Centre Network in Brussels.

Andreas Schlieper is a senior official in the Ministry of Economics of North-Rhine Westphalia in West Germany.

Paul Wäldchen is a senior official of the Directorate-General for Regional Policy of the European Commission in Brussels.

TABLES AND FIGURES

Tables

Figures

PREFACE

Local authorities, particularly those in 'less-favoured' regions of Britain, have become increasingly concerned with the economic problems of their areas, devising new structures and new policy measures aimed at economic 'rejuvenation'. Part and parcel of the concern with economic rejuvenation has been the interest in promoting new technologies, in terms both of new products and of use, and in the innovation process; and the initiatives of the European Community in the fields of regional, SME and employment policies and of technology promotion have been increasingly recognised as relevant to local economic strategy.

The book seeks to address some of the key issues facing local government in the related areas of economic rejuvenation, technology and innovation policies and seeking EC support. Three specific themes will be addressed:

1. What can British local authorities learn from experience of technology and innovation policies elsewhere, notably in Western Europe, but also from the Massachusetts experience? How have such issues as technology transfer and the role of SMEs been tackled elsewhere, and with what effects?
2. Which developments at the EC level are most relevant to technology and innovation policies at the local level? How is EC policy likely to develop in this field, and with what implications for local authorities?
3. What has been the role of EC funding in the development of local initiatives in Britain? What kind of new initiatives in technology promotion and innovation are emerging, and with what consequences?

In the 1980s two trends have been apparent across Western Europe in new technology and innovation policy: (1) a decentralisation of technology and innovation policy, with regions (eg. in France and West Germany) and municipalities playing an ever more active role; and (2) a shift of policy from just the provision of sites and basic infrastructure to a more 'service-oriented' approach of offering 'know-how' and 'brokerage' at the local level. In other words, there has been a change of actors and roles, with an increasing involvement of lower levels of government in technology and innovation policies. Britain has participated in this process but, from a European perspective, in an imperfect manner that suggests that much can be learned from cross-national comparison.

One aspect of the work of the Department of European Studies at the University of Bradford is a briefing function to policy makers and affected groups about developments at the EC and European level. The objectives are to speed up the process of learning about new European initiatives; to identify 'models of best practice' from which lessons can be derived; to spread a recognition that European comparisons are a useful device for learning about policy; and, more generally, to foster a cosmopolitan outlook in policy making. This volume shares these objectives. It is more specialised in its concerns than the earlier volume by my colleague Colin Mellors, Promoting Local Authorities in the EC. Like the forthcoming volume Local Authorities and Long-Term Unemployment: The European Dimension it focuses on central political issues that have involved an increasing interaction of local and EC officials and a growing awareness of the local importance of the European dimension. The book should be of interest to all those involved with the development of local government, whether as officials, elected members or teachers of local government courses. In addition, public policy courses and EC courses will find much of the material relevant to their own concerns.

In the face of an occasionally harassed editor, my wife Ann has displayed great reserves of patience. This volume has benefited both from her advice and from her loving support. My particular thanks are also due to the secretaries in the Department of European Studies - Beryl Bromley, Jean Davison, Win Healey, Ele Hey, Betty Jones and Jennifer Kenyon. Together they have worked cheerfully, patiently and hard for an editor who can rarely resist making last-minute changes to a manuscript. Also, I am grateful to Corinne Menage, of the French Cultural Delegation in Manchester, and to Dr. Gerhard Murjahn, of the Goethe Institute in Manchester, for their support, without which this book would not have been possible.

Kenneth Dyson

Chapter One

INTRODUCTION

Kenneth Dyson

One of the most interesting political developments since the 1970s has been the erratic but gradual shift of ever more local authorities from an identification of their role in purely national terms towards a new interest in trans-national relationships. In practical terms the shift has meant no longer just dealing with Whitehall and with neighbouring local authorities. It has involved striking up and fostering new relationships within the European Community, notably the European Commission, and with other local and regional authorities in 'partner' states of the EC. The phenomenon has also been notable in regions of industrial decline whose local authorities perceive the big 'structural' funds of the EC (notably the European Social Fund and the European Regional Development Fund) as increasingly relevant to their problems. For the political scientist the emergence of local authorities as international actors (albeit in a manner restricted by the rules and attitudes of central governments) provides an interesting new phenomenon for study; for local actors it is a cause for some reflection about the way in which such activities are being, and might be, conducted and developed. The origins of this process of 'internationalisation' are complex and deserve a brief sketch.

1. The impact of protracted economic crisis post the oil crises of 1973 and of 1978/9 has been felt not only on the economic base of local areas, particularly as mounting unemployment, but also in the form of 'local fiscal crisis'[1]. Fiscal retrenchment at the centre, legitimated by a newly resurgent neo-liberal ideology and the need for budgetary discipline, has coincided with mounting demands for service provision and a weakened local revenue potential. In this context, caught up in a dizzy vortex of political and financial pressures, and anxious to protect and renew their economic base, local authorities have had an incentive to seek out new friends. This process has emerged at a time when other changes have made new trans-national relationships possible.
2. Britain's entry into the European Community in 1973 seemed at first to present problems of policy adjustment and structural change essentially within central government. Over time, however, local authorities learnt to appreciate the relevance and importance for their own new and

developing economic policy initiatives of the large and fast-growing 'structural' funds of the EC, notably the European Social Fund (with a 270% increase of budget between 1978 and 1983) and the European Regional Development Programme (in its first ten years 1975-84 its annual budget increased eightfold to 7.8% of the total EC budget). By the mid 1980s they were appointing EC liaison officers in increasing numbers, seeing the European Commission as a willing 'listening post' and useful partner and facilitator (compared to Whitehall), and beginning to envisage 'European cooperation' in terms that went beyond the Commission's 'troughs of gold' to include relationships with other EC regions and local authorities with which there was a community of shared interests and a need to share and pool information and experience[(2)].

3. Superimposed on the effects of entry into the EC and of being caught at the hard 'implementation end' of central government's neo-liberal strategy, were some even more profound structural changes in the international economy and Britain's relative position[(3)]. These changes involved notably the rapid emergence of 'newly industrialising countries' as major producers of manufactured goods (eg. steel, shipbuilding, textiles); the spectacular trading successes of societies (like Japan) with a 'knowledge-intensive' production process and portfolio of products; and the 'globalisation' of an increasing number of markets (like consumer electronics). Local authorities, along with other national actors, and the EC itself, needed to learn to think on a global scale. This new learning process about the scale of the problems of economic adjustment, as it began to take shape at the local level, lubricated a new and more intimate relationship of local authorities to the EC Commission and to 'partner' regions and localities in Western Europe. Local and regional economic problems could be increasingly defined in terms of broader European anxieties about 'technology lag' (eg. in the application of microelectronics), as developments in high-technology trade suggested that industrial supremacy could crumble at alarming speed and that collaboration seemed the most effective response to vulnerability[(4)].

In the case of British local authorities a key role in generating a new political interest in the EC has been played by the combination of the impacts of economic recession (in particular, its very differential spatial impacts) with structural changes in the world economy (including the long-term failures of central government's economic policies). At the same time, as first and foremost an 'economic community', the EC has shared the concerns of local authorities. In addition, for reasons of institutional interest and European ideology, the Commission has been keen to promote close working relations with local authorities in general.

The consequence is that a new network of local-EC relations has come into existence; in turn that network has itself become absorbed in programmes (like SPRINT, Strategic Programme for Innovation and Technology Transfer) whose aim is to create further mechanisms for transnational cooperation.

It must be emphasised at the outset that this area of local authority-EC interaction, and more generally of local and regional economic policy, is inseparable from longer-term national problems in the UK that have accumulated over decades. National economic and industrial policies have failed to arrest the relative decline of manufacturing industry so that by the mid 1980s the latter had become too small and too 'low-tech' to support viable and strong economic growth in the long term. On several indicators there were grounds for alarm:

1. Over decades Britain had experienced a progressive collapse of its share of world trade in manufactures, from textiles to telecommunications. Import penetration had been rising steadily; between 1965 and 1979 the volume of imports roughly tripled relative to domestic production of manufactured goods.
2. The higher the research intensity required in a sector, the faster British companies had lost ground. Thus there was a tendency for the technological content of manufactured imports to rise relative to that of exports. Because 'high-tech' products involve a high 'value-added' component, a further deterioration in the balance of trade in manufactures was to be expected. In fact trade in manufactures moved from a surplus of £3.6 billion in 1980 to a deficit of £8.5 billion in 1986.
3. Britain's relative performance in industrial research and development expenditure had been historically poor (see tables 1.1 and 1.2). For the period 1981-83 Britain's R&D expenditure fell by 0.7% per annum, whilst that of her main competitors grew between 2-8% per annum. In industrial R&D expenditure fell by 1.4% per annum in Britain; it rose in France by 3%, West Germany by 3.2%, the United States by 4.7% and Japan by 10.6%(5). Notably, Britain was dropping further behind in the robotics race(6). Britain's position in advanced technology had become one of the weakest in Western Europe(7).
4. Britain's training and skill levels had lagged behind those of her major competitors for decades, from management down. Firms were not only backward in investing in training; they were also quite complacent about it. The 'skills gap' between Britain and other advanced industrial societies has been identified in particular at intermediate levels and management levels(8).

Table 1.1: Growth Rates of Industrially-Funded R&D

Country	1967-83	1967-75	1975-83
Japan	10.8	10.6	10.9
USA	4.1	2.4	5.7
W. Europe	4.4	4.3	4.5

Source: OECD, quoted in Pari Patel and Keith Pavitt, 'Is Europe losing the technology race?', Research Policy, no.1 (1987)

Table 1.2: Intra-European Variations in Industry-Financed R&D in 1983

Country	Percentage share of European total	Proportion of value added (%)	$ per capita	% growth p.a. 1967-83	Defence as a % of GERD
W.Germany	35.6	1.86	96.4	5.64	4.3
France	18.7	1.15	57.7	5.80	21.4
UK	16.6	1.22	49.5	1.08	29.2
Italy	8.5	0.60	25.0	5.12	3.4
Switzerland	5.3	n.a.	136.8	1.80	1.5
Sweden	5.5	2.18	109.4	6.59	10.7
Netherlands	4.7	1.18	54.9	2.01	1.5
Belgium	3.8	1.33	64.9	6.53	(*)
Denmark	1.1	0.82	35.4	5.34	(*)
Ireland	0.3	0.51	13.6	7.45	(*)

GERD = Gross expenditure on R&D
*In Belgium, Denmark and Ireland, defence R&D accounted for less than 1% of GERD

Source: Pari Patel and Keith Pavitt, 'Is Europe losing the technology race?', Research Policy, no.1 (1987)

These failures of private-sector and national political action precipitated a growing involvement of local authorities in economic development issues. At the same time they provided severe constraints on the effectiveness of local political action. Local economic strategy could hope to be a useful complement to national and private-sector strategies. It could never realistically be expected to act as a substitute.

ECONOMIC GEOGRAPHY AND PUBLIC POLICY FOR REGENERATION

The background to this book is provided by three fundamental and complex phenomena: firstly, the geography of relative economic depression presents a new and ever bleaker picture in Britain and elsewhere in the EC, with regional imbalance greater than at any time since the period between the two wars and the 'North-South' divide emerging as a major political issue by 1987; secondly, increasing importance is being ascribed to the growth effects of technology-based industries (like electronics, computers and computer services, telecommunications, scientific instruments, office machinery, pharmaceuticals, biotechnology and aerospace) and to the role of technology diffusion and innovation capability in solving the problems of industrial decline; and, thirdly, the European Commission is seeking to carve out a greater role in regional economic development, more recently by harnessing technology and innovation policies for this purpose. At the EC level regional disparities have mounted against the background of four factors: (1) enlargement, with Portugal's income per capita around half of the EC average and Spain's at 75%; (2) above average rises in the labour force in the southern and western states - like Ireland, Italy and Greece; (3) differing rates of adjustment to the decline of traditional manufacturing industries; and (4) inadequate coordination of national and Community regional policies. Faced by these regional disparities, and new north-south rivalries for aid within the EC, the Commission attempted to persuade member states to double regional funds by 1992. ERDF's significance for Britain is apparent in table 1.3.

The 'dismal' nature of Britain's economic geography has been revealed in a succession of official publications: in Regional Trends, 1986; in the UK Regional Development Programme 1986-90; in the Department of Employment's job census, 1987; and in the European Commission's Second Periodic Report on the Social and Economic Development of the Regions of the Community, 1984[9]. According to the latter, using a broad geo-political comparison, 29 of the 33 British 'regions' (as defined by the European Commission) fell below the Community average in terms of unemployment and economic output. A more refined picture of the economic geography of 'divided' Britain is offered in Regional Trends (1986). In this report the affluence of Greater London and the rest of the South East contrasts sharply with the situation in the North, the North West, Yorkshire and Humberside and the West Midlands. The latter regions are characterised by lower rates of company formation, the highest levels of long-term unemployment in

Table 1.3: European Regional Development Fund, 1986 (Ecu m)

	Commitments	Payments
Italy	813.63	701.43
UK.	513.33	468.35
Spain	640.88	314.30
Greece	309.65	302.88
France	259.25	200.36
Portugal	380.84	188.78
West Germany	82.53	88.23
Ireland	125.13	77.04
Belgium	19.14	21.61
Denmark	11.12	18.89
Netherlands	28.29	11.83
Luxembourg	0.97	0.13

Source: European Commission

England, lower rises of earnings for manual workers, substantially lower weekly household income and average spending per head, a relative decline of gross domestic product per head, rising crime rates and low standards of educational achievement. They are also areas of 'outward' migration, with the additional problem that the bulk of this migration is composed of the employed and skilled rather than the unemployed and much of it is intra-corporate. Hence inter-regional migration is not serving as a natural equilibrating mechanism for regional imbalance. This 'broad-bush' picture of 'two nations' becomes even grimmer when the periphery of Scotland, Wales and in particular Northern Ireland is added: in 1984 GDP per head in Northern Ireland was 78.3% of the UK average, compared to 117% for the South East. However, right at the heart of the somewhat crude characterisation of the 'North-South' divide lies the regional mismatch between job opportunities and the unemployed. Tables 1.4, 1.5, and 1.6 summarise the major disparities.

Whilst these figures broadly support the picture of a 'North-South' divide, this model does in fact need major qualification and refinement. In fact the South West has a lower GDP per head than the North West and Scotland. The South-East Economic Development Strategy, drawn up by several Labour councils in 1987, speaks of a South-South divide, with the coastal towns and the eastern Thames corridor suffering general decline. Within a single region there are totally different local labour markets (compare, for instance, small business expansion around Warrington with the empty factories of Kirkby in the North West). Contrasts in unemployment are marked within as well as between regions, not least in the context of an 'urban-rural shift', underway since

Table 1.4: UK Unemployment, April 1987, by Region

Northern Ireland	18.3%
North	15.0%
Wales	13.1%
North West	13.7%
Scotland	14.0%
West Midlands	12.1%
Yorkshire and Humberside	12.3%
East Midlands	9.9%
South West	9.0%
East Anglia	8.2%
South East	7.8%
United Kingdom	10.9%

Source: Department of Employment

Table 1.5: Regional Disparities in the UK

	Regional Employment (% change June 1979-June 1986)	GDP per head (1985: UK Av=100)
Scotland	-10%	97.4
North	-14%	92.9
Yorkshire & Humberside	-12%	91.8
North West	-16%	96.0
Wales	-17%	88.9
West Midlands	-10%	92.3
East Midlands	- 2%	95.7
East Anglia	+ 9%	100.7
South West	- 2%	93.9
South East	- 2%	125.7 Gt. London 107.7 Rest of S.E.

Sources: Department of Employment and Economic Trends

Table 1.6: Regional Manufacturing Output and Employment Change

	Percentage Change in Output 1979-83	Contribution of Manufacturing to total output (per cent)		Percentage Change in Employment 1979-84	Confirmed Redundancies per 1000 employees 1979-82
		1979	1983		
South East	- 6.1	23.9	22.0	- 17.5	28.1
East Anglia	- 3.0	27.2	25.2	- 14.5	31.0
South West	- 4.5	24.6	22.9	- 16.7	42.1
East Midlands	- 12.4	34.3	30.4	- 19.7	42.8
West Midlands	- 23.3	40.2	34.1	- 28.5	47.5
Yorkshire-Humberside	- 18.3	32.1	27.3	- 28.0	61.5
North-West	- 19.3	35.6	30.0	- 29.0	65.2
North	- 15.7	32.1	28.6	- 29.8	64.3
Wales	- 20.0	26.2	21.1	- 33.0	84.3
Scotland	- 14.0	27.8	24.1	- 27.7	69.2
Great Britain	- 13.3	28.2	24.0	- 23.6	49.1

Notes: Output measured as gross domestic product (GDP), net of stock appreciation, at 1980 prices. Employment change measured from mid-year to mid-year

Source: Economic Trends, Department of Employment and Manpower Services Commission

the 1950s, that has seen the emergence of small towns and rural areas as sites of employment growth[10]. Conurbations in both North and South are suffering from this process; whilst towns like Bracknell, Milton Keynes, Winchester, Basingstoke and Horsham are the big 'job gainers'. The country towns, with typical populations of 100,000 to 150,000, are becoming the magnets for new economic activity. Official reports, and not least the academic literature, have indeed come to see the problem of the decline of industrial regions as complex and multidimensional and as requiring fundamental and long-term structural changes. The problem involves not only the decline of manufacturing industries (like heavy engineering, textiles, steel and shipbuilding) but also regional imbalances in the growth of the service sector (eg. business services, banking and finance, retail distribution) and in the impact of the new information technologies (eg. office machinery and data processing equipment manufacture). Thus, according to the job census of January 1987, more than two-thirds of service jobs created since 1979 have been in the South East; over the previous three years 47% of jobs created in Britain were located in the latter region, with Scotland, the North West, the North and Yorkshire and Humberside together accounting for only 14%.

Similarly, as table 1.7 illustrates, high-technology business location has strongly favoured sites in the South (eg. Berkshire and Hertfordshire). The ten top counties for 'high-tech' location are to be found in a narrow belt between Hertfordshire and Bristol; only Leicestershire, Warwickshire and Lancashire outside the South have an above average concentration of 'high tech' amongst British counties. High-technology business location reflects the shift from urban centres towards rural areas (eg. East Anglia), notably new towns and attractive residential areas, and a pronounced clustering around London. Three axes of development radiating from London are to be found - towards Cambridge, towards Swindon down the M4 and towards Southampton and Poole[11]. Wales and Yorkshire and Humberside possess a notably low representation of 'high tech', the latter having only about a quarter of the concentration found in the South East outside London. Moreover, Yorkshire and Humberside, the North West, the West Midlands and the East Midlands have actually lost substantial numbers of 'high tech' jobs in the 1980s[12]. Firms in many of the traditional industrial regions have reacted to new technology by the adoption of new manufacturing <u>processes</u> that have generally been labour displacing rather than job creating. They have not participated anything like as strongly in the job-creating production of new technology <u>products</u>. Regionally, microelectronics usage in products is highest in East Anglia (21% of factories) and lowest in the North (6%). In production processes, it is highest in the North (60%) and lowest in the West Midlands (39%)[13]. In 'official diagnosis' the problems of the traditional assisted areas are no longer simply attributed to an over-dependence on older industries. They include: an overdependence on externally-controlled branch factories; low innovation potential; a poor capacity for new firm formation; an insignificant business service sector; inadequately developed research and development activity; a lack of concentration of financial institutions; and a relatively 'headless' occupational structure, that is to say, a small proportion of professional and managerial employment[14]. Uneven spatial development had, in other words, complex qualitative dimensions. It had also major political implications, with differences in the movement of votes in the regions being the most significant feature of the general election of June 1987 (as table 1.8 shows).

Table 1.7: Ranking of Counties by Relative Concentrations of 'High-Tech'

Top Ten Rank	County	Score (GB=100)	Bottom Ten Rank	County	Score (GB=100)
1.	Hertfordshire	244	1.	Scottish Islands	27
2.	Berkshire	195	2.	Powys	32
3.	Gloucestershire	171	3.	South Yorkshire	34
4.	Surrey	168	4.	Dyfed	34
5.	Hampshire	158	5.	Shropshire	37
6.	West Sussex	155	6.	West Glamorgan	39
7.	Avon	155	7.	Lincolnshire	42
8.	Isle of Wight	153	8.	Grampian	42
9.	Dorset	148	9.	North Yorkshire	44
10.	Somerset	139	10.	Central Scotland	45

Note: scores are computed by measuring the proportion of 'high tech' in total employment in each county, and comparing the county score with the average for the UK

Source: I. Begg and G. Cameron, 'When the Chips are Down South', the Guardian, Wednesday, June 3rd 1987

Alongside these changes in spatial patterns of employment and growth and in official diagnosis of the general character of the regional problem, two significant changes took place at the level of regeneration policy perception since the 1970s. Together they generated a new set of expectations of local political actors, alongside a new vocabulary of public policy ('small and medium-sized enterprises', 'start-ups', 'science parks', 'innovation centres', 'venture capital', 'transnational cooperation networks', 'regional networks' etc.) 'Silicon Valley' and 'Route 128' acquired a certain mythology for policy makers, the reality of which is unpacked in Tony Jowitt's chapter. An interesting example is provided by the idea of the science park, associated since the 1960s with the University of Stanford in the United States, and since 1972 with the University of Cambridge. It generated a new movement from 1982. By the end of 1986 28 university-based parks were in operation in the UK,

Table 1.8: Movement of Votes by Regions in the General Election of June 1987

	All seats in region				79 marginals		
	Con	Lab	All		Con	Lab	All
North	-2.4	+7.1	-3.8	.....	+1.2	+5.6	-6.8
North West	-2.0	+5.2	-2.8	.....	-1.5	+1.7	-0.6
Yorks	-1.2	+5.4	-3.9	.....	-0.9	+7.4	-5.4
W. Mids	-0.6	+2.1	-2.5	.....	+2.0	+2.6	-4.3
E. Mids	+1.5	+2.1	-3.1	.....	+3.9	+3.2	-5.9
E. Anglia	+1.1	+1.1	-2.5	.....	+1.6	+0.3	-1.5
South West	-0.6	+1.5	-0.5	.....	+2.2	+0.3	-2.1
South East	-1.2	+0.9	-1.8	.....	+3.7	+3.0	-6.6
London	+2.5	+1.5	-3.2	.....	+3.3	+1.0	-3.8
Wales	-1.2	+7.6	-5.7	.....	-1.4	+8.4	-8.1
Scotland	-4.3	+7.3	-5.3	.....	-3.1	+6.2	-7.2
Overall	-0.2	+3.3	-2.9	.....	+0.9	+3.6	-4.8

Source: The Press Association

with £92 million of public money committed and 412 tenant companies. France's two oldest and most prominent science parks, Sophia-Antipolis (near Nice) and Meylan-ZIRST (near Grenoble) had respectively 212 and 79 tenant companies (see the chapter by Dormard). These changes amounted to a new 'policy formula' for regeneration that has been embraced at local, regional and EC levels and, with varying degrees of enthusiasm, at the national level in Western Europe (on the latter compare, for instance, Dormard's chapter with those on the UK). Public policy began increasingly to be grounded on acts of faith in new technology and small firms(15). In contrast to the classical approach, a new 'bottom-up' approach - pursued not least by the European Commission - encouraged a more positive role for local authorities in economic regeneration.

1. Public policies have been increasingly based on the perception that, at worst, the traditional 'exogenous' regional policies of central governments have failed or, at best, are inadequate (eg. because not 'cost-effective')(16). Thus between its peak in 1975-6 and 1982-3 expenditure on regional policy in Britain declined by 41% in real terms (with, in 1982, the formal suspension of the Industrial Development Certificate (IDC) that had constituted the 'prohibitive' side of the regional policy system). The relative decline of regional policy had its origins in several factors: (1) recession was having pervasive national effects and reducing the volume of mobile manufacturing investment that could be induced to relocate by regional policy instruments; (2) national support programmes (like sectoral schemes, R&D support and new schemes to support small businesses like the Loan Guarantee Scheme and the Business Expansion Scheme) were being expanded; (3) the mounting scale of public investment in individual projects (eg. in 1987 aid of £450 million to British Aerospace towards the development costs of the A330 and A340 series of jets) could equal total regional spending in a year; (4) the emergence of big infrastructural projects added further to the attraction of the south (notably the Channel tunnel, the regeneration of London's Dockland and the building of a third London airport at Stansted); (5) the phenomenon of 'jobless growth' in the manufacturing industries severely compromised the effectiveness of a regional policy traditionally oriented towards manufacturing industry; whilst (6) after 1979 a Conservative government, ideologically committed to 'neo-liberalism', was keen to achieve cost-effectiveness and 'value-for-money' by targeting regional development grants more precisely to job creation and to emphasise the contribution that factors other than regional policy could play in regional industrial development (eg. growth of self-employment, greater

labour mobility and wage adjustment, with larger inter-regional wage differentials acting as a means of 'natural adjustment' to alleviate spatial imbalances). Accordingly, following a major review, the 1983 White Paper - Regional Industrial Development - emphasised the social rather than economic goals of regional policy *per se*, its very title also indicating that the government's review had not simply been concerned with regional policy: and the UK Regional Development Programme 1986-90 argued that improvements in the national economy have a more profound effect on the regions than can be achieved by regional policy 'even with the assistance of the (EEC regional) fund'. The latter programme warns that 'none of these (initiatives) is likely to yield quick results. Regional prosperity cannot be achieved in the absence of national prosperity'. Emphasis was placed on fostering an 'enterprise culture' and on measures of 'self-help', like the proliferation of enterprise agencies on the model of the St Helens Trust through which trained people act as agents, consultants, financial brokers and problem-solvers for small businesses.

In part responding to this new political and policy situation, and in part to the inadequacy of traditional 'exogenous' regional policies to prevent the growth of regional economic disparities in any case, a new policy rationale for regeneration began to emerge at the subnational level, not just in Britain but elsewhere in Western Europe, and one that was to receive the blessing of the European Commission The new policy rationale emphasised the need for local and regional action to mobilise indigenous resources for the purpose of regeneration. Stress was now placed on the role of local and regional authorities in developing new ways of harnessing the indigenous development potential in their areas. In fact some British local authorities played a pioneering role in developing these ideas (eg. the Greater London Council). This indigenous potential was to be developed in two main ways: by aiding both firms in traditional sectors (eg. textiles, machine tools, metals) and the growth of new technology-based firms; and by a more 'programmatic' approach that included area infrastructure schemes essential for local economic regeneration (including training, tourism, rail and road access, telecommunications, water, sewerage, gas, electricity). Within this new policy formula particular attention was given to the role of small and medium-sized enterprises (SMEs) as a flexible and dynamic source of innovation and economic renewal. A fundamental question has been how best to deliver this aid, a question that is handled in several of the chapters in this volume (eg. by Peter Aitken). Two aspects have been: (1) a new concern for 'technology transfer', in order to accelerate the transfer into practical commercial forms of ever more rapid scientific and technical advances; and (2) an emerging recognition that both the question and the answers have a European and not just national dimension. The first concern involves regional and local authorities in striking up new or refashioning old relationships within their communities (eg. to institutions of higher education, to chambers of commerce and to local financial institutions); the second concern means seizing the new opportunities offered by the European Commission's role. Thus, the new ERDF rules, which came into force on 1st January 1985, underlined the renewed importance to be attached to promoting the indigenous development potential of regions; the SPRINT Programme, as launched in 1986, confirmed the Commission's aim of strengthening the infrastructure of assistance for SMEs; whilst STRIDE (Science and Technology for Regional Development in Europe) sought to aid the establishment of innovation centres and similar organisations in areas of industrial decline. Indeed the Commission consciously adopted an animateur role, stimulating general innovation through business improvement services and new mechanisms for diffusing 'state-of-the-art' technologies (see the chapter by Waldchen). Local authorities were having to learn a new game of 'partnership' and one that was complex because it meant bringing together local and European dimensions within the constraints set by national governments. Above all, the new game required deep-seated cultural change not just on the part of a wide variety of actors at the local level but also within local authorities themselves, at official and elected levels. The capacity to effect that kind of change posed perhaps the greatest challenge and question mark for the new policy formula. It also required central government support; local authorities often had trouble implementing strategies inspired by the EC because of the lack of this support.

2. Public policy has begun increasingly to reflect an awareness that 'the technological resources' of a locality, region or country are central to an improvement of its competitiveness. In this sense it is necessary to 'intellectualise business processes' by ensuring a ready supply of, and recognition for, technologically-educated people with 'up-to-date' ideas (see the chapter by Schlieper). As business becomes more 'knowledge-intensive' and subjected to an increasing rate of market and technological change, so the risks from conservatism and parochialism in the business structure of a region or locality mount. Correspondingly, 'awareness' issues and the circulation of ideas and information become central on the agenda of local and regional action, as public policy is challenged by the

increased pace of developments in technology. In particular technology transfer needs to be speeded up, both vertically and horizontally. Vertically, the rapid drop in the time span from a scientific breakthrough to its translation into commercial products has shortened the learning process for business. The 'NIH syndrome' ('not invented here') that Prutec, the venture capital arm of the Prudential, has found to be a major problem in British companies is an increasingly short-term and ultimately very costly luxury. Horizontally, the circulation of ideas and information amongst firms must be improved.
Britain lacks either Japan's structure of interlocked 'corporate families' (the so-called Keiretsu like Mitsubishi, Sumitomo and Mitsui) or West Germany's 'organised capitalism' in the form of a more developed system of chambers of commerce and of an elaborate and intimate bank-industry nexus [17]. In this sense, because of structural deficiencies in the British market economy, a greater burden falls on British local authorities in the field of technology transfer issues. Moreover, in taking on this task they lack the more refined and sensitive modes of intergovernmental interaction that are possible in a federal system like that of West Germany (see Schlieper's chapter) or in France (see Dormard's chapter). In the absence of little prospect of significant reform in bank-industry relations, in the system of chambers of commerce or in intergovernmental relations within the UK the idea of regional development agencies, borrowed from Scotland and Wales, might seem to have a particular and more direct appeal for England. Indeed, in 1987 a former Conservative Secretary of State for Trade and Industry, Leon Brittan, identified himself with this latter proposal, as did the Association of Chambers of Commerce. They were seen as a more effective alternative to the less powerful and under-resourced regional development companies, like the Northern Development Company, that the government sought to encourage. Meanwhile, within the present structure local authorities have begun to occupy themselves with the idea of technology transfer and innovation centres and the complex and difficult task of seeking to attract university, business, financial and governmental support. They have found that support is most readily forthcoming at the European level, from the European Business and Innovation Centre Network (see the chapter by Malan) and the European Commission (see the chapters by Aitken and Waldchen). Also, on reflection, local authorities recognise that the transnational perspective offered by the EC's initiatives offers the best antidote to the dangers of parochialism at the local and regional levels.

CHALLENGES TO, AND QUESTIONS FOR, PUBLIC POLICY

These two perceptions - of the need to mobilise indigenous resources and of the importance of 'technological' resources - have provided some important new challenges to public policy development. Three challenges in particular have received considerable attention in recent debate about local and regional regeneration.

1. The importance of reducing barriers to the flow of information by means of new local, regional and transnational 'networks'and liaison mechanisms has been increasingly recognised. In practical managerial terms, however, tackling the problem of external communication both with sources of scientific and technological knowledge and with geographically distant markets presents new difficulties for local policymakers. In the first instance, it implies a new relationship with academic institutions, as well as with the business community. Higher education is not only a repository of scientific and technological skills; it is also valuable as part of a 'global' knowledge system, not least about corporate and policy developments. Accordingly, harnessing of the technological, social scientific and language resources of higher education is an essential component of a regeneration strategy (see the chapters by Jowitt and by Howells and Charles). New opportunities need to be developed for the transfer of people and ideas not only by means of science parks, innovation centres and the introduction of technology innovation officers (as well as more informal local and regional mechanisms) but also by strengthening transnational cooperation at both business and official levels. A successful forging of these new types of domestic and international relationships means overcoming cultural as well as institutional difficulties. The open question is whether, or to what extent, these difficulties (and often prejudices) will be subordinated to the 'imperatives' of the new policy formula. A key part of the answer undoubtedly lies in the quality of local and regional leadership and involves a major supplementary question -does such leadership exist? Major issues of structure, recruitment and training are raised.
2. 'Demand-pull' as well as 'technology-push' has a role to play in regional and local regeneration; and a feature of demand in areas of industrial decline is that it tends to be for conventional 'low-technology' goods. Thus a lack of demand for new telecommunications services (eg. facsimile, electronic mail) may lead to an under-investment in the infrastructure that is likely to be a necessary condition for regeneration. But how does one stimulate demand for new

high technology products and services in the region? Clearly, an innovation-oriented procurement policy on the part of local authorities has a key part to play (as the Commission's SPRINT programme recognises), and an effort can be made to coopt other public authorities into a 'concerted' policy. However, it is much more difficult to ensure that such a procurement policy is matched by a qualitative change of demand within the private sector. Here a wide range of initiatives is required, covering such areas as technical consultancy and training, and addressing the basic entrepreneurial problems of the area (see the chapters by Blackburn and Kennedy and by Schlieper).

3. There is general recognition of the importance of venture capital, in the form of equity participation and 'hands-on' management in new ventures rather than just loans, so that the risks involved in new technology investment can be mitigated[18]. Local enterprise boards, like the West Midlands Enterprise Board (the largest of its type), have been much exercised by the problem of venture capital, have sought to encourage a more active role by the big commercial and merchant banks (eg. WMEB with Lazards) and have formed joint companies with some local authorities (like Bradford and Calderdale in the case of the West Yorkshire Enterprise Board) for the purpose of borrowing money to advance in venture or development capital deals. Meanwhile, since 1983 the EC has been supporting the European Venture Capital Association (EVCA) as well as financing the pilot project 'Venture Consort' (which gives direct capital aid to consortiums of venture capital organisations established in various EC states for transnational innovation projects among SMEs).
At the same time the scale of this problem, and its complexity, suggests a new role for local and regional financial institutions as well as the need for new regional development agencies specialising in venture capital for new activities, perhaps on the model of the Scottish Development Agency. 'Local' knowledge of financial institutions is clearly a key factor. Again, American and West German experience is instructive (see Jowitt's chapter and Schlieper's chapter). West Germany, for instance, has a regional structure of public savings banks that are statutorily required to devote themselves to local economic development; whilst in the United States private universities like MIT and Stanford have themselves been active in organising venture capital provision, setting a model for the public universities. Also noteworthy is Scottish experience. Scotland has maintained its 'fair share' of venture capital investment (in regional terms); it has its own indigenous financial sector, unlike the other UK regions[19]. Yet the importance of an adequate regional financing system is

being recognised in Britain at a time when 'globalisation' of financial markets is further eroding local and regional identities within the financial sector. Clearly an issue for national and EC policies is how to redress the regional imbalances that are likely in the provision of venture capital, as existing areas of 'high-technology' strength continue to attract further funding (see table 1.9). In 1985 59% of venture capital funds went into London and the South East. The East Midlands, Yorkshire and Humberside, the North and the North West combined received only an 8.3% share. Financial Britain remained centred on London where there was a lack of local knowledge of good business opportunities. A similar heavy bias in favour of London and the South East could be found in the Loan Guarantee Scheme. Between its inception in 1981 and 1985, 38% of acceptances were concentrated there, whilst an even bigger share of total monies advanced went there. In general, individual loans were higher in Britain's richest regions[20].

These changes of policy perception associated with the stress on 'indigenous development' and 'technological resources' raise other questions of a more fundamental kind that ought not to be avoided.

1. Are local authorities, and the EC itself, structured in the best ways to tackle these challenges? At one level policy redefinition has triggered off a new process of 'bureaucratic infighting' as officials seek, among other things, to secure status and power in any restructuring. Processes of energetic, time-consuming administrative politics seem on occasion to threaten the vitality and even the very existence of new policy initiatives for regeneration. Thus within the Commission the issue of who controls indigenous development policy (DG13 or DG16?) became a major problem (see the chapter by Aitken). At another level more fundamental structural issues might be posed. Problems of internal coordination and of external 'diplomatic' management are exacerbated by an English local authority structure that diffuses executive authority and does not provide the same opportunities to develop the 'strong' executive that can more often be found in continental European local politics[21]. The EC Commission is, in turn, locked into a complex, indeed convoluted, structure of EC decision-making that encourages 'policy inertia' and results in a continuous and debilitating process of frustrated expectations[22]. Official responses have not adequately coped with either of these questions: this criticism can be levelled at the Maud and Bains reports on management in English local authorities and at the Single European Act. Two developments at the Commission level are at least

Table 1.9: Venture Capital by Region (1985)

	By Amount (%)	By Company (%)
Greater London	35.5	23.2
South East (N)	14.0	13.7
South East (S)	10.2	10.2
West Midlands	7.8	6.8
South West	6.7	7.3
Scotland	6.6	11.7
East Anglia	6.4	5.7
Wales	3.9	8.6
Yorkshire & Humberside	3.2	3.7
East Midlands	2.1	3.7
North West	1.6	2.2
North	1.4	2.0
Northern Ireland	0.2	1.2

Source: Venture Economics (1986). Figures do not include money from Investors in Industry

encouraging. The genesis and role of the SME Task Force is considered in detail in Aitken's chapter. Also, the 'integrated operations' programme of the Commission represents a new effort to get its act together by coordinating some of the funds that go to the regions - the ERDF, part of the European Social Fund, and the much smaller fund for modernisation of agriculture. After the initial schemes for Belfast and Naples, Birmingham and Bradford were quick to undertake their own studies. However, even if localities and the Commission succeeded in their efforts, the question remained of just how far national government would endorse the approach.

2. Can local authorities overcome the language and cultural barriers that stand in the way of adopting a very different approach to decision making? The fundamental problems are perhaps cultural rather than structural, rooted transnationally in the legacy of Britain's 'island mentality' and a certain aversion to the learning and use of foreign languages as well as domestically in a highly developed pluralism and tradition of institutional autonomy(23). As a consequence, responses to new policy initiatives may be delayed and, when they come, perhaps partial and inadequate. Local authorities will need to look again at

their recruitment, training and promotion policies with a view to ensuring that 'the right people are in the right posts' and that new forms of interorganisational mobility are encouraged. Complex problems of personnel policy and politics will follow. Local authority personnel policies will need to achieve a new flexibility so that they are consistent with a key maxim of the new policy formula: that the transfer of people and ideas is the best means of putting technology to use.

3. Questions about political control are also raised as the drive by local authority professional officers to establish contacts and expertise at the EC level tends to leave the elected councillors behind. To what extent do local authority-EC relations reflect any kind of political strategy? Or is strategy in fact the outcome of what can be gained at the EC (and national) level by professional officers? On the whole these new patterns of relations are seen by local politicians as 'technical', 'outside their experience' and 'difficult'. Local authorities may even find themselves chasing money whose use they do not regard as effective as far as local economic strategy is concerned. The theory of a 'bottom-up' approach to local economic development turns out in practice to have strong 'top-down' features.

4. Most fundamental of all, are excessive expectations being generated about 'endogenous development', 'science parks' and SMEs? It seems that in practice, and here American and West German experience is relevant, science parks are strengthening existing centres of economic growth that would realise their innovative potential anyway because of the quality of their industrial and research structures(24). In particular, the employment effects of the location of high-technology firms appear in fact to be rather small(25). Where job creation has been significant, namely in self-employment, much of it has been concentrated in 'low-tech' services, involving little capital investment or even entrepreneurship(26). It can be argued that a stress on 'endogenous development' simply reproduces and reinforces existing regional disparities. In the process, areas of industrial decline are in danger of being drawn into an expensive and increasingly costly process of 'subsidy competition' in a vain effort to keep pace. As science parks proliferate in number with too little regional input, their impact is likely to be diffused. Indeed there is likely to be a mismatch between much of the work coming from higher education and what the area can use. In Britain the science park movement has had two notable features: (1) the regional dimension has been lacking, with most parks created in areas that do not qualify for regional assistance (hence they are cut off from sources of ERDF aid); and (2) there has been an almost complete lack of interest in the

parks by the private financial institutions. A combination of powerful local actors with a strong research infrastructure - as found in Meylan-ZIRST near Grenoble - is not to be found in Britain; also absent is the presence of central government's will to decentralise research and training facilities, as in the case of Sophia-Antipolis near Nice (see the chapter by Dormard). The idea that small firm growth is the answer to high unemployment is also seriously misleading; many of the jobs created are part-time, low-paid and in poor working conditions, and most are created in prosperous areas(27). In short, technology transfer exercises emerge as a means of containing relative depression, with new types of spending programmes needed to create significant employment.

One might even be tempted to see an element of symbolic gesture in the new policy formula: on the one hand, material benefits are implied; on the other hand, an 'affective' appeal is made that helps define and reinforce community solidarity, and ideological payoffs are gained. In other words, following this line of argument, the short-term political gains from the new policy formula are likely to exceed the material economic gains. In the longer run, however, the absence of delivery of material benefits will produce a loss of credibility for the policy formula and launch a new process of policy redefinition. This process might well involve relearning some of the strengths of traditional 'exogenous' policies. It may not be a case of 'plus ca change, plus c'est la meme chose' but of recognising that the 'new' policy formula for regeneration had 'thrown out the baby with the bathwater'.

NOTES

1. L. J. Sharpe (ed), The Local Fiscal Crisis in Western Europe (Sage, London, 1981).
2. C. Mellors (ed), Promoting Local Authorities in the European Community (IULA, London, 1986).
3. See eg. K. Dyson and S. Wilks (eds.), Industrial Crisis (Basil Blackwell, Oxford, 1983).
4. M. Sharp and C. Shearman, European Technological Collaboration (Chatham House Paper 36, Routledge and Kegan Paul, London, 1987).
5. P. Patel and K. Pavitt, 'Is Europe Losing the Technology Race?', Research Policy, no.1, 1987.
6. J. Northcott et al, Robots in British Industry: Expectations and Experience (PSI, London, 1986).
7. M. Sharp and C. Shearman, op.cit.
8. See eg. G.D.N.Worswick (ed), Education and Economic Performance (Gower Press, Aldershot, 1986) (especially for the work of S.J. Prais and I. Jones); Competence and Competition (NEDO Books, London, 1986); The Making of Managers: A Report on Management

Education (NEDO Books, London, 1987); and A. Ovenden, Competitiveness in UK Manufacturing Industry (BIM, London, 1987).

9. See also R. Martin and R. Rowthorn (eds.), The Geography of Deindustrialisation (Macmillan, London, 1986); and A. Amin and J. Goddard (eds.), Technological Change, Industrial Restructuring and Regional Development (Allen and Unwin, London, 1986).

10. S. Fothergill and G. Gudgin, Unequal Growth (Heinemann, London, 1982); A. Champion et al, Changing Places (Edward Arnold, London, 1987).

11. See eg. K. Morgan and A. Sayer, Microcircuits of Capital: 'Sunrise' Industry and Uneven Development (Polity Press, London, 1987); and D. Keeble and E. Weaver (eds.), New Firms and Regional Development in Europe (Croom Helm, 1986).

12. I. Begg and G. Cameron, 'When the Chips are Down South', the Guardian, June 3rd, 1987; P. Marsh, 'The Lure of the Silicon Glen', Financial Times, November 12th, 1986.

13. See Amin and Goddard, op.cit. Also Microelectronics in Industry: Promise and Performance (PSI, London, 1986).

14. Department of Trade and Industry, Regional Industrial Policy (DTI, London, 1983), pp.34-68. Also D. Massey, Spatial Divisions of Labour (Macmillan, London, 1984).

15. See eg. R. Rothwell and W. Zegveld, Reindustrialisation and Technology (Longman, London, 1985), especially chapter seven.

16. K. Morgan, 'Regional Regeneration in Britain: the Territorial Imperative and the Conservative State', Political Studies, December 1985, pp.562-5.

17. See K. Dyson and S. Wilks, op.cit.

18. On US experience see R. Premus, Venture Capital and Innovation (US Government Printing Office, Washington DC, 1985).

19. A.D. Bain and R.G. Reid, 'The Finance Sector' in N. Hood and S. Young (eds.), Industry, Policy and the Scottish Economy (Edinburgh University Press, 1984).

20. C. Mason, 'Venture Capital in the United Kingdom: A Geographical Perspective', National Westminster Bank Quarterly Review, May 1987, pp.47-59.

21. K. Dyson, 'Local Government Reform Reconsidered: Paradigm and Perspectives', Local Government Studies, April 1977, pp.135-49.

22. H. Wallace (with A. Ridley), Europe: The Challenge of Diversity (Chatham House Paper 29, Routledge and Kegan Paul, London, 1985).

23. See generally K. Dyson, The State Tradition in Western Europe (Basil Blackwell, Oxford, 1981); also W. Wallace, Britain's Bilateral Links Within Western Europe (Chatham House Paper 23, Routledge and Kegan Paul, London, 1984).

24. On West Germany U. Hilpert, 'Technologieparks und der Mythos von Silicon Valley' in J. Hucke and H. Wollmann (eds.), Stadtpolitik and Technologieentwicklung, forthcoming 1987.

25. E.J. Malecki, 'Science, Technology and Regional Economic Development: Review and Prospects', Research Policy, 10, 1981, pp.312-34.

26. A. Rayan and R. Pearson (eds.), UK Occupation and Employment Trends to 1990 (Butterworth, 1986).

27. D. Storey and S. Johnson, Small and Medium-Sized Enterprise and Employment Creation in the EEC Countries (University of Newcastle, 1987).

Chapter Two

RESEARCH AND TECHNOLOGICAL DEVELOPMENT IN THE 'LESS-FAVOURED' REGIONS OF THE EUROPEAN COMMUNITY: A UK DIMENSION

Jeremy Howells and David Charles

The regional problem in the United Kingdom appears to be one of the most persistent in the whole of the European Community. In part this situation is a reflection of the poor national economic growth performance of the UK since its entry into the European Community (EC). However, it is also a reflection of the widening of the gap in economic affluence between the prosperous south-east and the rest of the country. The real extent and scale of the regional problem in the UK has been highlighted in the DTI report to the Commission of the European Communities (CEC) entitled 'United Kingdom Regional Development Programme 1986-90' which has been reported in Hansard (27th October 1986, p.33). The report notes that, of the poorer regions identified by the Commission within the Community, over one-third are in the UK. However, more particularly it finds that of the 40 most deprived areas in the whole of the European Community, 28 were found to be in the UK.

Within the UK, and elsewhere in Europe, there has been a growing recognition that the level of research and technological innovation in a local area or region is a major long-term influence on its economic growth and development. It is seen that regions or localities can only sustain satisfactory long-term growth if firms or plants established there are able and prepared to adjust continually to technological change. The rest of this chapter will investigate this association between research and technological development (RTD) and economic growth at the local and regional level, specifically looking at the UK situation. This analysis is followed by a brief review of the location of research and technology within Britain. The chapter will then outline the national and European context for RTD, reviewing particular policy shifts and constraints, before concluding with some major issues that need to be addressed when developing RTD initiatives at a local or regional level.

THE LOCATION OF RESEARCH AND TECHNOLOGICAL INNOVATION IN THE UK

Before studying technological sophistication in a geographical context, some reference should be made to the key characteristics and processes associated with technological innovation and development, and in particular to their contribution to local economic growth. Fundamental to our understanding of how technological innovation and sophistication varies over space are three main elements: research and development (R&D), process or capital innovations and product innovations. These elements will be briefly considered in turn.

Research and Development

An important component of technological innovation is R & D through which new products and processes are incorporated into the production process. Technological change does not generally occur by accident, but rather by the deliberate diversion of resources to activities, centred on R&D, that generate technological progress (Kennedy and Thirlwall 1972, p.13). Thus organised research activity undertaken by industry and, to a lesser extent, government is now the main generator of technological progress in Britain and other mature industrial economies (Little 1977, pp.87-91; Rothwell and Zegveld 1982, pp.46-8; Malecki 1982, p.21). On the micro scale of the firm it has also been shown that R&D can lead to an improved market standing and competitive position, generating future growth and profit, and can indeed be essential for long-term company survival and growth. The importance of R&D to both national and regional economic development has recently been translated into policies directed towards the fostering of industrial research via substantial aid schemes (Organisation for Economic Cooperation and Development 1982). On a specifically regional level, the Northern Region Strategy Team concluded that an important factor in the poor technological performance of indigenous manufacturing industry in the UK Northern Region was the low number of 'in-house' and detached separate R&D units located in the region (NRST 1977, Vol. 2, pp.110-16). This locational factor has had the effect of reducing the probability of technological advance for many establishments in the Northern region (Thwaites 1978, p.1).

Process or Capital Innovation and Technology

Developments in process or capital technology do not have such long-term significance in terms of output and employment as advances in product innovation and sophistication (see below). Nevertheless, changes in process technology represent an important cornerstone in the overall competitiveness, productivity and efficiency of manufacturing activity (Nasbeth 1974, p.294). It is often only by continual technological improvement in production systems that firms in certain industries are able to remain viable. Moreover, the adoption of new techniques in capital technology not only helps to modernise manufacturing processes but also has the advantage of involving lower risks, lower costs and shorter time scales than the majority of 'in-house' product innovation and development projects (Gibbs 1984, p.115). At the same time new process technologies may be product innovations for firms in the capital equipment industry and so may have a dual benefit to both vendors and users. In addition, the take-up of such new techniques may help to raise the firm's level of technological awareness, leading to further adoption of more sophisticated technologies and possibly also to internally generated innovations. Any lag by local firms or plants in the development and adoption of process technology is likely to have a direct impact on the competitiveness and growth of the industrial base in that area or region.

Product Innovations and Technology

For most firms and industries, however, product innovation and sophistication represent the most important single factors in ensuring their economic viability and future long-term health (Howells 1985, pp.1045 and 1057). The economic importance of product innovation is indicated by the fact that the main objective of firm-based industrial R&D is the generation of new, and the development of existing, products. This product orientation in terms of innovative activity has been confirmed by various studies of industrial R&D in both the American and the British economies (Bloom 1951; Gustafson 1962; Gerstenfeld 1970; Schott 1976). If product innovation and sophistication are crucial to the successful development of firms, they are also of major importance on a macro-economic scale in relation to government industrial innovation policy, on both a national and a regional scale. A policy orientation towards product innovation and sophistication has several potential advantages. It enables long-term sustained growth to be achieved, via the development of new industries and markets at the leading edge of technology. Such a policy also offers great potential for employment growth over both the short run and the long run. In addition, it shifts competitive orientation away from cost towards quality and innovativeness - an orientation better suited, and with more benefits for, mature industrial economies such as the UK. Moreover, this type of policy will, by its very nature, centre on indigenous technological development rather than relying on the 'importation' and transfer of mainly process technology.

Bearing in mind these main components and characteristics of technological innovation in the UK economy, it is necessary to review the spatial variations in industrial technological development. The discussion will concentrate on the three main elements outlined earlier, namely: R&D, process and product technological innovation. Finally, a brief mention of research being currently undertaken in the UK service sector is made.

R&D LOCATION IN THE UNITED KINGDOM

It was noted earlier that R&D represented an integral input to, and component of, industrial innovation and development. However, apart from a study by Buswell and Lewis (1970), which examined R&D in Britain at a broad regional level, very little research has been undertaken on the UK geography of R&D. More recently, a number of studies have examined various aspects of the location of research activity in Britain (Howells 1984; Buswell, Easterbrook and Morphet 1985; Gibbs, Alderman, Oakey and Thwaites 1985).

A study by Howells (1984) of the overall concentration of R&D activity within Britain and covering the period 1971-1976, found that, on an inter-regional basis, research employment was heavily concentrated in the South-East standard region. On an urban/rural county level, however, it revealed that R&D employment was spatially dispersed. With the availability of more recent data for 1981 it is evident that the employment shifts in the period up to 1976 have not changed fundamentally during the late 1970s and early 1980s (Howells 1986b). Thus, although in 1981 the South East's share of total research jobs in Britain fell back to 54.0% from 57.4% in 1976, the share for the three southern regions of the UK, including the South East, increased very slightly to 68.0% (compared with 67.9% in 1976). On an urban-rural level, dispersal continued, despite the fact that the conurbations increased their share of research employment in 1981 and thus reversed a decline that had occurred during the first half of the 1970s. Even so, it was the attractive but low-cost and less urbanised localities of Britain that overwhelmingly dominated the pattern of research activity growth.

The relative distribution of R&D employment across Britain is revealed on a more detailed Local Labour Market Area basis in Figure 2.1. It shows clearly that those areas with relatively high concentration levels of research employment are to be found in the residentially attractive suburban and less urbanised areas of southern Britain, within easy access of London. Outside southern Britain those localities with above average concentrations of R&D employees are restricted to a few suburban areas located near to major conurbations, for example in the North West, and to the location of major government-controlled research establishments (particularly associated with nuclear power and defence, like Dounreay, Sellafield and Malvern). It should be noted here that defence-related expenditure is of major importance in influencing the UK's R&D location (see later).

Research by Howells (1984) on the major factors influencing R&D location and based on a study of the UK pharmaceutical industry, stressed the importance of internal (within the firm) rather than external factors in the changing geography of industrial R&D in Britain. Although external locational considerations such as the residential attractiveness of an area and the availability of suitable labour are recognised as important, the internal corporate context of industrial R&D activity was stressed. The internal structure of companies and in particular good links between R&D and other activities of a firm, played a major, if not dominant role in the location of many industrial R&D units.

Figure 2.1: Employment in Research and Development in Britain, 1981: Location Quotients

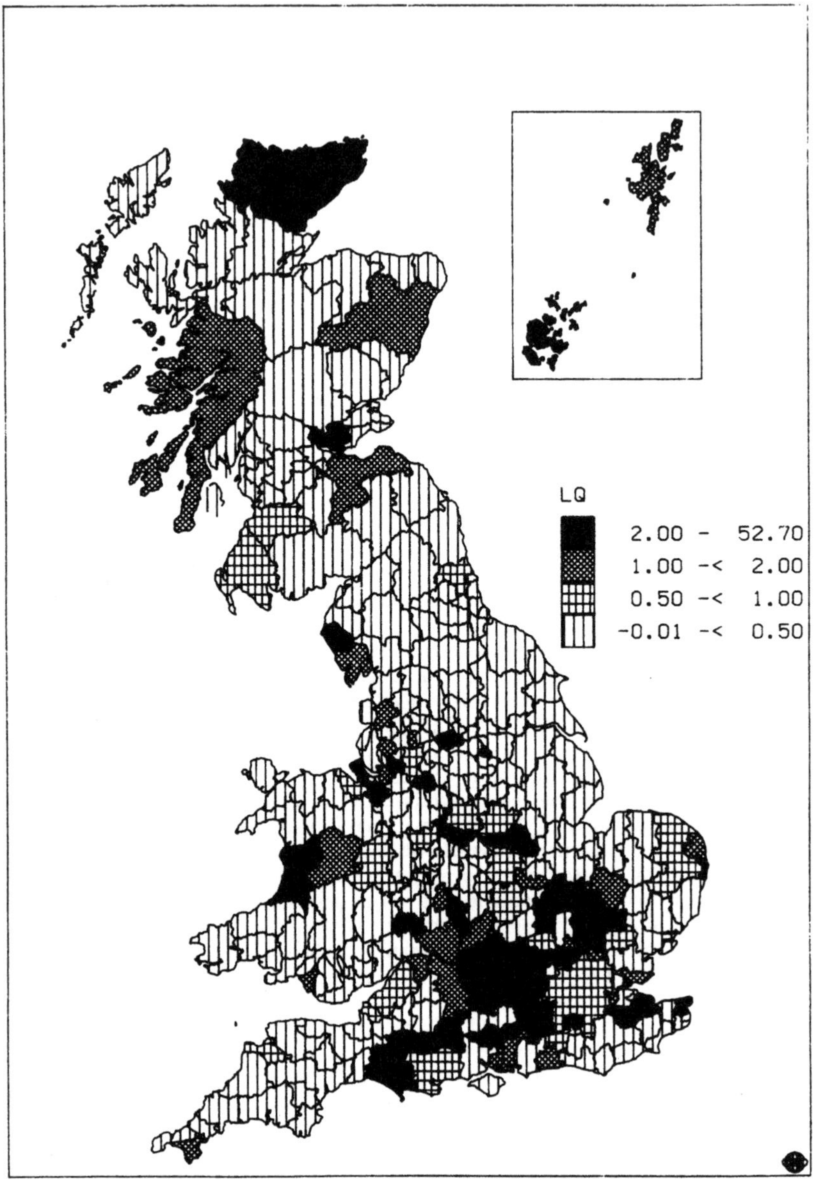

Source: Howells (1986b), p.475

LOCATION OF CAPITAL INNOVATIONS AND TECHNOLOGY

Several studies have shown that there appears to be much less geographical variation, particularly on a core-periphery regional basis, in the location of capital or process innovations. Research has shown that the peripheral, 'less-favoured' regions of the UK do not significantly lag behind the core South-East region in capital or process innovations (Thwaites, Oakey and Nash 1981, pp.36-49; Thwaites, Edwards and Gibbs 1982, p.10; Thwaites 1982, p.377) and in one industry recorded actually an advantage (Howells 1986a). The factors that were thought to explain this lack of spatial variability in capital innovation are associated with differences in the characteristics of capital and product innovations. Unlike in product innovations, where companies use their internal R&D resources to yield technological development, in capital innovations it was found that the vast majority of manufacturing establishments updated their production processes through the installation of machinery, the majority of which was purchased from external sources. As a consequence the availability of process machinery did not appear to be spatially constrained. For the small number of internally generated capital innovations, however, there was a more striking pattern of spatial variation, with significantly higher levels of 'in-house' process innovations in the South-East region of the UK compared with the peripheral North and North-West standard regions.

As far as other factors are concerned, industrial structure (that is, the mix of 'high' versus 'low' technology industries that an area possesses) does not play a dominant role in influencing the pattern of capital innovation and sophistication in manufacturing industry. Evidence from Oakey, Thwaites and Nash (1980, p.244) about the spatial incidence of industrial innovations, and subsequent work by Thwaites, Edwards and Gibbs (1982, pp.21-23), found that industrial structure played only a minor role in determining the pattern and rate of adoption of industrial innovations (see also Norton and Rees 1979). Finally, with reference to organisational factors, it appears that capital innovation or sophistication is influenced by factors that are associated with the manufacturing establishment itself (such as the type of production system it possesses and the presence and level of on-site R&D workers) rather than the characteristics of the controlling company.

LOCATION OF PRODUCT INNOVATIONS AND TECHNOLOGY

In the case of product innovation and sophistication research has revealed that there are major geographical variations in technological development. Studies in the UK have emphasised the dominance of the core South-East region over the Development Areas and 'other' regions in terms of the number of innovative manufacturing establishments present in each area (Oakey, Thwaites and Nash 1980, p.248; Oakey, Thwaites and Nash 1982, p.87). This feature is evident in Table 2.1, which is based on some 807 manufacturing establishments sampled from three UK industries: metalworking machine tools, scientific and industrial instruments, and radio and electronic components. It reveals that innovation in the Development Areas, and in particular within independent single-plant firms, was substantially lower than that observed in the South-East region, suggesting significant differences in product innovation between the South East and other parts of Britain.

Table 2.1: Establishment Location by Status: Incidence of Product Innovation (Percentage of Establishments Innovating)

Area	Single Plant Innovation	Group Plant Innovation	Total Innovation
	%	%	%
South East	85	91	88
Non Assisted Outside the S.E.	74	88	82
Intermediate	76	87	82
Development Area	55	87	73
Great Britain	78	89	84

Source: Thwaites, Oakey & Nash (1981) p.55

In relation to the UK pharmaceutical industry Howells (1985) found that spatial variation in product sophistication was evident on an urban-size rather than centre-periphery regional basis. Factories located in smaller urban centres were more likely to be of high-technology status than those situated in larger, industrially stagnant, urban conurbations. In part this situation arose because plants located in smaller urban centres had certain distinctive organisational characteristics, such as being more recently established and being in turn associated with high product technology status. However, over and above this feature, the analysis revealed that smaller urban locations are independently associated with higher product-technology, suggesting that particular small-town environmental attributes, such as greater availability of space for manufacturing operations and residentially attractive environments for highly trained workers, may also help to explain this pattern. By contrast, large city or conurbation environments were characterised by low product-technology plants.

The significant spatial variation found in product innovation compared with capital innovation has been seen as arising out of one major fact: that, because product innovations are mainly internal and confidential and more spatially immobile in nature, their incidence will more accurately reflect the indigenous potential of the innovative performance of a region or area (Oakey, Thwaites and Nash 1982, p.1082). This observation has been particularly accurate in the case of independent single-plant firms where the Development Areas strikingly lag behind the South East in product innovation. Research by both Oakey, Thwaites and Nash (1982, p.1082) and Howells (1985, pp.1056-7) indicates that the product innovation performance of the 'less-favoured' assisted areas of Britain would have been very much worse without the contribution of branch plants owned by multiplant companies. These branch plants were welcome additions to the production output of peripheral, 'less-favoured' areas of Britain. At the same time they were dependent on the technical support and infrastructure provided via intra-corporate linkages from the parent company. Hence their contribution to innovation was clearly not evidence of self-sustained indigenous innovation capability.

Apart from location itself, the organisational characteristics of the plants themselves influence their level of production innovation and sophistication. Thus, as has been noted above, if a manufacturing plant is part of a multiplant company, rather than just a single-plant firm, it has a much greater likelihood of being sophisticated in product technology. Not surprisingly, the research and technical infrastructure available to the plant were also important factors influencing the level of product innovation. Howells (1985, p.1055) found that it was the size of the corporate R&D inputs that were of prime importance in determining the level of product sophistication in a plant. Thwaites, Oakey and Nash (1981, pp.50-53) found that on-site R&D facilities were an important factor in the level of product innovation. Clearly, therefore, the organisational characteristics of manufacturing plants (and their controlling companies) have a major influence on the level of product innovation that a locality generates. These relationships between spatial variations in organisational characteristics of plants and firms and the level of product innovation in an area or region require further research.

LOCATION, TECHNOLOGICAL INNOVATION AND SERVICES

Research into location and technological innovation within the UK service industries, and more particularly the information economy (Hepworth 1986), has been even more limited than that for manufacturing industry, despite the facts that in 1984 some 64.8% of total UK employment was in the service sector and that it has been the major job generator during the 1970s and 1980s. This mismatch may be in part due to the belief that technological change in the service sector only passively follows technological innovation in manufacturing. In other words, technological developments in services tend to be seen as exogenous influences, emanating from a dynamic manufacturing sector, in particular in relation to information technology. However, service innovations do not necessarily have a subordinate role to manufacturing innovations. In fact certain information services provide a vital role in the development and application of new technology goods (the most obvious example being computer software). More generally, there has been a convergence in the development of goods and service innovations.

A study undertaken for the European Commission and assessing the impact of technological innovation on the location of UK service activity (Howells and Green 1986) offers evidence that the 'less-favoured' peripheral regions of the UK will significantly lag behind the 'core' regions of southern Britain in the introduction and growth of new and technologically advanced service activities. The study considered, for example, the introduction and growth of computer communication networks in the context of the location of information-related service activity on both an intra- and inter-corporate basis. Particular attention was given to the spatial pattern and development of Value-Added Network Services (VANS) in the UK. VANS are provided by companies, using private or public communication networks, and offer to the user a combination of the transmission of information and its manipulation. By 1990 the market for VANS in the UK alone is estimated at $1.4 billion. In fact, the core regions of the UK dominated the pattern of VANS growth in Britain, with the Northern region, Wales and Northern Ireland recording little or no development (Table 2.2). Similarly, on a broader level, a marked concentration of employment (Figure 2.2) and new firm formation in the computer service industry was to be found in the core South-East region of Britain. On the basis of initial research work at least, it appears that the distribution of technologically innovative service companies and activities in the UK is highly concentrated in the core area of southern Britain.

This section has not only stressed the importance of RTD to economic growth and development but also indicated that the spatial distribution of RTD is highly concentrated in the south-east of Britain. As such, it is expected that 'less-favoured' regions will significantly suffer from their low research and technology base. In addition, policies designed to stimulate RTD will also find it much harder to successfully operate because of this situation. It should also be recognised that there are other national and EC policy constraints that both determine the existing RTD pattern and framework in the UK and also influence the successful outcome of local and regional initiatives to stimulate RTD. Some of the key policy issues associated with this spatial pattern will be outlined in the next two sections.

UK REGIONS WITHIN A NATIONAL RTD CONTEXT

Any initiatives at the local and regional level must be aware of both the national and EC context for research and technological development into which such schemes have to fit. On a national level within the UK, acknowledgment has to be made of the structure of research and development in Britain, science and technology policy, industrial policy and regional policy. Individually and collectively, they will affect how and where research and technological development in the UK will occur.

Table 2.2: U.K. Registrations under the VANS General Licence by Region, 21 January 1986. Figures in brackets are numbers for 1 August 1985

Region	Number		Percent of U.K.total
South East and East Anglia	137	(81)	76.5
South West	17	(13)	9.5
West Midlands	4	(2)	2.2
East Midlands	3	(3)	1.7
Yorkshire & Humberside	3	(3)	1.7
North	-	(-)	-
North West	10	(4)	5.5
Scotland	4	(3)	2.2
Wales	-	(-)	-
Northern Ireland	1	(1)	0.6
U.K. total	179	(110)	99.9

Source: Howells and Green (1986), p.168; Compiled from data provided by the Department of Trade and Industry (TK3AAE)

National R&D Base

A key parameter in the development of RTD in specific localities is the overall size and growth of R&D in Britain as a whole. Prospects here are gloomy. Between 1981 and 1983 R&D employment in the UK fell by 4.6%, whilst there was a similar fall (in real terms) of R&D expenditure in industry over the same period from £1,661.2 million to £1,564.1 million. Not surprisingly, this decline is reflected in international comparisons where, between 1981-3, industrial R&D expenditure as a ratio of Gross National Product (GNP) in the UK fell by 2.4% compared with a rise in all our main OECD competitors (Howells 1986b). Public support for R&D is also set to decline. Total government expenditure on R&D in real terms (constant prices) is planned to fall by 6.1% between 1985/6 and 1988/9. Moreover, in terms of government expenditure on fundamental scientific research the UK comes bottom or second to bottom on all yardsticks applied when compared with other major funding countries (US, France, West Germany, Japan and the Netherlands). Within this overall trend of decline in the research base of the UK there are, as noted earlier, marked regional variations in R&D, with a heavy concentration of research activity in southern Britain.

A further macro-level constraint is provided by government expenditure patterns themselves. In the year 1984/85 51.0% of total government expenditure went to the Ministry of Defence. This

Figure 2.2: Employment in Computer Services (AH8394): Location Quotient, 1981

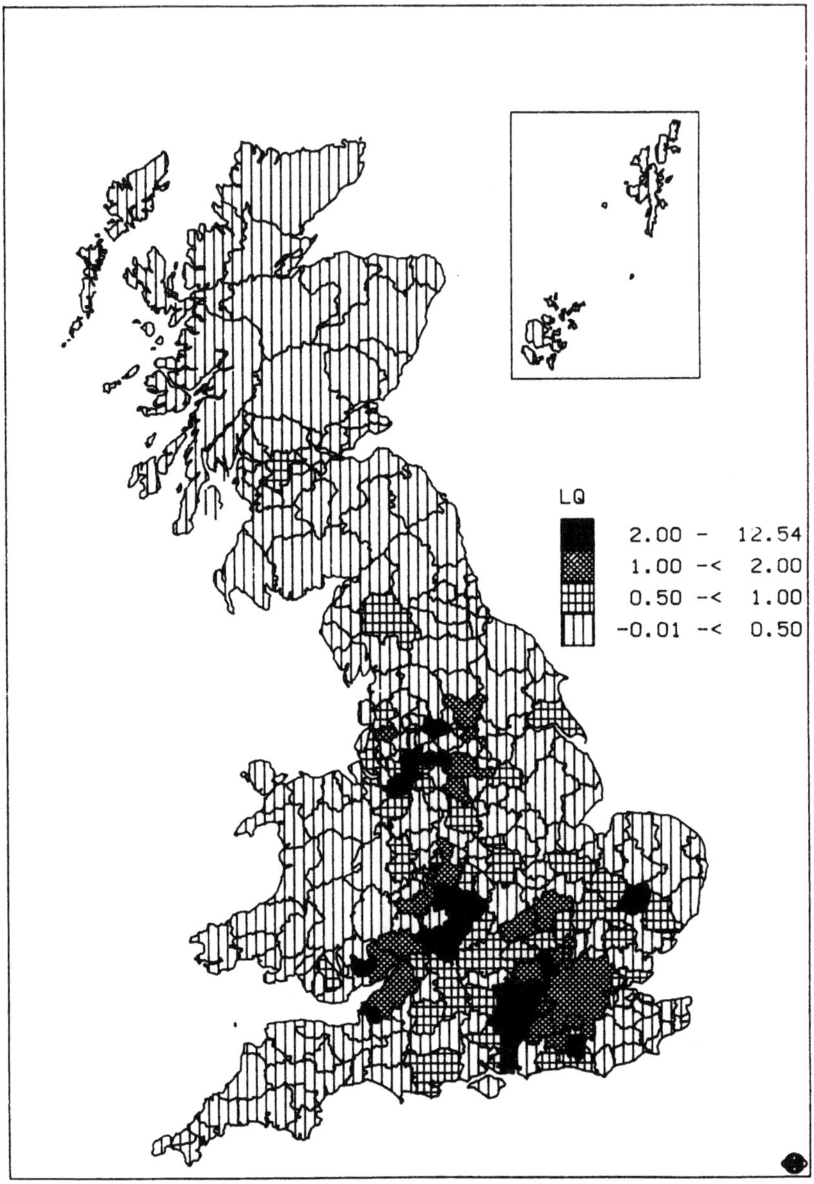

Source: Howells and Green (1986a), p.173

compared with 8.1% for the Department of Trade and Industry, the government department with research and technology transfer projects most directly geared to industry (Cabinet Office 1986, table 8). Indeed, within the planned decline in total government R&D expenditure, that of the Ministry of Defence is expected to rise slightly in real terms between 1984/5 and 1988/9 (0.9%); expenditure by the Department of Trade and Industry is set to fall by 37.8% (Cabinet Office, table 9). In regional terms the pattern of defence-related expenditure has been shown to be heavily biased towards southern Britain (Buswell, Easterbrook and Morphet 1985, pp.53-5). This pattern is evident in the actual distribution both of specific Ministry of Defence Scientific and Research Establishments, which are almost totally located in the south of Britain, and of companies receiving funds for contract RTD for the Ministry. On a wider scale government-funded research establishments (65.4%) overall were found to be concentrated in southern Britain, with the South East having 47.9%, East Anglia 8.9% and the South West 8.6% (Table 2.3). These figures may, in fact, underestimate the proportion of employment that is in the South East; most of the largest establishments are located there.

Any initiatives designed to expand research and technology in the peripheral, 'less-favoured' regions of Britain have to acknowledge that they will be highly constrained in both the industrial and public research pool of these localities.

Science and Technology Policy

Under the Thatcher government since 1979 the main strategy for stimulating industrial and technological change has been an indirect one of supporting the creation of a healthy dynamic environment for UK industry. In relation to RTD strategy and policy the most important government departments are the Department of Trade and Industry (DTI) and the Department of Education and Science (DES). The total R&D budget of the DTI is, as we have seen, very small in contrast to the overall government research budget and especially that of the MOD, and more particularly its significance is set to fall rapidly over the next few years. Nonetheless the DTI, excluding its expenditure on its own four research establishments, has had an important set of technology programmes (Table 2.4) which, though small in size, have had a significant impact on industrial research. It has also provided research aid via its 25% grants to individual R&D projects in companies, pre-competitive collaborative research programmes and technology specific non-project support schemes such as the MAP (Microprocessor Application Project) scheme.

The role of the DES is associated with more basic long-term research via its responsibility for funding research through its five research councils: Science and Engineering Research Council (SERC); Medical Research Council (MRC); Agricultural Research Council (ARC); National Environment Research Council (NERC); and the Economic and

Table 2.3: Regional Distribution of Government Funded Research Facilities[1], 1984

Region	Scientific & Industrial Research Establishments		Agricultural[2] Research Establishments		Total	
	No.	%	No.	%	No.	%
South East	111	51.9	23	34.8	134	47.9
South West	22	10.3	2	3.0	24	8.6
East Anglia	14	6.5	11	16.7	25	8.9
East Midlands	4	1.9	0	0	4	1.4
West Midlands	5	2.3	1	1.5	6	2.1
North West	7	3.3	0	0	7	2.5
Yorkshire & Humberside	7	3.3	2	3.0	9	3.2
North	9	4.2	0	0	9	3.2
Wales	10	4.7	0	0	10	3.6
Scotland	24	11.2	21	31.8	45	16.1
Northern Ireland	1	0.5	6	9.1	7	2.5
Total	214	100[3]	66	100[3]	280	100

1. This is defined as including research facilities operated or funded by the following government departments and nationalised industries - MOD, DTI, DoE, DTp, DEn, Home Office, DHSS, MRC, SERC, NERC, NCC, AFRC, MAFF, Northern Ireland and Scottish Departments, CEGB, British Gas, NCB, BBC, BSC, BR, UKAEA, LRT and WRC
2. In relation to agriculture, husbandry farms without a sizeable (>10 employees) research and technical staff are excluded
3. Does not total due to rounding

Table 2.4: DTI Technology Programmes, Expenditure 1981-86

	£ millions
Production techniques	90
Microelectronics applications	50
Information technology	150
Advanced instrumentation	35
Materials processing	65
Production and development of microelectronics	50
Biotechnology	15

Source: Wallard (1985), p.204

Social Research Council (ESRC). It is also involved in basic research via its relationship with the University Grants Committee (UGC) and the funding of other higher education institutes. Again, there is a planned cutback (constant prices) in government funding for both the research councils and the UGC for the period 1985/6 to 1988/9 (Cabinet Office 1986, table 9), after the already heavy cutbacks, particularly by the UGC since 1981.

A further aspect of government science and technology policy is the British Technology Group (BTG), formed in 1981 from the merger of the National Research and Development Corporation (NRDC; established in 1949) and the National Enterprise Board (NEB; established in 1975). The NEB has now been effectively wound up within BTG, with the majority of its assets being sold off (for example its remaining holding in Celltech) and all its staff being transferred to the rest of BTG. However, the operations of NRDC within BTG continue, associated with assisting researchers in the commercialisation and funding of innovative ideas and the wider financing of technological innovation in industry. Thus, in 1985 BTG spent some £10.8 million on projects to commercialise technology, with a total income of £22.4 million. However, there is a prospect that BTG will be privatised.

A final element in the science and technology strategy of the government is the individual programmes, such as the Alvey programme on information technology and the LINK scheme. The five-year Alvey Programme is to cost £350 million, of which some £200 million will come from the government. Its basic aim is to facilitate inter-firm and industry-university collaboration at the pre-competitive research stage, leaving commercial exploitation in the hands of individual firms. Similarly, the recently announced LINK scheme, run by the DTI, is designed to make strategic research by academics readily available for industrial exploitation through joint government-industrial financial support. The scheme will start with £4 million from government in 1987/88, and overall £200 million will be spent by the government (with money from the DES as well). Critics of this latter scheme argue that the funding is not new money but funds taken from elsewhere and that a substantial part of the overall scheme is dependent on private-sector funding.

Of concern to the 'less-favoured' regions of the UK is not only the continuing cutbacks in science and technology funding by government but also the fact that government support for science and technology has strongly favoured the prosperous, southern part of Britain. For example, in the case of the DTI the MAP funding which started in 1978 went primarily to companies located in the South East (Table 2.5), although it has only a quarter of all UK manufacturing industry. The only other region with a 'take-up' rate in excess of its share of UK manufacturing industry was the South West. All other regions were under-represented. There has also been criticism of BTG (and the previous role of the NEB) for not giving sufficient support to the actual development and production of technological innovation in the 'less-favoured' areas of Britain. Similarly, whilst there are variations in the Alvey programme between different types of project (such as VSLI, CAD, Man-Machine Interface and VAD), in all five main areas of technology firms in the South East overwhelmingly have the highest levels of participation in the programme (Rothwell and Beesley 1987, p.73). Major proportions of the funds have gone to the individual research facilities of GEC, Plessey and British Telecom, along with the other major firms. It is clear that a policy of selectivity and excellence will always discriminate in favour of the existing strengths, thus exacerbating regional disparities in RTD performance.

Industrial Policy

Less directly applicable, although still of significance to RTD in the peripheral regions of the UK, is the government's wider industrial policy and its spatial impact. A key element in the Conservative government's policy strategy is, as we have noted, its primarily indirect approach towards stimulating industrial development. This approach can be seen in its largely successful stimulation of venture capital funding in the UK, which is well ahead of that of the rest of the EC, and in its support of new and small firms. Two examples of such schemes are the Loan Guarantee Scheme (LGS) and the Business Expansion Scheme (BES). Under the LGS when it was first established loans made by the private banks to small firms were guaranteed for 80% of the value of the loan. Again analysis of the loan guarantees issued by region between 1981 and 1984 indicates the favourable position of the economically prosperous South-East region, in terms of both the number (37.6%) and the value (41.3%) of loans provided. Similarly, under the BES, introduced in 1983 to inject development capital into unquoted businesses across all sectors of industry, there has been a similar concentration in the South-East region. Thus for the financial year 1983-4 53% of all firms financed under the scheme were located in the South East (Rothwell and Beesley 1987, p.44).

Table 2.5: Regional Distribution of Firms Offered Grants under the MAP Scheme

Region	Percentage of firms
Scotland	4
North East	3
Yorkshire/Humberside	6
North West	9
East Midlands	7
West Midlands	8
South East	52
South West	8
Wales	2

Source: Northcott and Rogers (1985)

Regional Policy

Finally, regional policy can indirectly affect the adoption and take-up of new technology within the peripheral regions. Thus regional policy in the form of the availability of regional development grants (RDG) in the 'less-favoured', Assisted Areas of Britain is seen as being an important influence on process technology developments (Gibbs 1984; Howells 1986a). Until recently regional development grants in the UK have been geared to capital investment subsidies rather than specifically to job creation. The availability of such regional aid in the Assisted Areas of the UK is seen as having encouraged the wider and more rapid adoption of new process technology investment, although these incentives have assisted branches of multiplant firms. There has also been direct support for the formation, movement or enlargement of RTD units in the Assisted Areas through job subsidies under the Office and Service Industry Scheme (now replaced under the new RDG scheme). The aim of the scheme was to reduce regional imbalances in the type of jobs in Assisted Areas by increasing service-sector employment and improving the supply of business and technical services to industry in those areas. Although much of the actual takeup of OSIS was by the office-based services, there were also some examples of R&D units being expanded and other technically oriented services being assisted (software, technical consultancies). However, the scheme was very small compared to RDG capital grants and was of insufficient scale to encourage the movement of large RTD units unless such a move was already planned by the company (Gibbs et al, 1985). Even this advantage to the 'less-favoured' regions of Britain in the development and growth of research and technology is being diminished by cutbacks in expenditure and coverages of regional aid. In terms of current prices, spending on regional aid fell from £956 million in 1982-3 to £615 million in 1984-5.

UK Regions and National RTD: Conclusions

This brief review of the policy environment for RTD and its development in the peripheral, 'less-favoured' regions emphasises two serious handicaps that local and regional initiatives in research and technology have to face. Firstly, government support for RTD is declining over time; and, secondly, the funding that is made available by central government goes mainly to the prosperous south-east of Britain. The assumption that the growth of high-technology industry in southern Britain is due to 'natural' change factors has, therefore, to be re-evaluated in the light of the spatial variations in government expenditure on research and technology. A final issue is whether central government expenditure and support for RTD in the regions goes to the right sort of research and technology initiatives in terms of maximum benefits for local economic development. Often, even if RTD is conducted in a region, by an institution of higher education for example, the commercial exploitation may take place elsewhere in the UK or even abroad so that the net benefit to the region is minimal.

UK REGIONS IN THE CONTEXT OF EC POLICIES

In terms of RTD expenditure the contribution of the European Community is relatively small compared to a large economy such as the UK. Total European Commission expenditure on RTD is much less than UK defence R&D, for example, and only a small proportion of this expenditure will actually be spent within the UK. However, on an individual project basis the sums can be significant, especially if channelled to a small firm or a research centre in an area of low RTD capability. It must also be remembered that, as these funds go to firms and organisations located in regions, they will correspondingly either increase or decrease existing regional RTD disparities. In this latter sense, the funds present an opportunity to boost regional RTD capacities.

Support for High Technology (DG XII and DG XIII)

The primary focus of Community interest in RTD has been provided by a concern to establish a European scale of research effort both in basic research for important new technologies (eg. nuclear power) and in technologies underpinning European competitiveness in RTD-intensive industries. In recent years the latter has come to acquire a more elevated status over the energy research originally funded under Euratom, largely as a consequence of the declining competitiveness of European high-technology sectors in IT and manufacturing technologies. The inability of the EC to compete in such sectors presents severe problems for the future if Europe's manufacturers become squeezed out of high technology and into direct competition with the newly industrialising countries of South-East Asia and South America.

The EC has responded with a new Framework Programme for Technological Research and Development (CEC 1986a), not in force by February 1987 principally because of objections from the British government to the scale of proposed funding. It emphasises the increasing role of RTD in determining the ability to generate jobs and achieve economic welfare; it recognises that a leading position in technology is required to maintain economic growth and, therefore, strengthens support for industrial technology. The specific programmes to be funded under the branch framework, called lines of action, are listed in Table 2.6, and the most significant are those related to the competitiveness of industry and services, with an anticipated 60% of the total budget. Within this specific programme the largest areas are information technology (IT), telecommunications, industrial technologies and biotechnology.

Table 2.6: List of Community Actions

1. Quality of Life

1.1 Health
1.2 Environment

2. Towards an Information Society

2.1 Information Technologies

3. The Life Blood of the Large Market

3.1 Telecommunications
3.2 Integration of Telecommunications Technologies with Information and Broadcasting Technologies into New Services of Common Interest
3.3 Transport

4. Application of the New Technologies to the Modernisation of Industrial Sectors

4.1 Technologies for Manufacturing Industry
4.2 Science and Technology of Materials and Raw Materials
4.3 Technical Standards, Measurement Methods and Reference Materials

5. Continuation and Updating of Activities in the Energy Sector

5.1 Fission
5.2 Fusion

5.3 Non-Nuclear Energies and Rational Use of Energy

6. Biotechnology : a New Technological Crossroads

6.1 Biotechnology, Management of Agricultural Resources, Agro-Industrial Technologies, Science and Technology for Development

7. Exploitation of the Seabed and Use of Marine Resources

7.1 Marine Science and Technology

8. A Europe for Research Workers

8.1 Implementation of a Europe for Research Workers

Source: CEC (1986a)

ESPRIT (European Strategic Programme for Research and Development in Information Technology) is the best known of these sectoral programmes. It was launched in 1982 as the European response to the Japanese fifth-generation computer programme and the US defence programmes in computing and semi-conductors. The involvement of the 'club-of-twelve' leading European IT firms (GEC, Plessey, ICL, Philips, Siemens, Nixdorf, AEG, Thomson, Bull, CGE, Olivetti, STET) at all stages in the planning process was clearly important to the eventual industrial orientation of the programme, albeit at pre-competitive level. Its major support is concentrated on advanced microelectronics, software production, advanced information processing, office systems and computer-integrated manufacturing. The initial five-year programme was for 750 million MECUS of Community funding, with industrial partners generally putting 50% towards the cost of individual projects.

Regional Participation in ESPRIT

The nature of the ESPRIT programme, like Alvey, is responsive in that it must call for project submissions from firms, higher-education authorities and research organisations. The 'leading-edge' requirements of the programme dictate that the organisations receiving funding must be capable of competing in an international research environment. As these organisations are not widely distributed across the UK (as outlined earlier), the funds will go to those areas that are already relatively rich in funding. Thus, for example, 70% of all ESPRIT money goes to the 12 major European IT firms, which make up a similar percentage of the volume of sales of European-based firms within the Community. A glance at the UK participants in ESPRIT shows that the large firms obviously do well (such as GEC, Plessey and ICL), that there are a number of smaller firms many of which are located in the south east, and that amongst the higher-education institutions it is those institutions near to the firms' RTD centres in the south that are more likely to participate.

From the point of view of the 'less-favoured' regions there are several points of interest:

1. The local institution of higher education is the most likely local organisation to be able to get access to ESPRIT, especially if it has existing major industrial partners in IT. Knowledge of the ESPRIT network may, therefore, be available there, and links with local firms may possibly be established.
2. Some isolated firms in 'less-favoured' regions may have obtained access to ESPRIT. A local authority should know of this and use them as an example for other firms in its area.
3. Some participants are not purely IT firms but may contribute to the applications of IT; hence other large competent firms should be encouraged to seek participation.

Other EC Programmes

In a similar way to ESPRIT, the RACE (Research and Development in Advanced Communications Technologies for Europe), BRITE (Basic Research in Industrial Technologies for Europe) and BEP (Biomolecular Engineering Programme) programmes offer support in telecommunications, industrial technologies and biotechnology respectively. RACE is perhaps more concentrated than ESPRIT in the sense that the telecoms firms are essentially a subset of ESPRIT participants; whereas BRITE may be much more widely spread, being aimed at firms involved in such activities as lasers, joining technologies, testing, CAD/CAM, materials, membranes and production technologies. Thus many firms in traditional sectors where new technologies can be applied to improve their competitiveness may be able to get this valuable RTD support. The benefits may also go much beyond the technical 'know-how', as the international co-operation required by the EC programmes gives a firm an entree to a wider international network of possible customers, suppliers and collaborators as well as other technological information.

In order to foster the development of this international network, the Commission has also instituted a programme called SPRINT (Strategic Programme for Innovation and Technology Transfer) in order to particularly assist SMEs to develop technology in a more open European market. Thus, the Commission is assisting the formation of liaison mechanisms between advisory bodies in different countries, improving the circulation of ideas and information including the establishment of new data facilities, and undertaking studies and comparisons of 'best-practice' policy for innovation support with the formation of international working groups to examine policies and promote particular sectors (CEC 1986b). Although this programme is not explicitly regional, organisations based in 'less-favoured' regions may be able to benefit greatly from these linkages and information networks and help SMEs in their regions to take a more outward view of the Community as a market.

European Regional Development Policy and RTD

Although support for RTD is not a primary responsibility of the Regional Policy Directorate (DG XVI), it has been called upon to fund some technology-related initiatives in recent years (for details see the chapter by Waldchen). This process has in fact been very much passive rather than pro-active, with individual countries proposing RTD-related infrastructure investments which are eligible for ERDF support. For instance, in the case of 'measures to exploit the potential for internally generated development of regions', the Fund may give aid to regional applied research organisations or technology transfer organisations for SMEs. The Fund may also contribute to public infrastructure which may encompass RTD infrastructure in the form of buildings etc (CEC 1984). Examples of the use of these measures cover a wide range of policy options. Research centres have been built or equipped using ERDF support in Italy and Greece in regions where RTD was virtually absent. However, in notable cases this support has then provided the opportunity for further EC funding from specific RTD programmes such as ESPRIT. Although this latter funding must be won in open competition, it would not have been possible to achieve this situation without the initial funds for establishing the unit.

Another regional initiative sponsored by the European Commission is the European Business and Innovation Centre Network (EBN), which is discussed in detail in the chapter by Jack Malan. It seeks to establish BICs in local economies across Europe in order to provide an industrial and technological base for economic regeneration. Many of the BICs established so far are located in areas of industrial decline and provide services and facilities to stimulate enterprise, diffuse technological information, and support new firms with accommodation or common services (see the examples in the chapters by Blackburn and Kennedy and by Aitken).

Although the EC regional and indeed technological policy makers cannot make a major contribution to the total RTD capacity of UK regions, they can add a new dimension to existing or planned strategies in the regions, by providing a wider perspective and by allowing firms to gain access to a wider RTD community.

CONCLUSIONS

A number of key issues confront policy-makers who are involved in the design and introduction of RTD initiatives at a local or regional level. An obvious, though crucial problem is that most peripheral, 'less-favoured' regions will have a small or non-existent science and technology base on which local innovative activity can be built, and which may not be able to easily attract funds from competitive RTD programmes. Local authorities and regions that are seeking to develop their RTD base are also confronted with a highly complex and constrained research and technology policy environment. Even in Britain there is a wide range of different science and technology programmes, co-ordinated by a number of different government departments and agencies. This complexity is also replicated, to a lesser extent, at the EC level, where a number of different Commission directorates have responsibility for research and technology projects. The complexity of research and technology programmes and initiatives that are available is matched by the strong policy constraints for RTD initiatives at a local level that are imposed by national parameters. For example, increasing interest in RTD at a local and regional level is being focused on higher-education institutions which can have an important role to play in local economic development. However, power and influence over the universities lie outside the local or regional level. Any benefits that may be gained by local or regional RTD initiatives can be more than offset by national trends and decisions made at a national level.

Two points need emphasis. Firstly, most locally-based RTD initiatives have been generally related to property infrastructure, reflecting the existing policy orientation of both EC (particularly in relation to the ERDF) and national programmes, and the institutional capabilities of the local authorities. Secondly, national or Community RTD policies, centred on long-term, pre-competitive basic research programmes, often have little relevance to 'less-favoured' regions, which require more short-term applied research programmes and technology-transfer schemes. Indeed, increased participation by establishments in the 'less-favoured' regions in such national and EC programmes may actually have a detrimental effect on the development of research and technology in such localities. It commits scarce science and technology resources, particularly personnel, in the region to projects that often have very little direct relevance or spin-offs to the regions concerned.

Public policy must recognise two major needs. Firstly, more effective co-ordination is required between local authorities and regions in the RTD initiatives that they implement. Such coordination would help to avoid competition and duplication of effort between localities, to acknowledge the cross-boundary implications of many of the schemes and to provide a co-ordinated, multi-locality programme for a wider region. Its implications include specialisation of implementation of RTD initiatives between neighbouring local authorities. Secondly, at the Community level, recognition has to be made of the need for a more pro-active policy in contrast to the tendency of most EC regional programmes to be 'demand-responsive'. Otherwise those less co-ordinated and indeed less well-off localities and regions of the UK and Europe, in most need of aid for research and technological development, will in fact be the losers.

REFERENCES

Bloom, G.F. (1951) 'Union wage pressure and technological discovery', American Economic Review, 12, 5-24

Branch, B. (1974) 'Research and development activity and profitability', Journal of Political Economy, 82, 999-1011

Britten, N. (1980) 'Industrial dependence and technological underdevelopment: Canadian consequences of foreign direct investment', Regional Studies, 14, 181-199

Buswell, R.J. and Lewis, E.W. (1970) 'The geographical distribution of industrial activity in the United Kingdom', Regional Studies, 297-306

Buswell, R.J., Easterbrook, R.P. and Morphet, C.S. (1985) 'Geography, Regions and Research and Development Activity: The Case of the United Kingdom' in A.T. Thwaites and R.P. Oakey (eds.) The Regional Impact of Technological Change, Frances Pinter, London, pp.36-66

Cabinet Office (1986) Annual Review of Government Funded R&D, 1986, HMSO, London

Commission of the European Communities (1984) Council Regulations(EEC) No. 1787/84 of 19 June 1984 on The European Regional Development Fund', Official Journal of the European Communities, 27, L169

Commission of the European Communities (1986a) Proposal for a Council Regulation Concerning the Framework Programme of Community Activities in the Field of Research and Technological Development (1987 to 1991) COM (86) 430 final, CEC Brussels

Commission of the European Communities (1986b) 'The Sprint Programme', European File, 18

Charles, D.R. and Howells, J.R. (In progress) Public Research Establishments and Regional Economic Development in the UK

Fothergill, S. and Gudgin, G. (1982) Unequal Growth: Urban and Regional Employment Change in the UK, Heinemann, London

Gerstenfeld, A. (1970) Effective Management of Research and Development, Addison-Wesley

Gibbs, D.C. (1984) 'The influence of investment incentives on technological change', Area, 16, 115-120

Gibbs, D.C., Alderman, N., Oakey, R.P., and Thwaites, A.T. (1985) 'The Location of Research and Development in Great Britain', Final Report to the UK Department of Trade and Industry and the Commission of the European Communities, CURDS, University of Newcastle upon Tyne

Goddard, J.B., Thwaites, A.T., and Gibbs, D.C. (1984) 'Technological Change and Regional Development'. Paper presented to CURDS/ESRC Workshop, Newcastle upon Tyne, 28-30 March

Gustafson, W.E. (1962) 'Research and development, new products and productivity change', American Economic Association, Papers and Proceedings, 52, 117-185

Hepworth, M. (1986) 'The geography of technological change in the information economy', Regional Studies, 20, 407-424

Howells, J. (1984) 'The location of research and development: some observations and evidence from Britain', Regional Studies, 18, 13-29

Howells, J. (1985) 'Product sophistication, industrial organisation and location: the UK pharmaceutical industry', Environment and Planning, A17, 1045-1062

Howells, J. (1986a) 'Capital sophistication and regional development: organisation and pattern within the UK pharmaceutical industry', Tijdschrift voor Economische en Sociale Geografie, 77, 92-102

Howells, J. (1986b) 'Industry - academic links in research and innovation: a national and regional development perspective', Regional Studies, 20, 472-476

Howells, J., and Green, A. (1986 'Location, technology and industrial organisation in UK services', Progress in Planning, 26, 83-184

Keeble, D.E. (1980) 'Industrial decline, regional policy and the urban-rural manufacturing shift in the United Kingdom', Environment and Planning, A12, 945-962

Kennedy, C. and Thirlwall, A.P. (1972) 'Surveys in applied economics: technical progress', Economic Journal, 82, 11-72

Little, A.D. Ltd. (1977) New Technology-Based Firms in the UK and the Federal Republic of West Germany, Wilton House

Malecki, E. (1982) 'Federal R&D spending in the United States of America: some impacts on metropolitan economies', Regional Studies, 16, 19-35

Nasbeth, L. (1974) 'Summary and Conclusions' in L. Nasbeth and G.F. Ray (eds.), The Diffusion of New Industrial Processes: An International Study, Cambridge University Press, pp. 294-315

Northcott, J. and Rogers, P. (1985) Microelectronics in British Industry, Policy Studies Institute, London

Northern Region Strategy Team (NRST) (1977) Strategic Plan for the Northern Regions, Volume 2, Economic Development Policies, HMSO, London

Norton, R.D. and Rees, J. (1979) 'The product cycle and the spatial decentralisation of American manufacturing', Regional Studies, 13, 141-151

Oakey, R.P., Thwaites, A.T. and Nash, P.A. (1980) 'The regional distribution of innovative establishments in Britain', Regional Studies, 14, 235-253

Oakey, R.P., Thwaites, A.T. and Nash, P.A. (1982) 'Technological change and regional development: some evidence on regional variations in product and process innovation', Environment and Planning, A14, 1073-1086

Organisation for Economic Co-operation and Development (1982) Innovation Policy: Trends and Perspectives, OECD, Paris

Rothwell, R. and Beesley, M. (1987) 'United Kingdom Research and Technological Development Policy: Some Regional Impacts', Science Policy Research Unit, University of Sussex

Rothwell, R. and Zegveld, W. (1982) Innovation and the Small and Medium-Sized Firms, Frances Pinter, London

Schott, K. (1976) 'Investment in private industrial research and development in Britain', Journal of Industrial Economics, 25, 81-100

Thwaites, A.T. (1978) 'Technological change, mobile plants and regional development', Regional Studies, 12, 445-462

Thwaites, A.T. (1982) 'Some evidence of regional variations in the introduction and diffusion of industrial products and processes within British manufacturing industry', Regional Studies, 16, 371-381

Thwaites, A.T., Oakey, R.P. and Nash, P.A. (1981) Industrial Innovation and Regional Development: Volumes I and II. Final Report to UK Department of the Environment, Centre for Urban and Regional Development Studies, University of Newcastle upon Tyne

Thwaites, A.T., Edwards, A. and Gibbs, D.C. (1982) The Inter-regional Diffusion of Production Innovations in Great Britain. Final Report to UK Department of Industry and the Commission of the European Communities, CURDS, University of Newcastle upon Tyne

Wallard, A. (1985) 'The problematic relationship between research and policy' in M. Gibbons, P. Grummet, and B. Udgaonkar (eds.) Science and Technology Policy in the 1980's and Beyond, Longman, London, pp.191-206.

Chapter Three

INDUSTRIAL CHANGE, NEW TECHNOLOGIES AND EC REGIONAL POLICY

Paul Wäldchen

Industrial change has become a matter of increasing concern in the European Community. Whilst total industrial employment continued to grow until the early 1970s, there has been a reversal of this process since then. Between 1970 and 1983 industrial employment in the EC states decreased by over 17%. Projections for the period up to 1990, carried out by the Commission, point to a continuation of this trend[1]. If these facts are clear, their interpretation gives rise to controversy. Whilst some lines of thought, following for instance Fourastie's theories[2], might even welcome this phenomenon as a further step in Europe's move towards a 'post-industrial' society, other interpretations of trends in international trade stress the loss of industrial competitiveness of Europe with respect to its major industrial competitors Japan and the United States, on the one hand, and the newly industrialising countries, on the other.

A closer look at industrial statistics shows that employment decline in the Community was particularly high for some material-intensive production sectors (e.g. coal, iron, steel) and for labour-intensive sectors such as textiles and clothing, footwear and leathers. This development is not surprising, for it confirms Europe's traditional comparative disadvantage in raw-materials and labour costs. What is more preoccupying is the fact that in the field of high technology, which normally should be its strength, Europe seems to have lost ground as well.

The Commission, in its memorandum of 1985 prepared for the Milan meeting of the European Council, pointed out that since 1972 the annual growth rate in real terms of the production of high-technology goods in the EC states has not exceeded 5%, while the rate in the United States is 7.6% and Japan 14% [3]. In addition, Europe's declining industrial performance has eroded its trade surplus in high-technology products. Over a twenty-year period the export cover of high-technology imports into the Community fell from 190% to 110% (1983). In its communication to the Brussels meeting of the European Council in March 1985, on strengthening the technological base and competitiveness of Community industry, the Commission re-emphasised the view that, while it is not justified to speak of an overall loss of competitiveness or a universal technological gap there are worrying trends in several branches with a high technological intensity such as information technology, telecommunications, biotechnology and new materials[4].

The Community was not willing to accept this deteriorating trend; in the long run it would undermine the economic basis of its international competitiveness and prosperity. At the Milan and Brussels summits it recognised the central role played by technological advance in economic growth and industrial competitiveness and the importance of collective Community effort to offset challenges in both home and overseas markets.

EC POLICIES FOR RESEARCH AND TECHNOLOGY

By 1987 a European research community was already in being. In 1984 the first Community framework programme allocated nearly 4.5 billion ECU for the period 1984-87 for scientific collaboration at the Community level. The ESPRIT programme on information technology, costing 750 million MECU over 4 years (1984-88), was perhaps the best known example of this new common policy for research and development. Other programmes for the stimulation of research and development for established manufacturing industries (BRITE) and advanced telecommunications technologies (RACE) were also launched, together with initiatives in agriculture, biotechnology, new materials and energy[5]. 1985 saw the launching of the 'Technology Community', followed in 1986 by its formal confirmation in the European Single Act and by the Eureka initiative which embraces more of Europe than the EEC member states.

The European Single Act provided a new political and legal basis for the development of the Community's scientific and technical strategy. It was intended that Community activity in the field of technological R&D would be conducted in a series of programmes at different levels, namely:

1. A unanimously approved multiannual Framework Programme, which is to provide the basis for the balanced overall development of Community actions.
2. Specific programmes, adopted by a qualified majority, which are concerned with particular objectives, designed to promote cooperation betwen all the partners and open to participation by non-member countries.
3. Supplementary programmes in which member states will participate on a voluntary basis.

The Framework Programme, which was still awaiting approval by the Council of Ministers in May 1987, proposed the adoption of seven lines of action adapted to the new requirements of the 1990s and covering the following topics: (1) management of resources (particularly in agriculture); (2) management of energy; (3) competitiveness of industry and services (information technology, telecommunications, etc); (4) quality of life ('Europe against cancer', the fight against AIDS, safety, environmental protection, etc.); (5) science and technology for development; (6) Europe's scientific and technical potential; and (7) general support for scientific and technical development (innovation, scientific networks, machine translation, etc.).

THE EC AND THE REGIONAL IMPACT OF INDUSTRIAL AND TECHNOLOGICAL CHANGE

How do these sectoral policy developments relate to and influence the regional problems and policies of the Community? Systematic analysis of this question became an integral part of Community regional policy. Every three years the European Commission publishes the so-called 'periodic report' on the social and economic situation of the regions of the Community, in which the principal features of regional development from a Community perspective are presented. Being aware of the fact that other policies may play as important a role as regional policy itself, the Commission has adopted the principle of carrying out continuous evaluation of the regional impacts of Community economic and sectoral policies.

The Regional Dimension of Industrial Change

As the second periodic report shows, the decline of certain industrial sectors has had a particular strong regional impact. At the forefront was the textiles and clothing sector. This sector had lost jobs since 1950 and at an ever accelerating rate. Annual loss between 1950 and 1960 was 0.8%; between 1960 and 1970 it was 1.7%; and between 1970 and 1980 it was 3.4%. The impact is particularly important for regional development in the Community since textiles and clothing is, in terms of jobs, the largest manufacturing subsector and geographically widespread. It is interesting to note that the textile areas in north-west and central Europe have been worst hit, while, on the contrary, employment in the peripheral regions has actually increased in some cases [6]. In second place came shipbuilding. Here too there was a continuous decline in employment since the 1950s. In contrast to the textiles and clothing sector, the shipbuilding sector was smaller and not so geographically widespread. The worst decline in employment was evident in the UK shipyards, followed by France and Germany. In third place was the iron and steel industry. Decline in this sector was more recent. Between 1955 and 1974 employment increased by some 100,000. During this period the integrated coastal steelworks were developed, importing their raw materials and largely exporting their finished products. Since 1975, however, there has been a major change: overcapacity and falling prices have led to the need for major capacity reductions, involving closures and reductions in employment. All member states' steel industries are affected, although over a long period the UK's losses were especially high there too.

This analysis would seem to suggest that in some cases (textiles and clothing in particular) peripheral regions have done better than the traditional industrial regions of central Europe. Certain other factors must, however, be taken into account:

1. In some of the least-favoured peripheral areas official job statistics do not give an accurate picture of the sectoral employment situation, as they are influenced by special social security systems(7).
2. Their industries are generally young and supported by government intervention.
3. The economies of these regions are indirectly protected by monetary adjustments. The continuous devaluations of the Italian lira and the Greek drachma, for instance, have without any doubt contributed to maintaining competitiveness in the principal industries of the countries concerned, both inside and outside the Community. There is, however, a clear macroeconomic cost of such a policy: it does not contribute towards the convergence of economies of Europe but rather reinforces the danger of 'l'Europe a deux vitesses'.

With respect to the regional dimension of total industrial decline, a study carried out for the Commission showed that over the period 1974-1982 this decline has been widespread in its territorial impact because almost three quarters of the Community's level III regions registered some decline in industrial employment (8). Severe decline, however, with an annual rate of more than 2% p.a., affected mainly the traditional industrial regions of the Community, particularly the North, the North-West and the West Midlands of England, parts of Scotland, Wales and Northern Ireland, Lorraine and Nord-Pas-de-Calais in France, the Saar and parts of the Ruhr in West Germany, the western part of the Netherlands, and Wallonia in Belgium. With the accession of Spain and Portugal to the EC, areas such as the Pais Vasco, Asturias or Setubal have to be added.

Reduction of industrial employment as such does not, of course, automatically imply regional problems. The transformation from sectoral problems into regional problems depends on the general economic and social structure of the region and its flexibility of reaction. Strong development of the service sector or a reduction or a slower growth of labour supply, due to the demographic structure, can compensate for the reduction in industrial employment. For these reasons, not all the above-mentioned regions characterised by particularly high job losses in industry have an equally high unemployment rate: thus the West German and North Italian regions have much lower rates than the British or Spanish regions.

The Regional Dimension of Technological Change

As technological change is a broad and complex phenomenon, it is not easy to assess its regional impact. In its regional impact assessment approach the Commission has, therefore, focused till now on one sector that has received particular attention, namely new information technology (NIT). Assessments of other sectors, such as research and technology, were in preparation by 1987.

Studies for the Commission showed that there was a close correlation between the level of socio-economic development and the level of NIT equipment: more highly developed and more central regions are far better equipped than less developed and more peripheral regions [9]. A similar pattern appears in the use of NIT services: the higher density of population and level of economic activity in the more central regions of the Community favours the use of these advanced services, whilst sparsely populated and low-activity areas discourage intensity of use. The predominance of small- and medium-sized firms in those areas is often a further hindering factor. As regards the future, all the evidence available to the European Commission points to the tendency for advanced telecommunications developments to follow demand. This tendency will be further reinforced by the fact that in more and more countries, like Britain, the telecommunications organisations responsible for NIT services either are being privatised or at least have to apply principles of commercial management. So, unless corrective action is taken, the development of the infrastructure for the new technologies will tend to follow established demand patterns and concentrate in the most developed regions of the Community, in the same way as railways and roads in the past. This process would be all the more regrettable as telecommunications services are, by definition, much more 'distance independent' than were the classical means of communication in the past. Responsible planning authorities are in fact provided with a new chance to improve the traditional geographical pattern of communications infrastructure equipment and service supply.

WHAT IS THE EC REGIONAL POLICY'S RESPONSE TO THE TECHNOLOGICAL CHALLENGE? HOW DOES IT RELATE TO LOCAL AUTHORITIES' INITIATIVES?

Regional policy is responsible neither for the development of advanced technologies as such nor for innovation policy in general. It must, however, devote major attention to these fields when it turns out that they constitute essential conditions for successful development or reconversion of regions. In its first phase the European Regional Development Fund was just responding to national requests for cofinancing projects; no special attention was paid to research, advanced technologies or innovation. Since 1980, in the course of repeated revisions of the ERDF Regulation, more specific approaches were successfully introduced by the Commission:

1. Within the 'non-quota section' the approach of the so-called 'endogenous potential development' was developed. This approach puts major emphasis on innovation and technology transfer; measures of this type appeal in particular to regional and local authorities.
2. Since 1985 the new instrument of 'Community programmes' tried to link the development of 'less-favoured areas' closer to Community policies, including those for research and advanced technology as just described.

Development of Endogenous Potential

The approach of developing endogenous potential was evolved post-1979, after the second oil crisis. It became increasingly clear that in a protracted period of recession or low growth there is little sense in region policy relying exclusively on the traditional strategy of creating infrastructure and attracting one or more branch plants to a region (i.e. waiting for a cure to come from elsewhere). As geographically mobile investments are scarce in such a period, only the needs of a few regions or zones could be met in this way. An alternative strategy was to mobilise factors already available in the region - endogenous potential. Generally, this potential is found in small- and medium-sized firms or craft industries and also in tourism or unused natural resources.

Which activities does the European Commission support under this strategy, and by what measures? In general support is given to those activities which precede or follow industrial investment and for which SMEs do not have 'in-house' facilities comparable to big enterprises. These facilities include market research, consultancy for improvement of business organisation and production, promotion of technology transfer, common services and production and easing access to risk capital. Secondly, there are measures to support the improvement of the physical environment through the conversion of old factory buildings into workshops where space and services can be provided for young entrepreneurs in order to facilitate their entry into the business world.

Three important features of this concept of support should be highlighted:

1. In contrast to the classical approach of regional policy, development of endogenous potential is a 'bottom-up' approach. It allows local and regional authorities to be involved in the reconversion or development efforts and to take initiatives ('forces vives'). As a matter of fact, this approach cannot be efficiently applied without strong support from local authorities and agencies of all kinds.
2. The approach fits into the concept of general innovation which does not depend on high performance in a specific technical area but on broad acceptance and implementation of innovation and its integration into the regional or local

economy.

3. Through its support mechanisms the EC furnishes aid to the different elements for endogenous potential development without prescribing to national and regional authorities how to organise them. The European Commission refrained from such prescriptions because the individual situations, structures and cultures within Europe are too different for a single approach to be imposed. There can, however, be no doubt that a carefully considered, inter-related a-priori organisation of the various elements deserves to be encouraged because it tends to be more efficient. For this reason the Commission supported the establishment of Business Innovation Centres (BICs).

The concept of endogenous potential has been applied by the Community since 1980. Within the framework of the so-called 'non-quota' section of the European Regional Development Fund four specific measures were established for the reconversion of areas of industrial decline (shipbuilding, iron and steel, textile and clothing and fishing areas). Almost all countries of the Community have benefitted from these measures. Given the broad acceptance of this approach within member states and by the Commission, it was taken over, on the occasion of the Fund revision on 1 January 1985, from the 'non-quota' section into the general Fund section in order to allow for a broader application. Thereafter national governments could apply it at their own request. At the same time the Commission continued to apply and develop it within the new instrument of 'Community programmes'.

Community Programmes

According to Article 7 of the new Fund Regulation, the second new instrument, Community programmes, aimed to provide a better link between the Community's objectives for structural development or conversion of regions and the objectives of other Community policies. Community programmes are, generally speaking, a continuation of the special measures of the 'non-quota' section. They differ in so far as they link regional policy not only to certain classical industrial policies (steel, textiles etc.), for which the EC in the light of Community treaties has a special responsibility, but also to new developing policies of the Community including those confirmed within the Single European Act (research and technology development; environment). The programmes STAR and VALOREN, adopted by the Council of Ministers in November 1986, which deal with advanced telecommunications and with the exploitation of endogenous energy potential, constitute a first application of this approach.

The STAR programme is based on the idea that advanced telecommunication services, which the Community is aiming to establish on the lines of a commonly defined strategy in Europe over the next ten years, offer, if properly administered, a unique chance to link 'less-favoured' peripheral regions of the Community better to central markets. This idea is supported by two facts. Firstly, certain advanced telecommunication services are distance-independent and therefore, for the first time in the history of communications, will diminish or abolish the disadvantage of distance to remote areas. Secondly, the cost of modern means of communication (eg. by 'broadband' cable) will be considerably lower than that of any comparable means of communication known up to today. In order to ensure that regional and local economies draw the maximum advantage from these new factors a series of promotion measures has been provided by the STAR programme. By mobilising local and regional initiatives these measures should create the critical mass of demand which is necessary to justify the infrastructure cost and the lack of which is often a hindrance to undertaking the investment.

The VALOREN programme starts from the fact that those member states of the EC that have the severest difficulties in implementing the general objectives of Community energy policy (reduction of dependence on oil, of consumption of energy in general, stronger exploitation of renewable energy forms etc.) coincide to a high degree with member states characterised by the severest regional problems. At the same time they have a considerable unused potential in the fields of renewable energies and the rational use of energies. The VALOREN programme aims at mobilising this potential. The field of local energy resources is one in which the usefulness of a strategy of indigenous development can be particularly well demonstrated. In many cases the local energy resource taken individually is not competitive with energy supply from outside. By considering resources and users in a local and regional context and by combining different users in a network, competitiveness can be obtained, dependence from outside diminished and the local and regional economic base be reinforced.

PERSPECTIVES ON FUTURE DEVELOPMENT

In the immediate future the EC will apply and develop the instruments with which it has been provided in the framework of the revised Fund Regulation of 1985. Within this framework member states can apply for: (1) national programmes of Community interest which allow for a multiannual cofinancing of regional and local packages of development or restructuring measures; (2) schemes for endogenous potential development, as described above; and (3) individual projects as in the past.

The Commission will propose further Community programmes based on Article 7 of the Fund Regulation. It intended to present in 1987:

1. Two programmes for steel and for shipbuilding areas. These programmes will put the new EC members, Spain and

Portugal, on the same footing as the Ten with regard to specific Community measures. They should also allow reinforcement of the existing special measures in those areas already covered and particularly struck by the continuing crisis in the two sectors in question.

2. A programme to provide a better link between the Community's regional policy and research and technology policy (STRIDE). The need for such a programme arises from, among others, the fact that research and technology capacities are distributed very unequally in the EC, hindering the 'least-favoured' countries from participating in the progress envisaged for the Community. This programme should, therefore, permit poorer and declining regions to improve their research and technology capability and thus enhance their economic development or restructuring efforts. It should assure a better participation of those areas in the major research and technology development effort which is at present undertaken within the Community by member states and the Community itself (see earlier).

On the whole, programme-financing should play an increasing role in the ERDF and gradually replace projects, up to a certain degree.

The further development of the European Regional Development Fund will largely depend on the outcome of the so-called 'cohesion' debate arising from the Single European Act, which by February1987 had been adopted by practically all member states of the Community. Being aware of the problems raised by the successive enlargements of the Community towards the South, as well as of the tensions that the achievement of a common internal market by 1992 may create, the Community has committed itself to a major effort to strengthen its internal equilibrium. It has undertaken in Article 130 D of the Single European Act to revise the existing structural funds with a view 'to clarify and rationalise tasks...', 'to increase their efficiency and to coordinate their activities between themselves...'. Within this discussion four major aims appear to be of particular relevance:

1. A considerable increase (absolute and relative to the total Community budget) of the financial resources available for structural policies and their medium-term programming within a coherent framework;
2. A further concentration of the financial means on the 'least-favoured' areas, entailing a new balance between 'least-favoured' areas and areas of industrial development;
3. A generalisation of the so-called 'integrated programmes' approach, including all structural funds, and trying to achieve a higher efficiency of Community intervention through synergetic effects.
4. More direct contacts between the Commission and regional and local authorities in planning and implementing

structural measures.

It is obvious that the 'cohesion debate' will affect all fundamental relations - North/South, developing/reconverting regions, centralised/decentralised approach - implied in Community structural policy. It is a major challenge to the Community, and the outcome may influence its path for a considerable period.

NOTES

1. European Commission, Second Periodic Report on the Social and Economic Situation of the Regions of the Community (Brussels, 1984).
2. Jean Fourastie, Le Grand Espoir du 20eme Siecle (PUF, Paris, 1958)
3. European Commission, Towards a European Technology Community (COM 85/350, Brussels, 1985).
4. European Commission, Strengthening the Technological Base and Competitiveness of Community Industry (COM 85/84, Brussels, 1985).
5. RACE, a programme for research in advanced telecommunications, is intended to permit the Community to stay in the forefront of communications technology. BRITE, a programme on basic research and industrial technology, aims to stimulate activity in the development and dissemination of basic technologies (new materials, computerised design, joining techniques) used by a number of traditional industries.
6. P. Keeble et.al., Centrality, Peripherality and EEC Regional Development (University of Cambridge, Cambridge, 1983).
7. For example, the existence of special employment maintenance measures, such as the Cassa di Integrazione in Italy.
8. Centre for Urban and Regional Development Studies, Industrial Decline in the Regions of the European Community (University of Newcastle, Newcastle, unpublished).
9. Centre for Urban and Regional Development Studies, The Effects of New Information Technology on the Less-Favoured Regions of the Community (Regional Policy series no.23, University of Newcastle, Newcastle).

Chapter Four

SMEs, RESEARCH AND DEVELOPMENT AND TECHNOLOGY POLICIES AND THE EUROPEAN COMMUNITY: ISSUES IN IMPLEMENTATION

Peter Aitken

This chapter provides a brief overview of the development of small- and medium-sized enterprise (SME) policy by the European Community (EC) institutions; an analysis of the emerging role of SMEs within various EC policies and funding instruments - with particular emphasis on technology support and research and development (R&D); a case study of the development and implementation of SME policy in the Strathclyde Region - with particular reference to the Strathclyde Business and Innovation Centre; and some concluding comments. Its objectives are to offer a better appreciation of the origins of present interest in SMEs; to show that an SME focus exists in virtually every Community policy area; to stimulate awareness of the problems of converting EC policy into practice in areas where a number of SME agencies already exist; and to awaken policy makers and analysts to the roles of some of the trans-national support agencies, such as the SME Task Force, the TII (the European Association for Technology Transfer, Innovation and Industrial Information), EVCA (the European Venture Capital Association) and EBN (the European Business and Innovation Centre Network). For this paper the European Investment Bank's (EIB) definition of an SME has been used: an SME is an independent firm with less than 500 employees whose fixed assets (net of depreciation) are less than 75m ECU (£45m) and in whose capital structure large enterprises hold no more than a one-third participation.

DEVELOPMENT OF EC POLICY FOR SMEs

Within this chapter, with its focus on the Community's recent SME policy, it is possible only to outline the development of the policy from its beginning in 1970. In that year the European Commission presented its Memorandum on Industrial Policy (the Colonna Report) to the European Council and the other consultative bodies. The comprehensive approach to industrial policy outlined in the Colonna Report was too much for the member states at that time and the broad policy proposals fell (Commission 1970). SME policy development continued, nevertheless, with a study begun in 1971 by the Economic and Social Committee (ECOSOC) on the Situation of Small- and Medium-Sized Undertakings in the European Community. This exercise was the first attempt at highlighting the problems facing SMEs, and it prompted the Commission to introduce appropriate assistance measures (ECOSOC 1974). The most significant development was the declaration of 1983 as the European Year of the Small- and Medium-Sized Enterprises (EYSME), an initiative designed to promote a greater awareness of the problems of SMEs (ECOSOC 1983). Early in 1984, the Commission responded to the interest in SMEs during EYSME by producing a review of existing Community policy with respect to SMEs (Commission 1984a). This initiative was endorsed by the European Council at its meeting in Brussels in March 1985, indicating that the formation and development of SMEs was to be one of the four fields of priority action.

The outcome was the establishment by the Commission in September 1985 of a working party consisting of representatives from all Directorates-General concerned with SMEs. It was charged with devising measures to promote the creation or the expansion of firms, to simplify regulations and to provide SMEs with support from Community financial instruments. The working party submitted its conclusions to the Commission in November 1985 (Commission 1985a). Early in 1986, the Commission made one of its Commissioners, for the first time, specifically and directly responsible for SMEs. In the same month a group of interested Commission officials was set up under the chairmanship of Mr Abel Matutes - the Commissioner who had been given responsibility for SMEs. Under his direction the Commission began to work on the preparation of a new Community policy for SMEs. Mr Matutes was on record as saying that his policy would not be one of direct subsidy to business but would use existing resources to help provide a new and better small-firms service. Also he was not interested in proposing projects that could be carried out better at the national level. 'It must be a policy designed together with small businessmen and not something which is imposed from above' (British Business 1986a). It is the need for contact with business that has prompted the call in March 1987 for the 28 pilot Community-funded Business Information Centres to provide a two-way flow of information (Official Journal 1987a).

In June 1986 an independent SME Task Force was established within the Commission with a staff of 20 and a provisional budget of 30m ECU for 1987. Its role was to co-ordinate all relevant activities within the Commission, as well as to help with the establishment, at European level, of the necessary machinery for solving SMEs' practical problems. Following earlier EC concern about the need to protect SMEs from excessive red tape and paperwork (first highlighted in the SME reports prepared by the European Parliament in 1977 and 1982) the Task Force paid particular attention to this area. Its objectives were: (1) to assess the implications of new Community proposals for enterprise, job creation and costs of compliance; (2) to see how simplification of existing legislation could help SMEs; (3) to simplify the administrative, fiscal and legal environment for SMEs by better co-ordination and liaison within the Commission and with SME representative organisations; and (4) to promote the convergence of national and EC policies.

This concern about reducing the impact of bureaucracy on SMEs led the Commission in 1986 to require that any proposal likely to affect SMEs should include a statement outlining such things as the likely impact on company competitiveness and employment. As part of this new programme an independent study was undertaken for the

Commission on the burdens imposed by existing Community legislation in a number of areas, including taxation, environmental and social legislation. This evaluation incorporated the results of interviews with businesses and contained a cost/benefit analysis of the effects on business of Community legislation. Its final report emerged in 1987.

At the beginning of August 1986, the Commission published its draft proposals for an Action Programme for SMEs (Commission 1986a). The programme laid down guidelines for Community action with respect to SMEs and set out a number of projects and courses of action for both the Community and the member states. The programme aimed, over a two-year period, to provide motivation for future action not only by the Commission but by all organisations - public and private - concerned with support for SMEs. In short, the Action Programme was the culmination of over a decade of developments aimed at shaping EC policies towards SMEs. In November the Council of Ministers adopted a Resolution on the Action Programme. This Resolution approved the main lines of policy and the strategy outlined in the programme. The caveat, however, was that agreement was subject to approval of individual proposals by the Council of Ministers, particularly their financial implications. The Commission was to report to the Council periodically on its operations in the programme; and to establish a standing arrangement to exchange information between it and the member states on schemes in progress and on plans to improve the business environment (Official Journal 1986a).

The SME Action Programme falls into parts, each serving one of two major EC objectives. The first part deals with Community action to provide a favourable environment for the creation and development of SMEs. This action involves positive measures to promote the spirit of enterprise as well as steps to render the regulatory framework in which businesses operate less bureaucratic and costly. The second part of the Action Programme will initially develop a set of six integrated projects intended to provide direct help for the creation and development of businesses. This exercise involves developing projects which introduce a special SME component to existing Community and national programmes. The six project areas are as follows: (1) training; (2) information; (3) exports; (4) creation of business and the promotion of innovation; (5) inter-firm and inter-regional co-operation; and (6) provision of capital.

Paralleling this activity, in August 1986, the Energy Section of ECOSOC published an Information Note on Techology, R&D and its importance to SMEs and the problems encountered in transferring technology to SMEs. The Section hoped that the report would distinguish between those aspects of technological assistance to SMEs that are the prerogative of the member states and those that should be encouraged and regulated by the Commission. The report was also seen as providing a checklist and stimulus for further discussion on the efficiency and prosperity of SMEs (ECOSOC 1986).

The interest in deregulation continued with the European Council at its meeting in London in December 1986. It not only endorsed deregulation activity but also sought action to ensure that existing EC schemes operate effectively for small firms; enable member states to learn from each other's experience; help the establishment of new small firms; and improve the access of small firms to new technology. On this last point, the Council noted the approval of the 1.5bn ECU innovation loan scheme (under the provisions of the New Community Instrument (NCI IV)) for investment in new technology by SMEs.

The Commission also began to implement measures to promote the development of SMEs through existing or new financial instruments by means of grants or loans. The process had begun with the EIB, the European Coal and Steel Community (ECSC), European Regional Development Fund (ERDF) and then the European Social Fund (ESF), and appeared most recently in the Agricultural Structures proposals and the Technology programme. The early focus of the SME activities stemmed undoubtedly from the 'indigenous development' measures introduced under the ERDF 'non-quota' measures. Most recently the Commission has been looking for new ways of financing innovation and enterprise, initially through the EIB and then by encouraging the development of the European venture capital sector, and now by entering the market directly to stimulate the use of private-sector funds with its 'financial engineering' activities (Commission 1986b). The development of this range of measures is discussed in detail in the next section.

REFERENCES TO SMEs IN EC POLICIES

This section illustrates the interest in SMEs contained in existing or pending EC legislation. For the purposes of presentation the policies are grouped as follows: (1) regional and employment policies; (2) industrial policies; (3) fiscal and legal policies; (4) energy policies; (5) research and development; (6) technology and innovation; and (7) education and vocational training.

Regional and Employment Policies

European Regional Development Fund

The ERDF provides grant aid to eligible infrastructure and industrial projects in the nationally-defined Assisted Areas. Under the 1984 Regulation, support of up to 50 per cent (55 per cent in some instances) is directed towards:

1. Community Programmes: intended to serve Community objectives and policies by promoting a regional dimension to sectoral policies or assisting in resolving serious problems in particular regions (see below).
2. National Programmes: are prepared by member state governments in conjunction with local and public authorities and statutory undertakings to serve both national and Community objectives (see below).
3. Projects: may be single or groups of projects above a 50,000 ECU threshold.

4. Studies: Article 24 of the Regulation provides for 50-70 per cent funding towards the cost of studies which relate to the operations of the Fund.

The Community Programmes are (initially at least) to provide a regional dimension to developing EC policy areas, such as environment and R&D. A feasibility study for the latter is already underway (Goddard 1987), and a study for the former is due to begin during 1987. The Commission is also hoping to bring forward a programme for Industrial Reconversion Zones in order to extend the 'non-quota' measures. Proposals for the first two Community programmes were approved in November 1986 (Official Journal 1986b). They are the STAR - telecommunications - and the VALOREN - energy development and saving - programmes. Article 4 provisions in both programmes contain specific references to increasing take-up by SMEs, and to providing support by means of studies and advisory services (Commission 1986d, 1986e).

By December 1986 four UK National Programmes of Community Interest (NPCI) had been approved - Shildon, Glasgow, the Mersey Basin and Tayside (Aitken 1986a). These programmes contain a co-ordinated set of measures directed towards infrastructural, environmental, tourism and employment projects.

Article 15 measures are intended to promote indigenous business development. They can be made as part of an NPCI or as applications in their own right. The proposals must be a consistent set of measures directed towards promoting and encouraging the development of SMEs. The Shildon NPCI, for example, contains an extensive set of proposals intended to encourage new business starts, provide aid to existing SMEs through business support and management training, and the construction of small workshops etc (Sedgefield District Council 1986). Approval to implement this package of measures, which contains items under both Article 15 and Article 19, was agreed in December 1986 (Johnston 1986). The Department of the Environment is keen to emphasise that the Shildon decision does not create a precedent. Five other Article 15 programmes have been approved. The first is for business development services associated with a food park in Morso in the north west of Denmark; the second is in Limburg province in Belgium and is to assist in the start-up phase of six business and service centres; the third is in Cork where the Business Innovation Centre received support for a range of business and technology initiatives; the fourth is for the Nord Tek programme which intends to promote the use and awareness of the new technologies in SMEs in North Jutland; finally, for Northern Ireland for support towards a range of business support, advisory and property initiatives, plus the construction and equipping of a technology centre (British Business 1987).

The ERDF non-quota (or specific) measures, progressively introduced between 1982-85 in certain steel, ship-building, textile and a limited number of fisheries areas, gave the Commission its first experience of multi-annual funding programmes. These programmes were intended to provide assistance towards environmental and SME business support measures. In the UK the business support measures (finance, marketing and technical advice) have been provided by private-sector firms or jointly funded development agencies. These programmes will cease during 1988, or sooner if the available funds are fully allocated (Aitken 1985). The ERDF Annual Report for 1985 pays particular attention to the success of the package of SME support measures introduced in Scotland in 1983, under the title of the Better Business Service. In the eligible areas in the Walloon region in Belgium approximately fifty companies have a 'technological innovation officer', 80 per cent of whose salary is paid for by the Regional Authorities and the ERDF. The officer is responsible for identifying the innovation potential within the business and implementing projects such as introducing new technology, purchasing a licence, research etc. The programme for the Walloon region also has provision for technical/economic studies. In the Mezzogiornio there is a programme aimed at distributing information about innovation in a wide range of areas to SMEs (Commission 1986c, p67). Particular provision is made for access to databases, publication of a technical bulletin and the organisation of seminars.

European Social Fund (ESF)

The 1984 Annual Report noted that a total of 179 applications were made for the vocational training provisions for persons employed in SMEs. Under the innovatory heading there was one SME/technology-related application involving projects from Calderdale Metropolitan District Council and the Institut de Gestion Sociale (Institute for Co-operative Management) in France to train specialists in new production and management technologies in order to promote the introduction and use of these new technologies by SMEs (Commission 1985b, p92, 93). In the 1985 report applications for retraining in SMEs as a result of the introduction of new technology increased substantially, while training in SMEs linked to Community R&D priorities increased by a third over the 1984 figures. The innovatory heading of the Fund had applications from most member states for projects to ensure the successful introduction of new technology in production and management in SMEs, for example from Strathclyde Regional Council, South Jutland Amtskommune (Denmark) and the Reggio Emilia Chamber of Commerce (Italy). In Belgium a separate programme dealt with the training of unemployed managers who intended to start a business in the advanced technology sectors (Commission 1986f, pp52-3, p98).

In a recent report on the Future of the Social Fund by the West German MEP Heinke Salisch (European Parliament 1986, p9) there are calls for better ESF assistance to be directed towards SMEs. The report also calls for a statement on which new technologies should be given priority in the ESF guidelines. The report's recommendations received an almost unanimous vote of support when it was debated in September 1986.

Industrial Policies

In February 1986, the Commission published a communication entitled

'Improving Competitiveness and Industrial Structures in the Community'. This report attempted to identify the key elements determining the Community's competitiveness and the factors likely to assist in its improvement. A section of the document referred to the role of SMEs, acknowledging the major contribution that they can make to 'growth and employment' (Commission 1986g, p3).

In July 1985, the Commission published its proposals for 'Stronger Community Structural Measures to Assist Steel Re-structuring Areas' (Commission 1985c). The aim was to promote alternative employment opportunities in the steel closures areas. Particular emphasis was placed on the role of SMEs in providing new jobs, encouraging the establishment of further Business and Innovation Centres (BIC) (see later), encouraging sub-contracting and assisting local employment initiatives. The Action Programme of 1986 (Commission 1986h) set out the steel measures in more detail and identified seventeen proposed priority integrated action areas, five of which were in the UK (Yorkshire-Humberside, South Wales, North Wales, North East, Strathclyde).

Fiscal and Legal Policies

In July 1985, the Council adopted Regulation 2137/85 which permits the establishment of a new form of association, to be known as a European Economic Interest Grouping (EEIG), from July 1989 (Official Journal 1985a). The EEIG is intended to encourage co-operation between companies (of up to 500 employees), incorporated in different member states, by enabling them to enter into loose relationships or groupings. The objective of the EEIG is to provide a wider market for the products or services concerned, encourage joint research, promote bulk buying of basic materials and joint tendering for contracts. Members will be free to join or leave the EEIG at will.

In June 1986, as part of the Commission's new initiatives to promote investment in SMEs, it was agreed that a European 'financial engineering' company - to be known as EUROCOFIN (ECF) - was to be set up by twelve long-term credit institutions in the Community in collaboration with the Commission, the EIB and the European Venture Capital Association (EVCA) (see below). The objective of the ECF is to support the more 'ambitious' SME initiatives (preferably trans-national) in the Community. It is expected that the company will be in operation from 1987. ECF will help small businesses to launch new initiatives against payment of a processing fee. The aim is to encourage the accessibility of Community and private financial instruments so as to offer, and to encourage the market to offer, new forms of financing, embracing innovative projects, technological projects and enterprise developments (Commission 1986b).

Energy Policies

Since 1978 the Commission has provided limited support for an annual series of energy demonstration projects. Although theoretically open to all companies, the complexities of the application process have tended to discourage applications from SMEs. In order to overcome this problem Article 5.1 of the revised Regulation of 1985 governing the projects permitted applications to be prepared and submitted on their behalf by independent technology advisers (Official Journal 1985b). In September 1986 a call was made for companies and experts to apply for designation as technical providers under the terms of the Energy Demonstration and Hydrocarbons Development Programmes (Official Journal 1986c).

A Commission Communication of 1986, entitled 'Towards a European Policy for Energy Efficiency in Industrial Firms', contained a number of references to the need for energy saving in SMEs, pointing to the success of the 'energy bus' test programme in this work (Commission 1986i, p25). The subsequent Council Resolution noted the Commission's intention to give a major emphasis to applications for demonstration projects support made by SME and industrial concerns generally (Official Journal 1986d).

Research and Development (R&D)

R&D was one of the main topics for discussion at the European Council meeting in Milan in July 1985. As an aid to discussion the Commission published a Memorandum entitled 'Towards a European Technology Community' (Commission 1985d). It indicated that SMEs had an essential part to play in this development strategy because of their adapatability and capacity for innovation. R&D programmes cover advanced information technology, telecommunications, bio-technology, materials research, transport, environment and energy research.

SME participation in R&D projects was first referred to in the Basic Research in Industrial Technologies for Europe (BRITE) programme launched in 1985 (Commission 1983a, pp13, 39, 78). This programme was intended to assist in increasing the competitiveness of established manufacturing industries such as machine tools, chemicals, motor vehicles, ship-building and flexible materials. The concern for SME participation has been carried through into the selection and evaluation process. The first call for applications attracted 559 proposals, of which some 18 per cent were from SMEs, 40 per cent from firms with over 500 employees and 42 per cent from research institutes and universities.

During the preparatory phase in 1983 and first two years of implementation of the European Strategic Programme for Research in Information Technology (ESPRIT) 866 proposals involving 236 partners were accepted. SMEs are involved in 53 per cent of projects, in 60 per cent of which they are undertaking more than 25 per cent of the work (these figures relate to numbers of projects not value). The areas in which they are best represented are software technology and advanced information processing, followed by office automation systems and computer integrated manufacture. Of the five sub-sectors in the programme, microelectronics is the area in which they are least involved because of the high level of investment required (Official Journal 1986e). In its review of the ESPRIT programme the Commission noted the impact of the programme on the technological base of the Community

(Commission 1986j).

The Second R&D Framework Programme (1987-91), with its emphasis on improving industrial competitiveness, envisages SMEs as having a role to play both in certain of the research programmes as well as in the application and dissemination of the results (Commission 1986k, pp23-24). The whole future of the programme was, however, brought into question during November/December 1986, with a continuing dispute between the Commission and the Council of Research Ministers over the size of the R&D budget.

To encourage SMEs to take part in Community R&D projects, the Commission introduced in 1983 the concept of 'expressions of interest' as a means by which SMEs could make contact with Commission services without embarking on the formal and potentially expensive application process (Official Journal 1983a). The second call for proposals under the BRITE programme issued a call for 'expressions of interest' in mid 1986. This process was to enable prospective applicants to get advice on the eligibility of their projects. In addition, the Commission indicated its willingness to help arrange partnerships based on the details provided. The call for proposals was made in January 1987 (Official Journal 1987b).

Technology and Innovation

In an attempt to improve the competitiveness of European products, a three-year plan was approved in October 1983 to develop trade in the new technologies and ensure their exploitation in the Community, particular reference being made to SMEs in this role (Official Journal 1983b). The 'Plan for the Trans-National Development of the Supporting Infrastructure for Innovation and Technology Transfer' was launched in January 1984, with three broad aims:

1. To ensure co-operation and cohesion between national industrial innovation agents, private and public alike.
2. To create, at Community level, shared or joint services in the areas of training, information and communication.
3. To secure information exchanges between member state governments on national and regional innovation measures.

As part of the implementation of the Trans-National Plan, the Commission has promoted the establishment of the European Venture Capital Association (EVCA), the European Association for Technology Transfer, Innovation and Industrial Information (TII), as well as the formation of the European Business and Innovation Centre Network (EBN) with assistance from DG XVI. TII, which was established in 1984, is a private non-profit organisation whose primary aim is the stimulation of innovation within enterprises (not just SMEs) and the promotion of technology transfer. It has over 200 members. EVCA aims to develop co-operation between venture capital companies in different member states. It had some 35 founding members, with portfolio investments of 1.5bn ECU. By mid-1986, membership had increased to 150. It aimed to support innovative projects with development potential on a European scale. In the spring of 1985, the EVCA announced that the Commission was to support a pilot scheme for innovative projects linking SMEs in more than one member state. This was termed the European Venture Consort Scheme (British Business 1986b). Despite the success of the scheme, and the support of an independent assessment of the need for further venture capital provision, the proposals for a European Venture Capital Fund remain to be implemented.

Proposals for business and innovation centres (BIC) in the Community began within the Commission's Regional Policy Directorate-General (DGXVI) during 1983. The concept was based upon the provision of high-technology managed workshops which could promote the development of innovators and ideas to the stage of commercial exploitation within a sheltered, supportive environment. In January 1984 DGXVI published its Model for Business and Innovation Centres (Commission 1984b). By November 1984 a non-profit organisation, the European Business Centre Network (EBN), was created by a group of twelve science parks and innovation centres. The Commission agreed to financially support the Network to the extent of covering any shortfall on its operating expenses until the end of 1987. The EBN model envisages the centres as being self-financing after 5-7 years, by means of rental income from letting of premises, consultancy fees and royalties from projects successfully launched through the BIC (Dekker 1985, 1987). By the end of 1985 thirteen centres had been established, with six in the ECSC priority areas and two in other steel closure areas, with a further twenty at various stages of development (Commission 1986h, p11). By early 1987, there were eight BICs in the UK. The target is to have 100 BICs by 1988, 25 of which will be in the UK (Hayton 1987). Under Budget line 543 (formerly 7731) the Commission provides grants of 50 per cent (generally up to a maximum of 150,000 ECU) to assist in the preparation and launch of a BIC. Funding is made available on a contract basis between the Commission and a sponsor. In January 1987, the Commission published a proposal for a further round of BICs during the period 1987-89. The proposal also calls for an extension of deficit funding for the EBN if required (Official Journal 1987c).

The Trans-National Plan provided also for the organisation of trans-national seminars to encourage new development; the organisation of group visits for heads of firms to technology fairs in other member states; and the establishment of links between technology and management advisory services to SMEs in different member states. By mid-1986 about 30 kinds of action had been taken. They can be grouped under four main headings:

1. Trans-national networks of specialists in all aspects of the innovation process, from the invention to the financing and marketing of new products and services.
2. Dissemination of information, including a communications link, between important technology transfer centres in the EC.
3. Trans-national conferences on technology transfer, of which there had been 40 by the end of 1986.

4. Exchange of information and experience, including the establishment of working groups on design, on innovation aspects of patents and on the rejuvenation of mature industries (Official Journal 1986f).

In August 1986 the Commission announced its support for several new projects under the Trans-National Plan. Amongst these was a one-year pilot scheme to establish a network of national experts on the rejuvenation of traditional industries. They will study the ceramics, textiles and shoe and leather industries and pass on their conclusions to small firms in these sectors. A number of UK organisations have been awarded support under these technology measures, including Calderdale MBC - for its Transfer in European Enterprise (TEE) Programme in conjunction with BICs in Enschede, Liege and Nancy. In Scotland the Scottish Development Agency (SDA) and the Lanarkshire Industrial Field Executive (LIFE) are also involved in projects.

The follow-up programme for the period November 1986-December 1988 was titled the Strategic Programme for Innovation and Technology Transfer in Europe (SPRINT) (Commission 1986l). SPRINT will act as a transitional programme while proposals are drawn up for a more consistent innovation programme from 1989. The priorities for action are: (1) support for liaison between advisory bodies, particularly SMEs; (2) the organisation of trans-national activities and dissemination throughout the Community of information on innovation and technology transfer; (3) the transfer to industry of the results from R&D carried out in the public sector or financed by the public sector; (4) initiatives to develop opportunities for co-operation between firms, particularly SMEs; (5) stimulation of supply of, and demand for, transferable technologies using data bases, technology marts and technology fairs; (6) promotion of innovation in the rejuvenation of mature industries; (7) training of those specialist consultants in technology transfer, innovation management and financing of innovation and related fields who provide services mainly to SMEs; and (8) the role of local authorities in the creation of a favourable environment for innovation (Ibid, Annex 1).

Educational and Vocational Training

In 1985 the Commission published proposals for a Vocational Training Programme (Commission 1985e) consisting of a network of demonstration projects (to be funded from the ESF), a research programme and a series of study visits and exchanges. These proposals recognise the needs of SMEs and encourage the development of new approaches to training that aim at familiarising and retraining management in the implications and applications of the information technologies (Ibid, p3). The Commission has asked the European Centre for Work and Society to co-ordinate the 66-project network, called EuroTecneT (Harrison 1986).

The linking of education and training with R&D and technology developments was assisted by the political commitment to a European Technology Community (Commission 1985e) and its recognition of the need for suitable technology training provision. This document refers specifically to the role of specialised SMEs in technology developments (Ibid, p3), suggesting that they are sometimes overlooked in national schemes.

The Commission proposals for the COMETT (Community Action Programme in Education and Training Technology) programme aim to encourage better links between universities and industry in the provision of advanced training geared toward the new technologies, through university-industry training partnerships, staff and student exchanges and joint training projects (Commission 1985f; Kirchberger 1986). Within this overall programme the development of 'open-learning' training and 'up-dating' systems are seen as important to the needs of SMEs (Ibid, p11). The proposal was formally agreed in June 1986 with a budget of 45m ECU and a call for applications made in December 1986 (Official Journal 1986h).

A CASE STUDY OF THE DEVELOPMENT OF A NEW TECHNOLOGY PROGRAMME IN STRATHCLYDE REGION

This section of the chapter focuses on Strathclyde Regional Council's response to the challenge of preparing a technology/R&D strategy. It is worth remembering that Strathclyde Region contains roughly half the population of Scotland and has an area of 5000 sq. miles. It includes within its boundaries the industrial areas of Glasgow, lower Clydeside and Lanarkshire (Young and Greig 1985), as well as extensive rural and island areas. The Regional Council is well versed in the implementation of locally-based economic and social initiatives (Moore and Booth 1986a). These local initiatives stemmed from the two key objectives agreed by the Council in 1976: (1) economic regeneration and employment creation; and (2) the need to alleviate poverty and deprivation. The initial emphasis was on alleviating deprivation. However, by 1980, as it became clear that the Scottish Development Agency was not going to undertake economic regeneration at the level required, the Regional Council became increasingly active on this latter front. Initiatives have included: (1) the provision of small workshop units, including the development of New Enterprise Workshops which combine premises with technical and business support; (2) the provision of business advice and information; (3) employment grant schemes/new technology training (using ESF monies); (4) area-based actions; (5) development of the role of the Further Education Colleges to meet local business needs; and (6) development and support for co-operatives and community businesses.

The Strathclyde Region has long been recognised as one of the most deprived in the UK and indeed in Europe, witness the findings of the EC's Periodic Reports on the Social and Economic Situation in the Regions of Europe. The Regional Council has taken every opportunity to use EIB, ESF and ERDF funds to tackle this problem (Keating and Waters 1985, pp69-70). In 1983 the Regional Council made a successful bid for support for an Integrated Development Operations (IDO) preparatory study (Chorley 1986). This study was undertaken during 1983/4 and submitted to the European Commission in December 1984. The study identified the three principal weaknesses in the local economy as: a dependence on heavy manufacturing industries with poor growth prospects and continuing employment decline; a lack of internally-generated growth, particularly through SMEs; and the absence of high technology growth sectors within the local economy, and a low rate of technological innovation in the existing industrial base. The study's proposals sought to ensure the maximum take-up and effectiveness of national technology schemes; to harness the resources and expertise of local universities, colleges and research institutions to promote innovation in local industry - particularly amongst SMEs that lacked in-house R&D capability; and to upgrade vocational training facilities, including buildings and major items of equipment to support ESF-funded programmes for private-sector firms training in the new technologies. These proposals were taken from the IDO report and submitted as an element within the Glasgow NPCI, which received approval in November 1985. The intensity of the problems in Glasgow was recognised with the award of 55 per cent support.

By late 1985 the Regional Council began to refine its activities in the development of a business and technology strategy, spelling out the implications for education, training, business development and technological innovation. By March 1986 the view was being taken that, in general, regeneration through the absorption of technology into the region's economy could take place in two ways: (1) through the formation of new businesses by individuals or teams from technological centres in academic institutions and existing firms; and (2) by the upgrading and general improvement in products and processes within existing businesses through the introduction of improved technology.

The Regional Council was aware that considerable, if fragmented, action was already underway. It was itself active through the local enterprise agencies, its New Enterprise Workshops (NEW) and its FE Colleges. The SDA provided support through its small business development activities, contributions to enterprise agencies, area projects and technology transfer role. This latter role is directed at larger companies, through joint ventures, such as Strathclyde Technology Transfer Ltd and the West of Scotland Science Park (Reilly 1986). Higher education centres, particularly Strathclyde University and Paisley College of Technology, were also active. The latter was involved through its role as a Better Technical Service provider, with small business training and support from its (in part) ERDF-funded resource centre (Glasgow Herald, 29 January 1987, pp12-13). Competing proposals for BICs were also being prepared by local enterprise trusts. The Regional Council sought to increase its contribution to promoting business and technology developments by building upon its own and other agencies' resources and integrating new initiatives into a framework of support.

Existing Infrastructure

The Regional Council began by reviewing the available resources to develop this programme. This review revealed that:

1. Research and education facilities existed on two levels: within higher education institutions and establishments such as the National Engineering Laboratory (NEL), Paisley College and Strathclyde University, where facilities existed for assisting in the testing and development of new products and processes; whilst more craft-orientated facilities were available in the New Enterprise Workshops and some FE colleges.
2. Financial assistance for the investigation and development of specific applications of technology to businesses was available through a variety of national- and EC-funded schemes - including the Better Business and Better Technical Services. The intention of these schemes was to supplement and draw out commitment from the companies themselves (Keating and Waters 1985, p76; Aitken 1985).
3. At the point of launching a prototype into full commercial production there were a number of venture capital sources as well as the conventional banks to which an approach could be made for start-ups and working capital.
4. A network of agencies offering business support existed in the region, principally the local enterprise agencies, the SDA, some local authorities including the Regional Council, both directly and indirectly through the network of FE college-based Small Business Centres, as well as banks and accountants.

Proposed Programme

The Council envisaged a programme with three parts:

1. Technology Agencies (TA). The functions of such bureaux would be: (a) to increase business's awareness of, and access to, schemes for technology transfer and the funding sources available for related consultancy, investment and training activities; and (b) to make known opportunities available to entrepreneurs and researchers for collaboration with large firms, academic institutions and venture capitalists. These functions were to be performed by officers working in the field with selected sectors or companies. In addition, seminars, conferences and exhibitions would be held to disseminate information and to promote co-operation between clients. Three alternative organisational arrangements were considered: (1) a Strathclyde-wide organisation operating from a central location with specialised field officers on an area or sector basis; (2) a network of three sub-regional agencies based on North Lanarkshire, West Strathclyde and Glasgow, each with a staff of three or four, backed up by a region-wide liaison group or central TA; and (3) a role for

individual enterprise agencies as technology agencies with an overall co-ordinating body to direct affairs at a regional level. Given the need to co-ordinate the technology and business development activities, the staff of the agency/agencies was envisaged as working closely with local enterprise agencies, the SDA, IDS and local authorities.

2. Business and Innovation Centres (BIC). The provision of such centres at this stage was based on the concept of a property-based facility - effectively a 'high-tech' managed workshop. Possible locations were thought to be the university or college campuses, or other public-sector institutions. There was uncertainty over whether there was a demand for 'high-tech' premises. If this demand was available, some link to the suggested configuration of TAs was considered a logical development. The difference between the client embryonic firms using the BIC and those using the existing new enterprise workshops, like Govan Workspace and similar developments, was seen as residing in the much higher use of technology and academic expertise and in the growth potential of the former. Close liaison between the staff at the BIC and the TA, both on a project basis and in overall terms, was seen as essential. Together these two organisations were seen as providing a comprehensive advisory service covering all aspects of business development, technological development and training. Considered alongside the BIC proposals were separate proposals for a specialised form of BIC to advance the use of CADCAM (Computer-Aided Design, Computer-Aided Manufacture) facilities in the Region.
3. 'Shop Windows'. An 'open-door' approach to technology was seen as essential to both broaden the possible range of products, processes and clients and reduce the Strathclyde Region's dependency on company managers who, in many cases, had already demonstrated a reluctance to recognise and grasp the opportunities available.

This proposed framework was considered by the Regional Council which approved the idea of a BIC with supporting TA network (Scotsman, 3 April 1986). The two major changes involved the abandonment of the 'shop-window' concept and the separation of the CADCAM centre from this programme as an independent development. In April 1987 it was announced that the Institute for Computer Integrated Manufacturing (ICIM) was to be established at the University of Strathclyde. The Centre has attracted £1.8 million from the private and public sectors.

Competing Proposals

Underlying this analysis by the Regional Council was a need to evaluate the competing proposals for BICs in the Region that had emerged during 1985. Two enterprise trusts, Lanarkshire Industrial Field Executive (LIFE) and the Ardrossan, Salcoats and Stevenston Enterprise Trust

(ASSET), realising that certain 'innovative' projects required intensive support beyond that normally available from the trusts, opened discussions with DGXVI of the European Commission for support for two innovation centres. LIFE went on to approach the Regional Council, the SDA and BSC(I) for support for a feasibility study of a centre (plus supporting technology agency) for Lanarkshire and had undertaken a preliminary review of the demand for such services in Lanarkshire. Armed with this review negotiation was underway for substantial EEC funding plus support from the SDA and BSC(I). ASSET had been arguing that, on the basis of its experience (including an innovation panel, a NEW at Stevenston and an ESF-supported Integrated Innovation and Business Development Training Programme), a Scotland-wide BIC with a supporting 'technology-agency network' and managed workshops is needed. A separate proposal prepared by the Technology and Business Centre at Paisley College of Technology entered the field in 1985 (Wylie 1986). Meanwhile the Regional Council's review of available resources led it to conclude in early 1986 that the best option was the development of a supporting technology agency network throughout the Region. This network, consisting of colleges, universities and some enterprise trusts, was seen as assisting in the identification of clients.

The Strathclyde BIC

Following discussions with various possible sponsors, Strathclyde Regional Council approved in April 1986 its support for a one-year BIC preparatory and launch phase to investigate: how best to provide assistance; what form the assistance should take; what market there is for this type of assistance in Strathclyde; and to prepare the five-year business plan. First-year pilot phase costs of £336,000 were to be split between the sponsors, with the SDA, SRC, BSC(I) and British Coal Enterprises providing £30,000 each, an additional private-sector contribution of £60,000 being sought, with the Commission providing £156,500 as a one-off payment under Budget line 7731. In September 1986 the Chief Executive and two members of the executive staff moved into the BIC premises in the Templeton Business Centre in the east end of Glasgow. By November all staff recruitment (six in total, including support) was completed. The objective was to set up a fully operational BIC by the end of 1987 with a five-year programme of development. To facilitate the operation of the BIC, it was established as a company limited by guarantee, with approved enterprise agency status. The members and directors of the company are SDA, SRC, BSC(I) and British Coal Enterprises.

Although the EC money provided was a one-off payment to launch the BIC, it was anticipated that significant further funding from the ERDF (particularly Article 15), SPRINT and other technology programmes (like the second COMETT programme) would be required to sustain the BIC at an appropriate level of expenditure during the subsequent five years. The purpose of the business plan that was to be prepared during the one-year pilot phase was to plan the programme of work and to define the shortfall of funds (if any). What remains to be tested is whether a regional network of property-based services develops or whether the service is provided on an intellectual network basis with only limited property provision.

During this preparatory year BIC staff will be working with a restricted number of clients selected in conjunction with local enterprise trusts, Strathclyde and Glasgow Universities, Paisley College, Glasgow College and other FE centres, local authority industrial development units, banks, accountants, and other companies. The emphasis at this stage of the programme was on providing a complete package of assistance both to companies with fewer than 200 employees and to individual entrepreneurs with innovative ideas, initiative and commercial ambition. All clients must have the potential for £1 million turnover with export potential, in a 3-5 year period. The BIC staff envisage spending 20-40 days per project. Two initiatives begun by the BIC are the marketing, design and exporting initiative (MADE) and the detailed investigation of the scope to launch a venture capital club.

Unlike the classic model of a BIC (best developed in Liege) the Strathclyde proposal does not envisage the construction of new workshops as a major part of the BIC programme. The latter would only proceed if demand had been established. Given the level of existing provision and proposals for other developments, the BIC is investigating possible 'added-value' and 'promoter' roles for the BIC in property and property management. The option of a centre and satellites as opposed to three or four BICs spread throughout the Region is to be fully investigated as part of the first-year preparatory phase.

In order to provide this service the BIC staff consists of specialists who provide: (1) project appraisal, involving initial technical, financial, marketing and management appraisal of projects/ideas; (2) product development and technology search, identifying and resolving business, technological and product-development problems; (3) marketing analysis, planning and product design, with market research and preparation of marketing plans, including test marketing and product design and packaging; (4) appraisal of prospects i.e. preparation of business plans, including risk appraisal; (5) funding i.e. arrangement of appropriate grants and seed/venture capital; (6) training support, with assistance with start-up training and re-training for staff and company executives; and (7) implementation assistance, helping with the solution of manufacturing and production engineering problems and generally monitoring progress (Hawkes 1987).

CONCLUSIONS

This chapter set out to trace the development of EC policy towards SMEs; to examine the range of measures directed towards SMEs in a variety of policies, but with particular emphasis on technology; and to examine the development and implementation of technology policy in Strathclyde Region.

SME policy at the EC level developed from an industrial policy initiative in 1970. This broad-based proposal attracted little support from the member states or interest groups but provided the basis for policy which was developed by ECOSOC and the European Parliament. Increasingly the emphasis has focused on the role the SME sector can play in job creation and innovation. The importance of SMEs within the Community has been recognised by the appointment of a Commissioner responsible for SMEs and the establishment of the SME Task Force. Measures to encourage SMEs have appeared in all the Community structural funds and lending instruments, initially under the EIB and ECSC global loans provisions, the ERDF non-quota measures, the ESF and, most recently, under the ERDF Article 15 provisions. Within both the Commission and sponsored bodies there has also been the growth of a number of support agencies whose activities affect SMEs. These agencies include TII, EVCA and EBN. Co-ordination of Community policies has generally been poor (not just for SMEs), though the situation is better in the 35 or so areas where Integrated Development Operations (IDO) studies have been prepared. The case study of Strathclyde Region has illustrated this latter point. Similarly, the proposals for the Integrated Actions for the steel areas should result in an expansion of small business development.

The policy section and the case study of Strathclyde have illustrated that the initial emphasis in EC SME policy was on the business start-up phase. In Strathclyde Region there have been the (part) ERDF-funded Better Business Services as well as Regional Council schemes to encourage additional employment in existing firms using ESF money. More recently ESF money has been directed to promoting self-employment through the training schemes run by the local enterprise agencies. Most recently there has been the extension into new technology and vocational training by the Regional Council and Strathclyde University. Paralleling these initiatives the Council has been investigating how more general technology and innovation initiatives under the Trans-National Plan could be developed.

The recently-established Strathclyde BIC, with its supporting network of technology agencies, has a central role to play in this process. The problem is linking the creation of technology appropriate to the needs of SMEs to the use made of that technology by SMEs to manufacture novel products, or develop processes and services for which there is market demand. The 'technology-agency' approach, as proposed by Strathclyde, is a model worthy of detailed monitoring and evaluation, particularly given its commitment to both start-ups and existing businesses, the latter being the area where the largest number of jobs is likely to be created. Its management and co-ordination role that brings together the various local providers may be a central element in preventing SME 'policy overkill' in Strathclyde. This role is important as the impact of general, far less technology- and innovation-oriented, programmes for SMEs, as part of the regional programme of local economic regeneration, has yet to be assessed (Moore and Booth, 1986b, p69).

The emphasis throughout this chapter has been on the Technology/Innovation programme. The R&D programmes, although they encourage participation by SMEs, and have produced figures to support their 'success', do so mainly by counting numbers not the value of the project (ECOSOC 1986, p43). An ERDF 'non-quota' measure in south-west France involved funding for specialist advisers and the creation of technology transfer centres to promote the results and industrial applications of basic research. Other means of linking SMEs with universities and research institutes are possible: as one of the services offered by BICs; by using other private-public technical support agencies, including perhaps Regional R&D Promotion Councils/Regional Development Companies; and through an enhancement of the University-Enterprise Training Programme (UETP) links developed under the COMETT programme.

This question of how to disseminate and exploit the results of publicly-funded R&D in the EC was the subject of a Community-sponsored seminar held in Luxembourg in September 1986 (Connell 1986). On the specific topic of university research, papers were given by speakers from Brunel University, NIHE in Limerick and Deloitte Haskins and Sells. It is worth making the following general points about university/industry links: the university partner must benefit in academic terms - by publishing papers, etc; the industrial partner must benefit by getting exploitable information, products or personnel from the results; collaboration must be genuine; and the work must be technically advanced in the area it covers. Drawing out new SMEs from academic institutions is difficult. Typically small technology ventures start as research spin-offs run part-time by academics. They are relatively risk-free initially but run up against lack of commercial, financial and management experience, with resulting problems in raising venture capital. Yet the transition from start-up to rapidly growing businesses with growth potential can be as little as 3-4 years (Connell 1986).

In the next phase of the SPRINT programme there is an emphasis on design and on the application of new technology in the 'mature industries'. These are areas that are important to industries in all traditional industrial regions. The widespread dissemination of the results of these deliberations is essential, but how this is to be done remains vague. Potentially it could be through: the network of technology advisers set up by the TII initiatives; the network of BICs; networks of technology advisers set up by the ERDF 'non-quota' measures; and networks established under the UETP agreements.

This problem raises the general question of responsibility for technology policy and SMEs. Is it the responsibility of DGXVI through its indigenous development actions, developed under the non-quota and Article 15 provisions, or is it DGXIII through the SPRINT programme with its references to using local authorities as agents in the innovative process through 'their role in the creation of a favourable environment for innovation on a local level', and the linking of regional technology/advisory organisations in both the private and public sectors? Indeed, the TII and EBN are talking about data links between participants, and 'ideas' data-bases, as well as access to general business and commercial data-bases. Both organisations potentially need to use the Business Co-operation Network (BC-NET) that is being developed by the BCC. The SPRINT programme refers to the training of technology transfer/innovation consultants, while the ESF, under the innovatory programmes, has been co-funding rather a similar sounding scheme in Calderdale MBC.

It is interesting to note that a DGXVI-funded Study of the Effects of the New Information Technologies (NIT) on Less-Favoured Regions of the Community, carried out in 1982/3, states that existing technology policy lacks the regional dimension and that regional policy lacks the technology dimension (Commission 1984c, pp169-174). The present position has developed since 1983, with the implementation of the non-quota programmes, the SPRINT programme and the establishment of BICs.

Underlying these questions is the role of the SME Task Force. The Action Programme addresses some of the questions with its references to developing inter-firm and inter-regional links by promoting BICs, links between universities and firms through the COMETT programme, and technology transfer/innovation under the SPRINT programme, as well as by emphasising the potential for developing joint ventures through the BC-NET. Co-ordination of action is crucial if the programmes are to achieve their full potential. The experience of actions such as those outlined for Strathclyde, which reviewed existing services in business promotion, training and the application of technology and then developed proposals to 'fill the gaps', could be a useful input to the future development of policy by the SME Task Force.

ACKNOWLEDGEMENT

The author is grateful for the comments and suggestions made on earlier drafts by his colleague Keith Hayton, the assistance received from Diana Hart at the EC Office for Scotland in the checking of document references, and the comments received from Douglas Martyn, Chief Executive of Strathclyde Business Innovation Centre.

REFERENCES

Aitken, P. and McEldowney, J. (1985) 'The Evolution of Small Firm and Local Employment Initiative Policies by the EC', paper presented at the 8th National Small Business Policy and Research Seminar, University of Ulster, 21-23 November

Aitken, P. (1985) ERDF Non-Quota Operations in Scotland, Briefing Note 6, The Planning Exchange, Glasgow

Aitken, P. and McEldowney, J. (1986) 'A Synthesis of EC Policy and Implementation Measures for SMEs', paper presented at the 9th National Small Business Policy and Research Seminar, Gleneagles, 24-26 November

Aitken, P. and Johnston, D. (1986) EC Policies and Practice in Relation to the Traditional Industrial Regions in Europe, Research Paper No 11, The Planning Exchange, February

Aitken, P. (1986a) ERDF-One Year On, Briefing Note 10, The Planning Exchange, Glasgow

British Business (1986a) 'Cutting Through the Red Tape', British Business, Vol 23 (8), 21 November, p.10

British Business (1986b) 'Cross Frontier Venture Scheme', British Business, Vol 22 (29), August, p.9

British Business (1987) 'EC Backs NI Technology Centre at Queen's College', British Business, Vol 24 (12), March, p.12

Budd, S. (1986) A Guide to the Maze, Inro Press, Edinburgh

Chorley, S. (1986) 'A View from a Regional Council: Strathclyde' in P. Aitken (ed), The ERDF - One Year On, Briefing Note 10, The Planning Exchange, Glasgow

Commission of the European Communities (1970) Industry Policy in the Community: Memorandum from the Commission to the Council (The Colonna Report), COM(70)100, CEC, Brussels, March

Commission of the European Communities (1983a) Proposal for a Council Decision on a Multi-Annual R&D Programme in the Field of Basic Technological Research, COM(83)350, CEC, Brussels, June

Commission of the European Communities (1984a) Community Policy with Regard to SME and Craft Industry: The Follow-up to EYSME, COM(84)263, CEC, Brussels, May

Commission of the European Communites (1984b) Model for BICs, Document XVI/37/84, CEC, Brussels, January

Commission of the European Communities (1984c) The Effects of New Information Technology on the Less Favoured Regions of the Community, Regional Policy Series No 23, CEC, Brussels

Commission of the European Communities (1985a) Report of SMEs and The Business Environment, SEC(85)1592, CEC, Brussels, November

Commission of the European Communities (1985b) Thirteenth Report on the Activities of the ESF (1984), COM(85)508, CEC, Brussels, October

Commission of the European Communities (1985c) Stronger Community Structural Measures to Assist Steel Re-structuring Areas, COM(85)384, CEC, Brussels, July

Commission of the European Communities (1985d) Towards a European

Technology Community, COM(85)350, CEC, Brussels, June
Commission of the European Communities (1985e) Vocational Training and the New Information Technologies, COM(85)167, CEC, Brussels, April
Commission of the European Communities (1985f) Proposal for a Council Decision on an Action Programme Community in Education and Training for Technology (COMETT) 1986-1992, COM(85)431, CEC, Brussels, August
Commission of the European Communities (1986a) Draft Resolution of the Council Concerning the Action Programme for SME, COM(86)445, CEC, Brussels, August
Commission of the European Communities (1986b) Financial Engineering, COM(86)723, CEC, Brussels
Commission of the European Communities (1986c) Eleventh Annual Report of the ERDF, COM(86)545, CEC, Brussels, October
Commission of the European Communities (1986d) Proposal for a Council Regulation - VALOREN Programme, COM(86)433, CEC, Brussels, July
Commission of the European Communities (1986e) Proposal for a Council Regulation - STAR Programme, COM(86)432, CEC, Brussels, July
Commission of the European Communities (1986f) Fourteenth Report on the Activities of the ESF (1985), COM(86)583, CEC, Brussels, November
Commission of the European Communities (1986g) Improving Competitiveness and Industrial Structures in the Community, COM(86)40, CEC, Brussels, February
Commission of the European Communities (1986h) Action Programme on Stronger Community Structural Measures to Assist Steel Restructuring Areas, COM(86)422, CEC, Brussels, July
Commission of the European Communities (1986i) Towards a European Policy for Energy Efficiency in Industrial Firms, COM(86)264, CEC, Brussels, May
Commission of the European Communities (1986j) ESPRIT - The First Phase, Progress and Results, COM(86)687, CEC, Brussels, December
Commission of the European Communities (1986k) Guidelines for a New Technology Framework Programme of Technological R&D, COM(86)129, CEC, Brussels, March
Commission of the European Communities (1986l) Communication from the Commission to the Council on the Extension and Revision of the 'Plan for the Trans-National Development of the Supporting Infrastructure for Technology Transfer', COM(86)483, CEC, Brussels, October
Connell, D. (1986) 'Bridging the Gap Between Academic Researchers and Industrial Corporations', paper presented at the European Symposium on the Utilization of the Results of Publicly Funded R & D, Luxembourg, September
Dekker, D.J. (1985) 'Industrial Redevelopment and Business and Innovation Centres in Community Regional Policy', in J.M. Gibb (ed), Science Parks and Innovation Centres: Their Economic and

Social Impact, Elsevier, Amsterdam, pp.70-75
Dekker, D.J. (1987) 'European Business and Innovation Network', in Bedrijvencentra: Exponen vauu Lokale Tewerkstellings-initiatieven, Koning Boudewijnstichting, Brussels, pp.66-86
ECOSOC (1974) Study of the Situation of SMEs in the EC, Document CES 714/74, Brussels
ECOSOC (1983) Inaugural Conference for 1983 - EYSME, ECOSOC, Brussels
ECOSOC (1986) Information Report on the Importance of Technological R&D to SMEs, Document CES 896/85, August
European Parliament (1986) Report on the Future of the ESF, prepared by the Committee on Social Affairs and Employment (Salische Committee), EP Working Document A2-80/86, session 1986-87, July
Goddard, J. (1987) 'Centre for Urban and Regional Development Studies (CURDS)', ESRC Newsletter, No 59, February, pp.33-34
Harrison, J. (1986) 'A Network for the Future', Transition, November, pp.28-29
Hawkes, D. (1987) 'The Strathclyde Business Innovation Centre' in P. Aitken (ed), A Guide to the EC Organisation, Operations and Funds, Briefing Note 14, The Planning Exchange
Hayton, K. (1987) 'Taking a Lead on Innovation', Planning, No 703, 30 January, pp.10-11
HMSO (1985a) Burdens on Business, Report of a Scrutiny of Administrative and Legislative Requirements, HMSO, London
HMSO (1985b) Lifting the Burden, Cmnd 9571, HMSO, London
HMSO (1986) Building Businesses ... Not Barriers, Cmnd 9794, HMSO, London
Johnston, B. (1986) 'Sedgefield Strikes Silver on Shildon Success', Planning, No 698, 12 December, pp.6-7
Keating, M. and Waters, N. (1985) 'Scotland in the EC', in M. Keating and B. Jones (eds), Regions in the EC, Clarendon Press, Oxford
Kirchberger, A. (1986) 'University Industry Co-operation in Training in the New Technologies - the COMETT Programme', Social Europe, January, No 1/86, pp.19-24
McEldowney, J. and Aitken, P. (1985) 'Small Firms and Local Employment Initiative Policies in the EC - Evolution and Contribution: Convergence or Divergence', in Local Initiatives in the EEC, European Centre for Work and Society
McEldowney, J. (1986) 'Local Business and Employment Initiatives: A European Perspective', The Planner, Vol 72 (5), May, pp.36-37
Moore, C. and Booth, S. (1986a) 'From Comprehensive Regeneration to Privatization: The Search for Effective Area Strategies', in W. Lever and C. Moore (eds), The City in Transition: Policies and Agencies for the Economic Regeneration of Clydeside, Clarendon Press, Oxford
Moore, C. and Booth, S. (1986b) 'The Post-Industrial Synthesis: Policies for Enterprise in Clydeside' in W. Lever and C. Moore (eds), The City in Transition: Policies and Agencies for the Economic Regeneration of Clydeside, Clarendon Press, Oxford

Official Journal (1983a) Call for Expression of Interest, Official Journal of the European Communities, Series S, No 135, 19 July
Official Journal (1983b) Council Decision on Transnational Plan for the Supporting Infrastructure for Technology Transfer and Innovation, Official Journal of the European Communities, Series L, No 353, December
Official Journal (1985a) Council Regulation No 2137/85 on the European Economic Interest Grouping (EEIG), Official Journal of the European Communities, Series L, No 199, July
Official Journal (1985b) Regulation Governing Energy Demonstration Projects, Official Journal of the European Communities, Series C, No 350, December
Official Journal (1986a) Council Resolution Concerning the Action Programme for SMEs, Official Journal of the European Communities, Series C, No 287, November
Official Journal (1986b) Council Regulations concerning the STAR and VALOREN Programmes, Official Journal of the European Communities, Series L, No 305, November
Official Journal (1986c) Establishment of File of Companies/Experts Capable of Providing Services in the Field of Energy Technology Projects, Official Journal of the European Communities, Series S, No 175, September
Official Journal (1986d) Council Resolution on Improving Energy Efficiency in Industrial Firms, Official Journal of the European Communities, Series C, No 240, September
Official Journal (1986e) Written Question No 2824/85 by Mr Jaak Vandemeulebrouke, Official Journal of the European Communities, Series C, No 314, p12
Official Journal (1986f) Written Question No 352/86 by Mr Lambert Croux, Official Journal of the European Communities, Series C, No 330, December
Official Journal (1986g) Notice Concerning Participation in the COMETT Programme, Official Journal of the European Communities, Series S, No 252, December
Official Journal (1987a) Invitation to Tender: Pilot Phase of European Business Information Centres Project, Official Journal of the European Communities, Series S, No 53, p.66
Official Journal (1987b) Call for Proposals for Participation in BRITE, Official Journal of the European Communities, Series S, No 21, January, p.43
Official Journal (1987c) Proposal for a Council Decision Concerning a Programme to Create and Develop BICs and their Network, Official Journal of the European Communities, Series C, No 33, pp.5-7
Owen, T. (1986) Mind Your Own Business, Eurofi, London
Reilly, A. (1986) 'Technology Transfer - The Role of the SDA', Planning Outlook, October 1986, pp.89-91
Sedgefield District Council (1986) NPCI Submission - Shildon, Bishop Auckland. SDC, Shildon, 2nd edition

Storey, D. (1982) Entrepreneurship and the New Firm, Croom Helm, London
Wylie, J. (1986) 'Strengthening the Links between Industry and Education', 120-Scottish Economic Development Review, No 8, pp.6-8
Young, R. and Greig, M. (1985) 'Strathclyde: A Region in Transition', paper presented to the Association of Traditional Industrial Regions of Europe (RETI) Conference, Leeds, September

Chapter Five

THE EUROPEAN BUSINESS AND INNOVATION CENTRE NETWORK

Jack Malan

In the 1980s Western Europe has witnessed a proliferation of the number of science parks and innovation centres. With the establishment of the European Business and Innovation Centre Network (EBN) in December 1984, a step was taken towards adding a transnational dimension to these initiatives. EBN had two basic objectives: (1) to help establish a series of new Business and Innovation Centres (BICs) in regions which qualify for assistance under the European Regional Development Fund (ERDF); and (2) to integrate existing and new centres into a network spanning the European Community.

It was expected that the EBN would ultimately consist of about 100 BICs. The purpose of EBN's network, in the short-term at least, was to ensure that those involved in setting up and running new centres learned from experience gained elsewhere and did not, therefore, have to reinvent the wheel. In the longer term, the main justification for promoting transnational co-operation between BICs lay in providing their client companies with the support structure needed to exploit the European market. By February 1987 EBN had 35 full members (start-up and operational BICs) and just over 70 associate members (multinational companies, banks, firms of consultants) which, along with the European Commission, actively supported EBN's aims[1]. Britain provided some one-third of the full members and also the largest number of associate members of any of the 12 EC member states. Italy, followed by West Germany and the Netherlands, were the next best represented among the full members, with Belgium playing a notable role in providing associate members. The Association's President was Vicomte Etienne Davignon, a former Vice-President of the European Commission and now chairman of Belgium's largest holding company; he was also a key figure in the Roundtable of European Industrialists whose membership overlaps with EBN's.

THE BIC CONCEPT AND EC REGIONAL DEVELOPMENT POLICY

It is important at the outset to explain precisely what is meant by a 'Business and Innovation Centre'. The idea of promoting small- and medium-sized enterprises as agents of economic growth is, of course, not new and features prominently in government policy in many countries. At a European level this idea is reflected in the new Regional Development Fund regulation which was introduced in 1984[2]. To quote from a recent paper prepared by the European Commission:

> It is now being realized that in order to succeed with the economic regeneration of the Community and in particular with its conversion and redevelopment areas, a new and much stronger emphasis must be given to industrial redevelopment and in particular to generating a vigorous private business sector based on or incorporating and receptive to various levels of technological advances. In view of the difficulties and drawbacks in attracting investment from elsewhere it has also been recognized that particular measures are necessary to exploit the potential for internally-generated regional development. These measures are of a micro-economic nature; they concern a particular area and take into account local characteristics and mainly consist of promoting and assisting new and existing firms. Resulting new activities will be additional and have growth potential only if they concern new products and processes, new technologies or new markets. Emphasis is laid therefore on small- and medium-sized undertakings and 'state-of-the-art' technology[3].

The concept of a BIC was formulated within this new framework as an instrument for promoting the type of new enterprises upon which the regeneration of the European Community's depressed regions ultimately depends, i.e. innovative, technology-based 'start-ups' with a high wealth- and job-creating potential. There are of course many other institutions, including science parks and innovation centres, which share this aim. Their approach is, however, seldom proactive or planned; similarly, they rarely offer the comprehensive range of facilities and services required to mobilise the full entrepreneurial potential of a locality. The purpose of a BIC is to fill this gap and to provide a mechanism for systematically transforming such potential on a selective basis, into a steady stream of innovative business 'start-ups'. Through intensive care, it will also aim to reduce the subsequent failure rate of these 'start-ups' to a minimum and to maximise their subsequent growth prospects.

A fully-developed BIC can thus be defined in terms of several basic functions. In brief these functions are systematically to detect, select and train potential entrepreneurs; to facilitate research, development and technology transfer; to provide the various professional services required to draw up a business plan and actually to launch a company; to help raise finance, including venture capital, which may come from a fund managed by the BIC itself; to provide incubator facilities and supporting services; and, finally, to ensure that the client company receives continuing assistance after its launch, if necessary through the direct involvement of BIC staff in the company's management. A full description of the BIC concept is contained in EBN's 'Manual of Best Practices' and other documentation[4].

It is not intended that a BIC should duplicate existing institutions such as science parks, innovation centres, managed workshops and

Table 5.1: BIC Procedures

Simulation on basis of experience Period: 1 year

Stage	Possible numbers of candidate or client entrepreneurs	Task	Method
1	PM	Promotion	Publicity
2	300	Initial Selection	Discussion
3	100	Candidates sign a contract by which they commit themselves to follow a programme	
		- Introduction to the programme - Basis of creation of a business	seminar/work session
	95	Self-evaluation by candidate of his/her entrepreneurial abilities and management knowledge	CBT (x)
	90	Guidance	
4		Training in weak areas	CBT (x) + advisers
5		Technology	advisers
6		Drawing up of business plan for the company	CBT (x) + advisers
		Specialist advice	
7	45	Finish drawing up business plans	document
8	15	Effective creation of the business	financing
		Financial advice	
9	15	Establishment	advisers

(x) computer-based or assisted training

Source: EBN, Manual of Best Practices, April 1986, p.62

enterprise agencies; rather, it should complement them. Similarly, although a BIC can be narrowly defined in terms of several functions, it should ultimately be regarded as the focal point of a federation of local interests, including not only other business promotion agencies but also local authorities, higher education establishments and the private sector. The objective of the BIC should be to bind these components into a managed entrepreneurial network and, within this network, to operate a system of accelerated natural selection and intensive care for the small number of innovative business 'start-ups' that are likely to have a significant long-term impact on the local economy.

THE IMPLEMENTATION OF EBN'S FIRST OBJECTIVE: ESTABLISHING NEW BUSINESS AND INNOVATION CENTRES

Support for the establishment of new Business and Innovation Centres has been provided by the European Commission since 1984 within the framework of the European Regional Development Policy. More specifically, under Budget Articles 774 and 7731, approximately ECU 3.0 million has been granted to help cover the costs of BIC business plans and pre-launch overheads.

Table 5.2: Grants 1986 (Article 7731) to BICs

BIC	Grant	Date
Teranto	100,000	19.03.86
Lancashire	85,000	19.03.86
Bilbao	147,000	27.05.86
Cheshire	75,000	27.05.86
Limerick	135,000	18.06.86
Galway	150,000	18.06.86
Heerlen	51,000	18.06.86
Dublin	150,000	25.07.86
Auvergne	130,000	25.07.86
Strathclyde	250,000	25.07.86
Cardiff	110,000	25.10.86
Alborg	62,500	13.11.86
Clwyd	150,000	13.11.86
Foggia	150,000	11.12.86
Turnout	98,000	11.12.86
Thebes	150,000	11.12.86
Setubal	147,000	11.12.86
Vercelli	150,000	11.12.86
Total Committed:	2,290,500	
Total Allocated:	2,900,000	

Source: Figures provided by DG XVI of the European Commission

The roles played by EBN in this programme are those of an agent or catalyst in the formation of BIC consortiums, and of an honest broker in subsequent negotiations between sponsors, who typically include local authorities, universities and the private sector, and the European Commission. The procedure for establishing BICs is outlined in a document that EBN and the European Commission have jointly prepared called the 'Programme of Work for a Business and Innovation Centre'. This forms an integral part of the contract signed by sponsors of a new BIC who receive funding under Articles 774 and 7731. The steps to be taken may be summarised as follows[5]:

1. Prior to signature of the contract with the European Commission the BIC sponsors, ideally from both the public and private sector, form an operating company. The chairman of this company should be the Managing-Director-designate of the BIC; he normally signs the contract on behalf of the sponsors with the European Commission. At this stage the Commission usually makes an 'up-front' payment equivalent to 30 per cent of the total value of the contract to the BIC sponsors;
2. Over the following three months or so, a First Interim Report is prepared by consultants. Depending on the country where the BIC is to be located, EBN can usually provide consultants, if so requested. In any event, the appointment must ultimately be agreed jointly by the BIC's sponsors and the European Commission. The purpose of the First Interim Report is to establish the feasibility of setting up a BIC in the locality concerned, and to assess its likely impact. This involves an analysis of various socio-economic factors and should lead to a clear identification of the prospective BIC's strategy and targets, which may be to concentrate on creating new enterprises or to specialise in helping existing entrepreneurs and small- and medium-sized businesses. The Report should also indicate how the prospective BIC will work alongside other agencies and organisations in its catchment area;
3. Assuming that the First Interim Report is accepted by the European Commission, a Second Report is then prepared. It involves drawing up a detailed business plan for the BIC itself. This process usually takes between 6-12 months and is sometimes preceded by a series of pilot projects and practical experiments. In any event, drafting the business plan will entail an in-depth examination of how each of the BIC's main functions is to be carried out, the premises and personnel needed, and the costs involved. It will also identify the source of funds, including European Community grants and loans. One consideration that the European Commission always stresses is that a BIC should be regarded as a business in its own right. Thus the aim in drawing up the balance sheet and the cash flow forecast, in the medium term at least, should be to break even;
4. Finally, after further discussions with the European Commission, the first and second interim reports are consolidated into a Final Report which, once delivered to Brussels, along with various Statements of Account, leads to the transfer of the balance

due under the contract to the BIC sponsors. Ideally, the launch of the BIC will follow shortly afterwards.

Judging by experience till early 1987 in the United Kingdom, the prelaunch costs of a BIC averaged about £150,000, most of which was spent on the business plan; up to half of this sum was usually covered by the European Commission under Articles 774 and 7731. Likewise, the capital investment and initial running costs of a new BIC, in the UK at least, usually totalled around £300-400,000. The length of time required to complete a BIC business plan was normally between 12 and 18 months. Experience elsewhere in Europe was similar.

Between becoming operational in 1985 and early 1987, EBN helped to negotiate 25 contracts with the European Commission under Articles 774 and 7731. The location of prospective BICs ranged from Alborg in Denmark to Bilbao in Spain. It was in Italy, Ireland and the United Kingdom, and more particularly in the Assisted Areas of these countries, that the majority of projects were concentrated. With the accession of Spain and Portugal to the European Community this pattern was, however, beginning to change.

Table 5.3: EEC Grants (1984 and 1985) for BIC Start-Ups

Country	ECU	%
Belgium	98,000	3.4
Greece	150,000	5.3
Denmark	62,500	2.2
France	210,000	7.4
Germany	100,000	3.5
Italy	500,000	17.5
Ireland	435,000	15.2
Luxembourg	-	-
Netherlands	51,000	1.8
Portugal	147,000	5.1
Spain	147,000	5.1
United Kingdom	955,000	33.5
	2,855,500	100

Source: Figures provided by DG XVI of the European Commission

Although by early 1987 it was too early to pass judgement on the 25 new BIC projects initiated over the past year-and-a-half, it was reasonable to assume that most would succeed. In 1987 this programme was to be continued under Budget Article 543. The BICs in the process of being started up from scratch would join 23 Centres which are full members of EBN and which, in some cases, were operational prior to the establishment of EBN itself. Few, if any, of these institutions approximated the EBN model of a BIC completely. All were, however,

Table 5.4: Start-Up and Operational BICs (EC Financed under Articles 774 or 7731)

Country	Negotiations	Contracted	Operational
Belgium	---	Turnout	Liege *
Denmark	---	Alborg	---
France	Bretagne *	Auvergne	Metz *
			Nancy *
Germany	Cloppenburg	---	Berlin *
			Dortmund *
			Essen *
			Hamburg *
			Saarbrucken *
Greece	Heraklion	Thebes	---
Ireland	---	Cork *	Limerick *
		Dublin	
		Galway	
Italy	Bologne	Bari *	Genoa *
	Cagliar	Foggia *	Giovinazzo *
	Milan	Taranto *	Valenzano *
	Naples	Varcelli *	
	Salerno		
	Terni		
	Trieste *		
Luxembourg	---	---	---
Netherlands	---	Heerlen *	Eindhoven *
			Enschede *
			Helmond *
Portugal	Lisbon	Setubal	---
	Oporto		
Spain	Barcelona	Bilbao *	---
	Oviedo		
	Valencia		
United Kingdom	Plymouth *	Barnsley *	Birmingham *
	Middlesbrough	Cardiff	Calderdale *
	Manchester	Derry *	Clwyd *
		N. Cheshire	Heriot-Watt *
		Strathclyde *	Lancashire *
			London *
			Newcastle *
			Rossendale *
Total	18	19	23
EBN Members*	3	10	23

Source: EBN

committed to the realisation of this concept, and many were receiving European Commission funding to this end. Taking the 'start-up' and operational BICs together, EBN was well on its way to achieving its objective of creating a network of 100 BICs in the European Community by the end of the decade.

THE IMPLEMENTATION OF EBN'S SECOND OBJECTIVE: CREATING A NETWORK OF BICs SPANNING THE EUROPEAN COMMUNITY

Creating a European network of BICs depended not only on building up a 'critical mass' of centres but also on consolidating links between them. The immediate objective of promoting transnational contact between BICs was, as mentioned earlier, to ensure that those involved in setting up and running new centres benefitted from experience gained elsewhere. To this end EBN organised a number of international conferences and seminars throughout Europe. Towards the end of 1986 the first meetings of BIC managers at a national level also took place, in Italy and the United Kingdom. These sessions proved particularly useful and would be repeated in the future on a regular basis. Promoting contact between BICs which are in the process of being established so that they can learn from one another was, of course, vital; for operational centres, however, the ultimate benefit of belonging to a European Network lay in providing their client companies with the means to exploit new markets. From EBN's point of view this function of the network was considerably more difficult to set in motion.

As a first step nine Business Innovation Centres participated in the European Commission's SPRINT Programme. Judging by the meetings held by early 1987, co-operation between these BICs would result in a number of client companies from different European countries being introduced to new business possibilities. In a few cases, this process might soon lead to cross-licencing, joint venture and distribution agreements being signed(6). With the support of EBN, a further six BICs applied to join the European Commission's scheme. A spin-off from these meetings is that a number of centres also reached agreement between themselves to share the cost of establishing stands at major international trade fairs, which is another way of providing client companies with new opportunities.

EBN hoped that its Database and Electronic Network, which was being set up for the Association by a Belgian bank, would speed up the process of consolidating cross-border links between BICs. In 1986 a prototype began to be developed by Banque Bruxelles Lambert, using an input of data on client companies by two full members, the Berliner Innovations- und Grunderzentrum in West Germany and Birmingham Technology Ltd. The database was to be used to store detailed information on BICs and their client companies. It was intended that this particular file should eventually be built up into a comprehensive international directory. The basic aim of the system was to enable BICs to identify client companies with the potential to collaborate transnationally, and a special programme was developed for this purpose. The database would hopefully not only increase the volume of information exchanged by BICs on client companies, thus improving the chances of identifying enterprises that could be matched up, but also render the whole process far more cost effective. Other files were to provide information on European Community programmes and sources of funding for BICs. The system had been tested by 1987 and was due to start operating on-line. All BICs belonging to the Association were to be linked up to it in 1987[7].

CONCLUSIONS

Various general conclusions about the establishment and operation of BICs could be drawn by 1987 from EBN's experience of putting the European Commission's programme into effect.

1. Although the grants made available by the European Commission for starting up BICs were relatively modest, they acted as a trigger and had a considerable multiplier effect by unlocking funds from other sources.
2. It was important that the sponsors of a BIC should, if possible, be drawn from both the public and the private sectors. Given the present spending constraints on local authorities, this partnership was often the only way of covering the initial capital investment and running costs of a new BIC. In any case, the active involvement of public and private sector interests was desirable as a means of ensuring that, once established, the BIC was managed as far as possible according to commercial criteria and with a view ultimately to becoming a profitable business in its own right. Similarly, the involvement of a broad range of interests from the outset could make it easier for the BIC to subsequently mobilise the local network of contacts needed to attract potential entrepreneurs and to enable client companies to flourish.
3. A considerable number of local companies from different European countries had, through their associate membership of EBN, committed themselves to supporting new BICs. In some cases, this involvement could be explained simply in terms of social responsibility, usually to offset larger-scale redundancies. But in addition, many major corporations were beginning to recognise that they might have a business interest in being more closely involved with small innovative firms, even if this interest was of a medium- or long-term nature. This process of recognition sometimes reflected the decentralisation of the larger company itself. Either way, the task EBN faced was that of persuading chief executives that BICs are an efficient and cost-effective vehicle for promoting such corporate strategies.
4. As far as the procedure for establishing BICs was concerned, there were many lessons to be learnt. Perhaps the most important lesson was that the success of the project depended more than anything else on the calibre of the Managing Director designate. It was essential that one person, who fully understood the BIC concept, should assume overall responsibility for launching the

centre. Similarly, he or she should be involved from the very outset and not be simply presented with a completed business plan by consultants to put into effect. The role played by the Managing Director designate should be regarded as a full-time job. For this reason, an appropriate allowance is usually provided under the European Commission's grant for establishing a BIC.

5. With regard to the operational centres belonging to the EBN network, although none as yet approximated to the BIC model completely, progress towards this objective was reasonably promising. Judging by the experience of two centres that were perhaps most advanced, Birmingham Technology Ltd and the Berliner Innovations- und Grunderzentrum, adoption of the BIC approach led to a relatively large number of innovative new enterprises being generated in a relatively short period of time. Similarly, through intensive care, it seemed possible to invert the failure rate for 'start-ups' which applies to the small business sector as a whole. In the case of Birmingham Technology, which had been operational for three years, the results were[8]: 2,800 applications; 29 'start-ups'; 2 failures; and 15 existing companies accepted as tenants. Consequently, 42 client companies were created along with 360 jobs. The results for the Berliner Innovations- und Grunderzentrum, which had been operational for the same length of time, were remarkably similar. Centres elsewhere in Europe, which have existed long enough to build up a track record, such as those at Limerick in Ireland and Liege in Belgium, seemed to be performing in a similar manner.

6. Given the cost of establishing and running a BIC it was perhaps not surprising, however, that none of the operational centres had yet succeeded in functioning without continued subsidisation of one kind or another. Attempts to generate increased income varied: Limerick, for example, took a royalty on the sales of its client companies; Birmingham Technology hoped to profit from the operations of its venture capital fund and had so far invested in the equity of thirteen of its tenant companies; other centres, such as Socran in Liege, tried to externalise their services and generate fee income by providing advice to small firms in the region as a whole. It was still far too early to judge which of these approaches was likely to prove the most successful.

As a general conclusion, it is important to stress that a BIC is a long-term development. Experience in the United States suggests that science parks and innovation centres have a gestation period of anything up to fifteen years. On this side of the Atlantic it may be possible, with the European Commission's intervention, to speed up the process. This, in any case, is EBN's purpose and the justification for the Business and Innovation Centre model. But although it is possible to identify the preconditions for the successful establishment of a BIC, their operations can, at this stage, only be gauged using intermediate performance indicators, such as the quantity and quality of new business 'start-ups'. It would be premature to attempt an assessment of the impact of Business and Innovation Centres on regional development in the European

Community in profounder terms[9].

NOTES

1. See EBN List of Members (Brussels, November 1986).
2. See Regulation 1787/84 published in the Official Journal No C169/1 on 28 June 1984.
3. Quoted from D.J. Dekker, 'Industrial Redevelopment and Business and Innovation Centres in Community Regional Policy', in J.M. Gibb (ed), Science Parks and Innovation Centres: their Economic and Social Impact (Elsevier, 1985).
4. EBN, Manual of Best Practices, 2nd Edition (Brussels, April 1986), pp.28-61; and EBN The Business of Developing New Business and Innovation (Brussels, 1986), pp.16-17.
5. See Programme of Work for a Business and Innovation Centre, pp.2-5, available from either EBN or the Commission of the European Communities (DG XVI).
6. See reports of Transfer of European Enterprise meetings and Brokerage Meetings, available from the EBN.
7. Further details about the EBN Database can be obtained from: EBN, 89 rue Froissart, B - 1040 Brussels.
8. See The Aston Science Park Experience, p.10. Paper available from Birmingham Technology Ltd.
9. Research is currently underway to assess the performance of Business and Innovation Centres and will be published as the 'Davignon Report' in 1987.

Chapter Six

NEW TECHNOLOGY POLICIES AT THE REGIONAL LEVEL IN FRANCE: NORD-PAS-DE-CALAIS AND PROVENCE-ALPES-COTE D'AZUR COMPARED

Serge Dormard

In recent years France has experienced a number of upheavals, both of institutional arrangements and of economic development. After two centuries of Jacobin centralisation, and of administrative continuity stretching back to the ancien regimé, a decentralisation movement finally achieved a breakthrough in 1982. In sharp contrast to political trends in England and Wales the role of local and regional authorities was strengthened. This major reform of 1982 was introduced by the new Socialist government (the first in the Fifth Republic), conceived and piloted by Gaston Defferre (as Interior Minister, now rechristened Interior and Decentralisation) and described by the Prime Minister Pierre Mauroy as a 'quiet revolution... the great achievement of President Mitterrand's term of office'. Regions were at last recognised as proper institutional entities with their own rights and duties. In particular, their role in economic affairs was strengthened. As a consequence the regions have become much more closely associated with the process of economic modernisation pursued by the French state. In this context a host of new initiatives have emerged in the field of new technologies since 1982.

The aim of this chapter is to outline the initiatives undertaken in new technology policies since 1982 in two French regions, which differ considerably in both economic and social terms: Nord-Pas-de-Calais (with two départements) and Provence-Alpes-Côte d'Azur (with six départements). Both had important regional capitals: the industrial city of Lille in the case of the former, and the port of Marseille in the latter. Also, both had local political leaders who were very influential in the Socialist government at the centre. Mauroy, the first Socialist Prime Minister, was mayor of Lille; Defferre, the Minister of the Interior, was mayor of Marseille. At the outset, however, it is necessary to analyse the general characteristics of the new institutional framework within which the French regions operate.

The law of 2nd March 1982 profoundly changed the institutional landscape of France in existence for the previous two centuries and indeed longer. Alongside the communes and the départements, the 22 regions became territorial units with their own distinctive competence. They emerged as a focus of deconcentration and decentralisation. One notable consequence was the end of the administrative 'tutelage' (tutelle), previously exercised by the prefect as the representative of the state and involving his right to review the wisdom and desirability of decisions as a routine matter. At the same time their sphere of competence was enlarged to incorporate areas earlier reserved to the central government - education, transport, urban development, professional training etc. There was, however, a considerable risk that the different administrative levels - communes, départements, regions and the centre - would develop incoherent and, to a greater or lesser extent, contradictory measures. Hence a number of legislative texts, publshed in 1985, sought to make more precise the distribution of competences between the different levels.

In economic affairs the regions could intervene freely to support local firms, whether by the use of financial asistance (employment premiums, tax concessions to attract new firms or encourage existing ones to expand, and loan guarantees), by becoming shareholders in the regional development bank in their area or by the creation of joint public-private enterprises. Against the background of a national economic planning process that was intended to be decentralised, the regions formed, alongside the state, a tier of planning. In this capacity they could formulate their own regional plans; they were also intended to be significant actors in the Ninth National Plan.

THE REGIONS AND THE NINTH PLAN

With the emergence of a majority for the Socialist Party for the first time in the history of the Fifth Republic in 1981, the national planning process was expected to become a main component in the new system of economic policy. The Eighth Plan (1981-85), which had been produced by the centre-right majority under President Valery Giscard d'Estaing, was rendered obsolete by the election of President Francois Mitterand and replaced by a Ninth Plan for the period 1984-88. The Ninth Plan put forward an ambitious modernisation strategy aimed at recapturing international competitiveness and accepting the imperative of industrial restructuring. Also, it confirmed the overriding importance of measures to ameliorate unemployment and proposed a priority programme for this purpose.

The law of 29th July 1982 on the reform of planning was linked to the law on decentralisation and established the instruments for a decentralised regional planning as well as reinforced the system of planning from the centre. More novel than the aim of putting national planning back at the centre of the political agenda was the Socialists' concern to achieve a greater participation of the regions in the implementation of the National Plan. Reliance was placed on a new exchange of information between the centre and the regions, on increased regionalisation of the budget, and on the signature of contracts between particular regions and the central government. In the new planning arrangements the regions were given three basic functions:

1. The regions were to participate in the work of the new consultative National Planning Committee, which took over responsibility for preparation of the Plan from the government in order to free the planning process from executive control.
2. The regions were to independently prepare their own regional plans, which would comprise two types of proposal: (1) economic development projects, with the objective of supporting and stimulating regional economic activity by public investment; and (2) regional spatial development directed in particular at the conurbations, the major employment centres and local areas of historic identity and involving the regions in assuming responsibility for encouraging local initiatives.
   For the implementation of its plan the regions were given several instruments, notably: (1) implementation programmes specific to each region and to be financed from its own resources; (2) new opportunities for economic and financial action (loan guarantee funds, equity financing, regional employment premiums and subsidies for new firms); and (3) planning contracts.
3. The regions were to agree planning contracts with the state. These agreements between the region and the central government: (1) establish the conditions under which the state and the regional council intend to cooperate at the regional level in order to realise the objectives of the priority programmes for the implementation of the National Plan; (2) determine the contribution of each of the partners to the implementation of the regional plan; and (3) determine the form, types and financial levels of assistance that the state and the region will apply in order to make effective the activities mentioned below.

Hence the planning contracts were above all relevant to all those operations requiring the cooperation of the national level and the regional tier, for instance joint development projects or industrialisation schemes. They were also of interest to those national policies whose translation into effective action required the support of sub-national authorities. Table 6.1 indicates the financial volumes that were committed for the duration of the Ninth Plan by the partners, state and regions, in the framework of the various planning contracts. One can see that they amounted to Fr.63 billion for the period 1984-88, the state accepting responsibility for nearly 60% of this commitment. Also, one can note that the two regions Nord-Pas-de-Calais and Provence-Alpes-Côte d'Azur accounted for the largest amounts of this commitment by the state (with the exception of the Ile-de-France around Paris).

Table 6.1: Financial Volume of the State-Region Contracts for the 5-Year Period from 1984 in the Ninth Plan

REGIONS	A		B		C		D	E
France	63.393	(100%)	37.811	(59.6%)	25.582	(40.4%)	1.180	1.5
Nord-Pas-de-Calais	6.400		3.950		2.450		1.628	1.6
Ile-de-France	15.602		7.137	(45.7%)	8.465	(54.3%)	1.559	0.8
Lorraine	3.921		2.979		0.942		1.465	3.2 (b)
Limousin	1.065		0.757		0.308		1.439	2.5
Picardie	2.627		1.776		0.851		1.430	2.1
Provence/Alpes/Côte-D'Azur	4.693		2.796		1.897		1.387	1.5
Franche-Comte	1.397		0.847		0.550		1.378	1.5
Poitou-Charentes	1.880		1.250		0.630		1.197	2.0
Alsace	1.800		1.100		0.700		1.147	1.6
Languedoc-Roussillon	2.157		1.381		0.776		1.118	1.8
Bretagne	2.618		1.804		0.814		0.969	2.2
Champagne-Ardennes	1.295		0.850		0.445		0.963	1.9
Midi-Pyrénées	2.220		1.433		0.787		0.954	1.8
Auvergne	1.225		0.775		0.450		0.921	1.7
Bourgogne	1.452		0.851		0.601		0.908	1.4
Aquitaine	2.400		1.470		0.930		0.903	1.6
Rhône-Alpes	4.500		2.980		1.520		0.898	2.0
Basse-Normandie	1.220		0.770		0.450		0.857	1.7
Haute-Normandie	1.388		0.865		0.523		0.841	1.7
Pays De Loire	2.063		1.180		0.883		0.704	1.3
Centre	1.470		0.860		0.610		0.651	1.4
Corse	Contract not signed in 1984		-		-		-	-

A: State-Region Contracts: Totals in Millions of Francs
B: State's Share: In Millions of Francs
C: Region's Share: In Millions of Francs
D: In Francs per capita (a)
E: State's Share/Region's Share (in Francs per capita)

(a) intensity of effects of contracts in each region; and (b) the region benefitting most from national solidarity

Source: Planning Commissariat

ECONOMIC DEVELOPMENT AND RESEARCH AND TECHNOLOGY POLICIES

Regional policy has been based on the increasingly accepted idea that, however important the endowment of natural resources and infrastructure is, modern economic development seems to depend more and more on the knowledge and innovative capacity of the indigenous population. This insight took practical form in the establishment, at the local level, of numerous institutions for training, for research and for technology transfer. The two areas of research and technology transfer have in turn provided the rationale for the creation of the regional technological poles.

Training

At the time of the preparation of the Ninth Plan almost all the regions had put training at the top of their priorities. Also, the new policy for spatial planning consisted of various measures to promote a more equal territorial distribution of training, notably in higher and technological education (and particularly in the case of university institutes of technology).

The Establishment of Regional Technological Poles

The regional technological poles were defined by a law of 15th July 1982, with the aim of assembling and concentrating in a single zone the range of 'high-technology' units: research centres, centres for advanced training and 'leading-edge' industries. It was then a matter of developing a system of dissemination for research, innovation and knowledge amongst the units. In particular, progress in research and technology was to be made available for the benefit of the whole range of regional companies. For this purpose the regions could organise:

1. Regional Centres for Innovation and Technology Transfer (CRITT). These centres were to promote the modernisation of the production structures of firms by the introduction of

new technologies. In collaboration with industry, each CRITT was to perfect innovatory processes and products. Local economic actors were to be provided with advanced ideas, pilot projects of applied research as models and appraisal. The CRITT made particular use of a network of technological advisers. By the end of 1986 more than 100 CRITTs were operating in the French regions. Many regions placed emphasis on the electronics sector and its industrial applications in automation of production, with Nord-Pas-de-Calais choosing microelectronics and Provence-Alpes-Côte d'Azur robotics. The two latter regions also selected biotechnology as a priority. These technological priorities were also incorporated in the state-region planning contracts.

2. The network of technological advisers. These advisers were to alert enterprises, particularly SMEs, to new technologies. They were responsible for seeking out for the latter scientific and technical partners who could help to integrate these technologies into their production process. By the end of 1986 more than 400 technological advisers were working in the French regions. The technological advisers worked in close collaboration with the chambers of commerce and industry on the task of encouraging firms to approach the relevant competent bodies on technological matters and the different funds for support of modernisation and innovation.

The efforts to increase research in France were considerably increased in the 1980s. In 1984 the regions committed Fr.380 million for this purpose; Fr.150 million of this sum were to support the provisions of the planning contracts. The latter represented an increase of 52% on 1983 and of 150% compared with 1981. For its part, the state spent Fr.340 million in 1984, and Fr.430 million in 1985, in the framework of the planning contracts.

The Development of the Technopoles

In the 1980s France experienced a wave of new science parks or 'technopoles' whose aim was to regroup in the one geographical area research activities, advanced training centres and innovative industries in order to create among these three elements the conditions for 'cross-fertilisation'. The first examples of this phenomenon had been available in the United States, with Route 128 and Silicon Valley (see the chapter by Jowitt). Since then one after another of the other industrialised countries sought to imitate the American model. Japan and then the West European countries (notably Britain) entered the race to establish science parks. France's first experience in this field had in fact been at the beginning of the 1970s with the creation of the Sophia-Antipolis complex (see below). With the 1980s such projects have multiplied. Each regional centre possessed or wanted to possess its own technopole : for instance, Bordeaux-Technopolis, Rennes-Atalante, Metz 2000, Nancy-Brabois and Grenoble-Meylan. Just as fifteen years ago each municipality wanted its industrial zone, so by 1987 the new movement had reached a stage at which each regional council wanted to establish a technopole. Without entering into the debate about how many of these technological 'parks' are really technopoles, or about the possibility that they are just another fleeting fashion, the rest of this chapter will examine critically the experiences in the two regions of Nord-Pas-de-Calais and Provence-Alpes-Côte d'Azur.

NEW TECHNOLOGIES AND THE REGION NORD-PAS-DE-CALAIS

Although the region Nord-Pas-de-Calais has for long been characterised by a process of industrial decline, the economic situation has deteriorated sharply since the mid 1970s. The regional plan of 1983 sought to establish the conditions for a new industrialisation based on the development of scientific and technical research and the creation of numerous technological poles.

The region Nord-Pas-de-Calais benefits from a demographic context that is quite distinctive in France. According to the census of 1982 nearly 3,932,900 people were concentrated on 2.3% of the national territory, giving a density of 317 inhabitants per square kilometre (the national average was 100). This fact connected the region strongly to the neighbouring countries of Belgium, the Netherlands and West Germany. However, in contrast to these countries, Nord-Pas-de-Calais proved once again to be characterised by an exceptional demographic vitality: the birth rate exceeded 16.2 per thousand, against 13.6 in France, scarcely 12 in the Netherlands and only 10 per thousand in West Germany.

The deterioration of the economic situation of the region began in the 1950s with the decline of the activities that had been the motor of its economic development for more than a century, coal and textiles. In order to appreciate the scale of these difficulties it is necessary to remember that in 1950 more than half of the industrial employees had been located in these two sectors. The policy of industrial decentralisation, which was put into effect from the 1960s, enabled the process of regional industrial decline to be slowed down, particularly as a consequence of the location of large automobile factories. However, the first oil shock, and especially the second, affected in particular the sectors that had till now been spared - iron and steel, shipyards, metallurgy and chemicals - and that were now to drag the region once again into the spiral of industrial decline. In the twelve years up to 1986, nearly 200,000 industrial jobs disappeared, a third of the total in 1974. Unemployment rose sharply to reach 14% of the active population, one of the highest rates for a French region. By 1986 annual net migration from the region was over 40,000 people.

The Regional Plan 1984-1988

Faced by this difficult economic situation, and recognising the industrial inheritance of the region, the regional plan of 24th June 1983 fixed as the regional aim for the period 1984-88 the establishment of the conditions for a 'new industrialisation'. This aim required:

1. The development of regional economic activity, by revitalising the traditional sectors (notably coal, textiles, chemicals), by developing sectors with potential (like food processing, maritime activities and transportation), and by weaving new activities into the industrial fabric of the region. However, the projected types of action appeared often confused, contradictory and at times unrealistic. Thus, in the coal sector simultaneous references were made to exports and to energy conservation, to development of coal and to research into new forms of energy (gas and solar energy). Curiously the regional plan looked forward to the construction of a large coal-powered station, forgetting that the nuclear power-station at Gravelines already satisfied almost the whole of the electricity needs of the region. One gains the impression of an industrial policy facing in all directions at once ('tout azimut'), that wants to conserve existing activities (even if their impact is negative) whilst supporting the most dynamic regional activities and seeking to develop the sectors with the strongest future potential. Taking into account the financial constraints on the region it is clear that such a strategy could not be practicable.
2. The development of human resources, implying an active policy of basic and continuing training. In effect the region had suffered for a long time from poor education and 'under-qualification' of its population.
3. This policy had to be linked to the development of scientific and technical research at the regional level and to the establishment of specialised 'poles' including training and technology transfer. Research support by the regional council of Nord-Pas-de-Calais really took off in 1974, since when it maintained a regular growth: Fr.1.9 million in 1974, 11.5 million in 1980 and 46.5 million in 1985. In total, over twelve years, nearly Fr.200 million were distributed to research teams and laboratories in the region. Up to 1981 the objective had been to promote specific research on themes of local interest or related to a particular regional policy, for instance lectureships in energy or coastal development. These interventions consisted primarily of assistance with the purchase of scientific materials or the construction of premises for scientific use. From 1981 the research policy of the French state underwent a new development, involving a larger scope for regional particularity. Also, the law of 22nd

July 1983 on the distribution of responsibilities between the communes, départements and the state allowed the region to 'determine multiannual research programmes of regional interest'. In addition, 'the region gives its view on the regional aspects of the geographical distribution of advanced training and research'. This new stage was characterised by a new political will at the regional level to establish 'multidisciplinary poles of know-how', comprising research laboratories, national scientific bodies and regional or national companies. These poles were based on the idea that training, research and technology transfer represented a whole that must be enabled to progress in a coherent and harmonious manner. Their essential task was to ensure the transfer of research results to regional companies in order to assist the industrial rejuvenation of Nord-Pas-de-Calais. This objective was made more precise and developed in the framework of the state-region planning contract of 1984.

The State-Region Planning Contract

On 27th April 1984 a contract was signed between the state and the Nord-Pas-de-Calais region for the duration of the Ninth Plan (1984-88). This planning contract had a range of components, beginning with various action programmes in the fields of basic and continuing training, of employment research, of communications and culture, and of economic development. Then, with special emphasis, it laid down the objective of promoting scientific research and innovation in the region. The importance of this latter objective led, in turn, to the signature of a special planning contract for this field on 24th October 1984. For the duration of the Ninth Plan it envisaged: (1) action for the comprehensive development of regional research; (2) the establishment of 'poles of research'; and (3) the 'technopole' of Villeneuve d'Ascq.

Action for the Comprehensive Development of Regional Research.

This action took two different forms:

1. The local development of national research bodies. A number of cooperation agreements were signed with important national research bodies for the purpose of formulating different development programmes for regional research: (1) with the National Centre for Scientific Research (CNRS) in order to develop the sectors in which regional research teams had attained a level of national or even international quality. The latter involved microelectronics, materials, advanced manufacturing technologies, scientific instruments, marine sciences, life sciences, medicine and social sciences. For the Ninth Plan CNRS's contribution was to rise annually to Fr.12 million, which would be additional to the Fr.10 million committed annually by the regional council; (2) with the

National Institute for Agricultural Research (INRA) in the field of the physiology of micro-organisms, which had already led to practical applications, as well as in such fields as agro-feeding processes, problems of soil impoverishment and the selection and production of sperms. INRA engaged in the enlargement of its complement of scientists and engineers in the region, the regional council bearing a financial cost of Fr.5 million for the duration of the plan; (3) with the National Institute of Health and of Medical Research (INSERM) in the field of clinical medical research, in cooperation with the regional university hospitals; (4) with the French Institute for Marine Research (IFREMER) in the fields of the exploitation of maritime resources and of coastal protection and development. The centre of Boulogne-sur-Mer was to be developed as a specialist in development of sea produce; (5) with the French Agency for Energy Control (AFME) in the field of research and training about new energy conservation techniques. For the Ninth Plan Fr.15 million were to be allocated to this programme, borne jointly by AFME and the regional council; and (6) with the Information Processing Agency (ADI), comprising in effect a 'regional information processing plan' and envisaging the provision of computers to educational institutions (Fr.16 million annually divided between the state and the region), the development of training and of research, and also support to SMEs for information processing equipment (Fr.3 million per annum).

2. Policy for scientific equipment. The intention was to help local research teams to acquire expensive scientific materials. For the period of the Ninth Plan almost Fr.100 million were allocated to this programme, with the state assuming two-thirds of the cost, the region 30% and the remainder to be financed by industry. An example was provided by the conception and construction of a laser spectrometer for the purpose of industrial control. Various regional firms (Société Huiles, Goudrons and Dérivés, Société Chimique de la Grande Paroisse) soon displayed their particular interest in this type of application.

The Establishment of Poles of Research.

From 1979 a pole of biological and medical engineering had been established, followed by the creation (after the decision of the interministerial committee for territorial development in December 1982) of three poles in the fields of advanced manufacturing technology, marine sciences, and transportation. By 1986 the regional council was collaborating with the state to establish and develop 14 poles, including research activities, training and technology transfer. Hence they were to be closely linked to the structure of CRITTs and the networks of technological advisers. Although most of these poles of research were based on Lille, the regional capital, others were to be found in Douai and Valenciennes and one in Boulogne-sur-Mer. In addition to advanced manufacturing, which will be looked at in detail later, the regional poles comprised:

1. Biological and Medical Engineering. Created in 1979, this pole amalgamates 40 research teams to be found in the universities, at the Pasteur Institute or at the Regional Hospital Centre. Its objective was to facilitate the transition to the stage of industrial production of new instruments or processes that could be used in the field of health. Examples included apparatus for detection of cancer tumours and for sight testing.
2. Microelectronics. The state was to invest a total of Fr.19 million in this pole during the Ninth Plan. Particular attention was given to development of research in the fields of electronic components and integrated circuits and to building up close contacts with the relevant regional companies, notably CIT Alcatel and Velec.
3. Biotechnology. In this high-growth sector a pole of research in anaerobiotic microbiology was established in 1983. In 1984 research in this field was supported by various partners (like the region, the Ministry of Research, DATAR) to the amount of Fr.4 million.
4. Marine sciences. Created at the end of 1982, this pole aimed to develop research activities on the sea and coastline of Nord-Pas-de-Calais. The principal areas for study were: (1) the aquaculture of Gravelines, making use of the discharge of hot water from the nuclear power station there; (2) the fishery and the development of sea produce by the IFREMER centre at Boulogne-sur-Mer; and (3) the quality of the coastal environment, along with the marine station at Wimereux.
5. The regional information processing network. Created in 1984, this network was to manage a training policy for the use of software as well as establish a software library, to be made available in particular for regional industry.
6. Transportation. Created in 1985 by the region, the Institute for Transport Research, the Universities of Lille I and of Valenciennes and EPALE, the Regional Grouping for Research in Transportation (GRRT) had the aim of developing research on the automation of guided transport.
7. Industrial and Food Engineering. Created in 1985 around INRA, this pole sought to develop research in the fields of pasteurisation and of cleansing of storage tanks.
8. By 1987 the following other poles were in the process of being established: (1) mechanics, for transfer and assistance with respect to problems of the behaviour of materials and structural calculation; (2) metallurgy and heavy mechanical engineering, to be developed at Valenciennes and specialising in the field of railway equipment; (3) coal combustion, gasification and carbon chemistry of coal at the Mazingarbe rig (Pas-de-Calais); (4) scientific instruments, in the fields of

new materials, electronic components, lasers, spectroscopy etc.; (5) medicine, on the themes of cellular and molecular genetics; and (6) documentation in human and social sciences.

The 'Technopole' of Villeneuve d'Ascq.
It might seem at first glance that Nord-Pas-de-Calais had succumbed to fashion in seeking to make Villeneuve d'Ascq, a new town situated to the east of Lille, the regional 'technopole'. However, a number of factors appeared favourable: (1) the location of three universities in its area; (2) a young population (an average age of 28 years), qualified (37% of the inhabitants had a technical diploma and 26% a university diploma), and composed essentially of managerial personnel and skilled service-sector employees; (3) the image of a 'modern' town, having opted for the introduction of new technologies (a 'cabled' town); and (4) the location of numerous economic activities. For instance, in the last two months of 1985 some 50 companies were formed in the new town; almost 20% of their activities involved information processing. At the beginning of 1986 the association 'Villeneuve d'Ascq technopole' was founded by representatives of the local commune, of the University, of the Ministry of Research and of industry (in the form of the regional chamber of commerce and industry). Its objective was to use the industrial, scientific and human potential of Villeneuve d'Ascq to create a structure favourable to contacts between the different actors in research and innovation, with a view to creating jobs, particularly highly skilled ones. A start was made with several projects that sought to make available to investors premises or common services (like secretariats, telex, and fax).

The Case of the Advanced Manufacturing Pole

This pole encompasses the whole range of new processes of automation of industrial manufacturing methods.

1. The organisation of the pole. The regional advanced manufacturing pole was created in 1983, in conjunction with the region of Picardie. For the Ninth Plan financing was to be increased to Fr.30 million, with one-third from the region and two-thirds from the state. The pole encompassed three types of activity: (1) training, located at the University of Valenciennes, was centred on an experimental factory workshop and on a computer-assisted manufacturing centre. Its cost was estimated at Fr.7.3 million for the period 1984-86; (2) research, situated at the University of Lille 1, was oriented towards robotics, computer-assisted design, automation of manufacturing industries, man-machine communications etc. An investment of Fr.8 million was scheduled for the first years of the Ninth Plan; and (3) technology transfer, situated at the Ecole des Mines (School of Mines) at Douai, involved robotics and computer-assisted design. The latter efforts were concentrated on the

mechanical industries, iron and steel and metallurgical industries, the textiles and clothing sector, plastics' reprocessing and food processing.

2. Regional instruments of assistance to firms. The region saw it as necessary to aid financially firms, notably SMEs, which decided to modernise their production process by automation. This intention found expression in the introduction (in collaboration with the state) of a range of support measures for regional firms:

1. The Regional Fund for Consultancy Aid (FRAC). Its aim was to provide financial assistance to SMEs that needed to use outside consultants for the modernisation of their production process. FRAC's intervention was extended to commercial activities (like diversification of services or products and exploration of new markets) and to personnel training. In 1985 the fund was provided with Fr.5 million, funded equally by the state and the region. When a consultancy did not exceed five days, FRAC could assume responsibility for up to 80% of the costs of the study in the form of a non-returnable subsidy (up to a ceiling of Fr. 25,000). The firms concerned had to have an industrial activity whose staff did not exceed 500 people and was to be independent of a large group and in a sound financial position. By the end of 1985 nearly 100 firms had made use of this procedure. Financial support was raised to Fr.8 million for 1986, again provided equally by the state and the region.

2. The Regional Advanced Manufacturing Plan (PPR). This plan was the consequence of an initiative taken by an interministerial committee on 14th December 1984 to help the two regions of Lorraine and Nord-Pas-de-Calais. Managed jointly by the regional directorate of the ministry of industry and research and the regional council, it was granted Fr.80 million in 1985 (with three-quarters coming from the state) and Fr.125 million in 1986 (thanks to EEC aid). The plan's objective was to assist regional firms to achieve industrial modernisation programmes requiring at least a 25% purchase of advanced manufacturing equipment. PPR's financing could not exceed 15% of the investment costs and took the form of an equipment subsidy or of an interest-free advance. The addition of this aid to the regional development grant, the regional employment premium and the regional new firms grant was not to exceed 30% of the investment (60% in the 'poles of conversion').

3. The Collective Action Fund. With Fr.7 million of financial support, shared equally by the state and the region, this fund offered assistance to programmes for a set of firms that sought to develop or introduce shared facilities for their technical or commercial activities. The assistance took the form of a subsidy or an interest-free advance that could represent up to 30% of the programme (50% in the case of

model programmes).

The Experience of URBA 2000

Announced in 1983, the URBA 2000 project aimed to regroup on a single site the whole range of new technologies, principally new telecommunications equipment and services, in order to apply them in an optimal manner to the largest possible number of economic snd social uses. The originality of the approach rested in substituting for a dispersed set of experiences a comprehensive and coherent project that would link together existing programmes in different departments, agencies and companies. It was expected to lead eventually to, for instance, revision of the rules for organising urban spatial development and to major modifications in the organisation of work.

Two sites were selected, Biarritz-Bayonne in the south (in the Aquitaine region) and the triangle Lille-Valenciennes-Lens in the north (in Nord-Pas-de-Calais). For the north several projects were of immense value and were rapidly fulfilled: like the launching of the biocarte ('health card'), the installation of terminals in retail shops (the move to 'cashless' shopping), the introduction of magnetic payment cards for buses (in Douai) and the creation of a 'picture bank' on textile materials at Tourcoing. One notable project was the satellite link between the headquarters of a refrigerated transport company and its vehicles spread across the whole of Europe. For each of its operations URBA 2000 brings together the partners, provides the solutions to technical problems but invests money only if they cannot manage to balance the budget. By 1986 URBA 2000 had committed Fr.140 million to its various activities.

A CASE STUDY OF PROVENCE-ALPES-COTE D'AZUR

It is both interesting and useful to compare the contents of the regional plan and the state-regional planning contract of Provence-Alpes-Côte d'Azur with those of Nord-Pas-de-Calais. Not least, and unlike Nord-Pas-de-Calais, Provence-Alpes-Côte d'Azur experienced a change of political majority as a result of the regional elections of March 1986. The Socialist Party lost its majority there. As a consequence, the assumptions on which regional planning had been based were in question. Despite this change of party political majority different regional policies seemed to converge on the idea of technological poles. Priority continued to be given, as we shall see, to the technological park at Valbonne-Sophia-Antipolis and the new park at Château-Gombert in Marseille.

At the census of 1982 the Provence-Alpes-Côte d'Azur region had 3,965,200 inhabitants, just as many as the Nord-Pas-de-Calais region, but with a population density of only 126 per square kilometre compared to 317 for Nord-Pas-de-Calais. This population is distributed very unequally, with a density of some 340 inhabitants per square kilometre in the département of Bouches-du-Rhône (which incorporates Marseille and includes 43.4% of the regional population) and only 17 per square kilometre in that of Alpes-de-Haute-Provence. Between 1962 and 1982 the regional population grew by nearly 41% against only 16.8% for the country as a whole. The birth rate was low (12.4 per thousand compared to 13.6 for France), the strong demographic growth being the product of an important migration, notably domestic, which the region experienced. By contrast, the unemployment rate was higher than the national average, in March 1985 12.7% of the active population against 10.3% for France as a whole. In the département of Var it exceeded 14.3%.

The Provence-Alpes-Côte d'Azur region is characterised by an important tertiary sector, particularly due to tourism, accounting for nearly 70% of the active population in the region compared to a national average of about 57%. Certain départements, notably Alpes Maritimes, have attempted for some years to provide themselves with less seasonal activities than tourism. Great efforts have been made to create highly skilled jobs, by attracting 'leading-edge' industries (like IBM and Texas Instruments) or by developing technological parks, as at Sophia-Antipolis in Alpes Maritimes. The secondary sector seemed under-represented, manufacturing industry accounting for only 25.4% of the active population in the region against 34.6% in France as a whole. Moreover, it was essentially concentrated around the Marseille conurbation - Marignane, Martigues, etang de Berre. In the midst of this very thin industrial fabric some very large industrial firms were, nevertheless, emerging: in aerospace (Aérospatiale at Marignane), in shipbuilding (Arsenal de Toulon or Chantiers navals de La Ciotat et de la Seyne-sur-Mer) and in chemicals (Naphtachimie at Martigues).

The Regional Plan

Proposed by the Socialist president of the regional council, Michel Pezet, and voted on 13th December 1983, the plan for the Provence-Alpes-Côte d'Azur region laid down five priorities for the period 1984-88:

1. Job creation by an active policy of economic development and a sustained policy of planning work time.
2. Improvement of the level of qualifications in the work force by changes in basic education and by developing professional training.
3. Basing regional development on research and innovation, notably in the priority sectors, by improving the effectiveness of the relations between the worlds of research and of industry.
4. Regional spatial planning focused on public transport policy and on land and property development.
5. Improvement of the quality of daily life, notably by town-planning and housing policies.

Also, as in Nord-Pas-de-Calais, special emphasis was given to training and to the development of research and innovation. The ambition was to make the whole region a technological pole on a national and even international scale. This ambition was to be realised by means of new technological parks (Château-Gombert) and by the creation of technology-transfer structures to operate between research centres and industry (see later).

However, with the change of party political majority after the regional elections of March 1986, and the replacement of the Socialist Michel Pezet by the liberal Jean Claude Gaudin, this regional plan could no longer be considered as representative of the regional objectives for the next years. Even so, on issues of new technology policy few modifications were to be expected on the part of the regional council; indeed, a consensus was emerging amongst the different political actors about the objectives for this field of policy.

The Planning Contract and Technological Development

The state-region planning contract, which was signed on 7th May 1984, included 29 articles organised around the five priorities of the regional plan (see above). On issues of technological development article 15 determined the joint programme of action between the state and the region for the next few years. Two types of action were envisaged:

1. To give to the Provence-Alpes-Côte d'Azur region a technological pole with elements of an international stature. This pole was to link together the activities of research, of advanced technical training and of industrial production in the 'leading-edge' sectors where the region had the available potential of important laboratories and researchers: in particular, robotics, biotechnology, chemicals, meteorology and instrumentation, and new materials.
2. To establish appropriate technology-transfer centres between research and training units and companies. Large financial sums were allocated for this purpose: more than Fr.67 million for the duration of the Ninth Plan, of which Fr.39 million were borne by the state.

In order to understand these developments in a more detailed and concrete way, it is useful to examine the cases of robotics and biotechnology.

1. Robotics was based on the International Institute of Robotics and Artificial Intelligence at Marseille (IRIAM), a public-private company created by the public authorities of the region (like Marseille city and the regional council), industrialists and financial institutions. It served as a technology-transfer structure for local firms and public authorities. IRIAM brought together different types of activity: training, conference organisation and supply of materials and of software. It could conclude agreements

with interested companies. Up to the end of the Ninth Plan IRIAM intended to support the creation of firms in the following sectors: maritime, agriculture, architecture and construction, and health.

2. In biotechnology the potential of the region was considerable. With more than 1,000 researchers and technicians working in this field, Provence-Alpes-Côte d'Azur was in second place amongst the French regions. Three sites could be identified: Nice-Antibes, Marseille and Cadarache. However, the regional industrial fabric related to biotechnology seemed very weak by comparison with the research potential. The only active companies were CIRD at Sophia-Antipolis, VIRBAC at Carros near to Nice, IMMUNOTECH at Marseille-Luminy and some companies in the area of Grasse. Also, the biotechnological pole created in 1983, jointly by the Ministry of Research and Technology, the regional council and the regional chamber of commerce and industry, had limited its activities to information (bibliographies, documentation), to training (notably organisation of courses and placements) and to consultancy (provision of expertise, including market and feasibility studies). However, in order to improve its effectiveness, contacts were established with the biotechnology CRITT at Toulouse.

Generally, in the absence of a satisfactory industrial fabric, the technology-transfer structure estabished in the Provence-Alpes-Côte d'Azur region had, at least in the short term, only a limited effectiveness. As a consequence, the regional policy makers placed even greater hopes in the regional technological parks - Sophia-Antipolis and, more recently, Château-Gombert.

The Regional Technopoles: From Sophia-Antipolis to Château-Gombert

The Sophia-Antipolis complex provides the archetypal French-style technological park, uniting on one site training and research activities and technologically advanced industries with the aim of achieving a 'cross-fertilisation'. If comparative references were made at the time of the start of the operation, to Route 128 in the United States or to Akademgorod in the Soviet Union, the French approach remained distinctive. At the beginning, in 1969, there was a simple private-law association, calling itself Sophia-Antipolis, sustained by a personality, the director of the prestigious National School of Mines (École Nationale des Mines) in Paris, in search of a decentralised location. Then, in 1970, the département of Alpes Maritimes committed itself to assist the association and, by guaranteeing the raised loans, facilitated the purchase of the necessary land. In 1972 the state gave its agreement in principle to the completion of the complex, which grew larger and thus made explicit its international stature. In 1974 the chamber of commerce and industry of Nice and the Alpes Maritimes became the director of works for the complex. In parallel, the state involved itself more deeply by producing, in 1974, a twenty-year plan for developing and financing the site. The development of the 2,500-hectare complex was divided up as follows: 750 hectares were scheduled to receive activities that aimed eventually to create 20,000 jobs, 150 hectares were destined for housing and for services, and the rest was protected and developed as green space.

Each year about Fr.40 million have been invested in the operation by all the interested public bodies, like the state and the département of Alpes Maritimes. Between 1972 and 1986 a total of more than Fr.2 billion had been invested on the site by the public and private sectors. By 1986 some 2,000 inhabitants lived in the midst of the Sophia-Antipolis complex. Nearly 500 housing units had been built, with an annual construction rate of about 150 units. However, in the absence of satisfactory cultural and social infrastructure, a substantial proportion of the personnel working on the site preferred to live in Nice, a distance of about 20 kms. In about 15 years some 95 institutions comprising 6,000 people had settled on the site. They included research centres or schools - like the National Advanced School of Mines (École Nationale Supérieure des Mines), the National Centre for Scientific Research (CNRS), the Office of Geological and Mining Research (Bureau de Recherches Géologiques et Minière), and the French Agency for Energy Control (Agence Française pour la Maîtrise de l'Energie) - as well as the registered offices of numerous firms, French and foreign. American multinationals, such as Dow Chemical and Digital Equipment, were present on the site, as well as French multinationals like Télémécanique, L'Oréal and Thomson-CSF. At the same time the initial ambitions had not been completely satisfied. Despite the variety of assistance available (different premiums, fiscal inducements, subsidies for land purchase etc.) firm creation remained an unusual feature of the site. Also, 'cross-fertilisation' was not so fruitful as had been expected. Its founders continued, nevertheless, to hope for the establishment of at least 400 firms between 1986 and the end of the century.

More recently the Provence-Alpes-Côte d'Azur region has added another 'technological pole', that of Château-Gombert in Marseille. It was essentially the product of the political rivalry within the region between the city of Nice, under Jacques Medecin, and the city of Marseille, whose Socialist mayor, Gaston Defferre, was also Minister of the Interior and Decentralisation. The Château-Gombert complex was seen as the counterweight in the west of the region to the complex at Sophia-Antipolis. For the implementation of this project four actors were brought together: the region, the département of Bouches-du-Rhône, the chamber of commerce and the city of Marseille. On 180 hectares of land to the north-east of Marseille the new pole was to house all the engineering schools of the chamber of commerce, regrouped around a Mediterranean Institute of Technology (IMT), an industrial zone of 70 hectares, as well as property development (on 15 hectares). A first development programme, covering 50 hectares and scheduled to be implemented in the Ninth and Tenth Plans, incorporated the whole of the IMT project and half of the urban centre. The investment committed for the Ninth Plan amounted to Fr.333 million (with Fr.86.5 million from the state, Fr.60.9 million from the region, Fr.43 million from the chamber of commerce, Fr.39.2 million from the département of Bouches-du-Rhône and the city of Marseille, and Fr.93.7 million from a public-private syndicate including the city of Marseille and the chamber of commerce). Besides the mobilisation of educational resources, the principal mission of Château-Gombert was to encourage technology transfer. For this reason it was intended to establish the regional branch of the Agency for the Development of Automated Production (ADEPA) and of IRIAM (which was discussed above). IMT was planned to become operational in 1988.

CONCLUSIONS

French experience with new technology and innovation policies is simply too recent to enable any definitive assessments of the results. At one level the two regions of Nord-Pas-de-Calais and Provences-Alpes-Côte d'Azur appear very different in economic and sociological terms. At another level, an examination of their new technology and innovation policies yields several conclusions:

1. Both regions accorded a central position to new technologies in their future economic development. Neither wished to risk being marginalised in the new industrial revolution
2. The priority activities for the two regions appeared often identical, notably robotics, biotechnology and electronics. The same phenomenon can be observed in the other French regions.
3. In the 1980s local and regional initiatives have multiplied to the point where it seems that new technologies have become the object of political 'gamesmanship' and competition, externally but also, to an increasing degree, internally within each region.
4. At the same time each region has chosen an approach best corresponding to its own traditions and particular advantages. Nord-Pas-de-Calais, with a developed industrial structure, preferred the approach of technology-transfer centres; Provence-Alpes-Côte d'Azur, with a less developed industrial structure, opted for 'technological parks'.
5. Even so, the regional differences on matters of scientific and technological development did not seem very important. In order to encourage new technology development, whether indigenous or 'imported', each French region had to resort increasingly to other factors, factors that seemed ever more qualitative and subjective. As new technology policies become commonplace, the role of cultural factors is likely to become more and more important. Hence a new opportunity emerges for the regions that have known how to conserve their historical and cultural identities.

REFERENCES

This chapter was translated from the French by Kenneth Dyson.

DATAR (1983) Rapport d'Activité and (1985) Rapport d'Activité, Paris

Delpierre, M. (1986) 'L'Evaluation du Pôle Productique Nord-Pas-de-Calais: Le Rôle des Milieux Environnants dans la Diffusion de l'Automatisation Intégrée de Production', University of Lille II, July

Janvier, Y. (1985) 'Economie et Pratiques Territoriales de Développement: Les Rôles des Technopôles', Espaces Prospectifs, 2, June

Laborie, J.P., Langumier, J.F. and De Roo, P. (1985), La Politique Francaise d'Amenagement du Territoire de 1950 à 1985, La Documentation Françcaise, Paris

MRT, MPAT and MEN (1985), Atlas des Pôles Technologiques Regionaux, La Documentation Francaise, Paris

Region Nord-Pas-de-Calais (1985), Recherche et Développement Technologique : La Politique du Conseil Régional, Conseil Régional, Lille

Region Nord-Pas-de-Calais (1984), Contrat de Plan entre l'Etat et la Région Nord-Pas-de-Calais pour le IXème Plan 1984-1988, Conseil Régional, Lille

Chapter Seven

CASE STUDIES OF LOCAL TECHNOLOGY AND INNOVATION POLICIES IN WEST GERMANY: SUCCESS AND FAILURE

Andreas Schlieper

This chapter provides case studies of local technology and innovation policies in the Federal Republic of Germany's most populous state (Land) and the traditional heartland of its heavy industries - North-Rhine Westphalia (Nordrhein-Westfalen).

North-Rhine Westphalia lies in the west of the Federal Republic and borders on Belgium and the Netherlands. It is the most populous federal state with 16.8 million citizens. Almost a third of the population of the Federal Republic lives there. The core area of the Rhenish-Westphalian industrial landscape is the Ruhr region, one of the richest bituminous coalbearing areas of the world and long one-sidedly characterised by mining, steel and iron-making industries. Meanwhile other industries have come, such as electronics, chemicals, synthetic fibres, paints, aluminium smelting and petroleum processing. There are also textiles and automobile manufacture, mechanical engineering, cement and glass works and large breweries. Between Köln (Cologne) and Bonn, in the Ville upland, the Federal Republic's largest brown coal deposit is mined. North-Rhine Westphalia's lively economic activity is reflected in its densely knit network of transport facilities linking the many cities: Köln, Essen, Dortmund, Düsseldorf, Duisburg, Bochum, Wuppertal, Bielefeld, Gelsenkirchen, Solingen, Leverkusen and Paderborn, to name but some.

The state of North-Rhine Westphalia was formed in 1946 mostly of areas which had belonged to Prussia since the early 19th century but had formed no political unit. Party-political power relationships in the state have changed frequently. Both Christian Democrats (CDU) and Social Democrats (SPD) have ruled partly in coalition with the Free Democrats (FDP) and on occasions alone. From 1958 to 1962 the CDU had the majority in the state parliament (Landtag), the SPD has had it since 1980. In 1987 its head of government, Johannes Rau, was a deputy chairman of the SPD and unsuccessful Chancellor-candidate of the SPD in the January election. Under Rau's leadership, North-Rhine Westphalia was keen to present an image of a 'model' SPD state.

North-Rhine Westphalia is one of the ten federal states of the Federal Republic of Germany. In the West German federal system there is a quite complicated division of labour between the federal level and the state levels which is regulated more or less consistently in the so-called 'Basic Law' or constitution of 1949 (the Grundgesetz). This division of labour leaves a certain scope for independent policy-making at the state level, notably in educational or cultural policy where the states have 'exclusive' jurisdiction. A more limited scope for autonomy of action is available in the field of economic policy. The scope for economic policy is limited both in legal terms and - even more strikingly - by financial constraints.

These limitations on economic policy leave two main fields of political activity for the state level:

1. Structural policy (Strukturpolitik) which, in this context, means in particular regional policy. In the 1980s, especially after the SPD lost power in Bonn in 1982, a big dispute emerged about whether the Federal Republic needed an 'industrial policy' and about which level of government should be responsible for it. Usually, an industrial crisis has a strong regional impact; the steel crisis, for instance, is concentrated on certain towns (like Duisburg) or regions (like the Ruhr). The federal government under Chancellor Helmut Kohl (CDU) claimed that the problems in these regions are 'regional problems' and should be tackled by the state authorities. In return the states, notably North-Rhine Westphalia, point to the fact that they do not have the financial resources and the adequate political instruments to solve industrial crises and the resulting social consequences. By 1987 this dispute between North-Rhine Westphalia and Bonn had reached a critical point, as the state's budgetary position deteriorated.
2. The other field of economic policy where the state government can act more or less deliberately is technology policy. The state government of North-Rhine Westphalia - like most of the other state governments - offers a wide range of financial subsidies and aid programmes to encourage technological development. There are programmes to increase R&D activities at the universities as well as at the enterprise level. The state government supports transfer and consulting activities and institutions like technology transfer agencies, technology parks or agencies that try to up-grade the technological standard in SMEs. For this latter reason an agency by the name of 'ZENIT' (the Centre for Innovation and Technology in North-Rhine Westphalia) was founded in 1984. It is supported by the state government, the State Bank (Westdeutsche Landesbank) and a special technology-oriented association of SMEs. In addition, the state government assists the application of new technologies especially in small and medium-sized enterprises. Overall, North-Rhine Westphalia's technology policy attempts to assist all three stages of technological development - invention, innovation as well as imitation (or application) - and to focus the policy on small and new firms.

POLICY INSTRUMENTS AND ORGANISATION

Policy making for new technologies and innovation needs to keep in mind a two-dimensional perspective: there are problems of designing the various instruments of policy and of the organization of policy.

Instruments

With respect to the instruments of economic policy - or, to be more precise, of regional economic policy - a world-wide 'state of the art' has been developed since the mid 1970s. In nearly all of the traditional industrialised areas and regions in Western Europe a 'multi-targeted' strategy is used, something that might be called a 'strategy network'. Governments and administrations have become aware of the fact that they have to operate in a complex and complicated society where all sub-systems are linked to one another and all influence each other. Investment decisions of private enterprises, for example, do not depend on financial criteria alone; there are technical and legal criteria as well, and there are even emotional or psychological components which cannot be influenced by financial subsidies alone. Thus, a regional strategy must use a whole bunch of different, hopefully consistent approaches. Of course, a main component of such a strategy should focus on capital, technology and management skills (the latter are one of the most important 'bottle-neck' factors for economic growth and development in the traditionally industrialised regions, not least in West Germany). At the same time it is crucial for the efficiency of a regional strategy that it is directed towards the qualification of the workforce; this means 'start-up' training as well as further education, 'skill-development' training and re-training. A third part of the above-mentioned 'regional strategy network' must cover the regional infrastructure, its improvement and renewal. In this context 'infrastructure' means in the first place the 'business-related' infrastructure like the information and communication system. However, remembering the various criteria of an investment decision, and especially the more emotional or psychological components, a 'business-related' infrastructure involves also the overall attraction and 'quality of life' of a region. Improvement of the leisure or shopping facilities of a region and its image will contribute to economic development. In this sense environmental policies are important because they not only open up the potential for further economic development; also, they improve the image and the attraction.

Such a 'multi-targeted' strategy attempts to improve the general - or rather regional - framework for economic activities. At the same time it becomes involved in the economic activities themselves and covers more or less the whole economic circle: R&D to create new technologies, transfer to distribute the knowledge, application to shift technologies into products or production processes, subsidies to provide sites and capital for investment, creation of new markets (by public procurement or by laws and regulations especially in environment protection) and even sales promotion for international markets.

Organisation

Most of the Western European countries have had to live with the problems of declining industrialised regions so long that we can now identify the various problems and their interactions quite well. Also, after more than a decade of regional economic crisis we know quite well, too, what to do and which instruments to use. And we even have - as mentioned earlier - an idea of some international standard, an ability to refer to 'best practise'. This situation opens up, however, a much more interesting question: if we know what to do, we can now devote attention to the issue of 'how' it should be done, and 'who' is going to do it. In other words, the central questions revolve around the organisation of regional economic policy and especially a strategy of decentralisation. What appear to be at first sight - from the national or regional perspective - quite similar problems of economic decline and unemployment turn out to be very differentiated at the local level. The same rate of unemployment is the result of very different causes; even more importantly, the endogenous potential and the regional and local pre-conditions for overcoming economic decline are different. In general, these differences cannot be identified by the state government. Even if it could do so, the state government cannot tackle these differences with sufficiently differentiated and sensitive programmes or instruments. New technology and innovation policies must move away from the myth that the central level can identify and tackle regional or local problems. The prime function of the central level of government is to provide general programmes, money and strategic guidelines that serve as a means of adjustment amongst the regions.

North-Rhine Westphalia operates a 'three-target' policy: (1) to reduce over-capacities in the steel and coal industries and make the reductions socially acceptable; (2) to modernise the remaining capacities in order to become internationally competitive; and (3) to build up new structures by means of new technologies, new qualifications, new products, and new enterprises. These new structures should themselves be consistent with three guidelines: (1) they should fit into the already existing regional or local structure; (2) they should contribute to the solution of regional problems and accommodate regional needs; and (3), most importantly, they should be competitive in international markets. These targets and guidelines are based on the key assumption that decisions about which technology, which product, which skills and which enterprise should be supported cannot be made only at the state level. Effective policy implementation requires the assistance and the co-operation of, as well as initiatives by, the local and regional level.

It might have been noticed that the word 'local level' has been used up to now and not the words 'local authority' or 'local government'. This usage aims to stress that a decentralised policy has to include not only the local public institutions, but all economic actors like enterprises, banks and trade unions, as well as the Labour Office, social and environmental institutions, the Factory Inspectorate, even the churches, not to mention all the more or less 'business-related' institutions that could fill half a book. In order to show how this strategy of decentralisation has been practised in North-Rhine Westphalia (and how it has sometimes failed) three examples will be presented. All three cases are related to technology parks. This relationship is no coincidence because from the early 1980s onwards technology transfer and application were considered the most important 'bottle-neck' factors for local and regional development.

THE CASE OF AACHEN

The first example is the city of Aachen (or 'Aix-la-Chapelle'). It has a population of some 200,000 inhabitants and is situated in the west of North-Rhine Westphalia, close to the Belgian and Dutch borders. Aachen is a very old city with a long urban tradition; in the medieval period it was the coronation city of the German emperors. Because of its coal resources - both lignite and pit coal - the Aachen region developed into an industrial region during the 19th century. In fact, it was one of the most important and advanced German industrial regions at the turn of the century. Already by that time the city of Aachen had become the centre of an isolated agglomeration area and had developed a more service-oriented economic structure. To a certain extent it can be compared to the Pittsburg region in the United States. In 1870 the Technical University was founded; later it proved to be the most important potential for structural change. When the first structural crisis, the decline of the textile industry in the 1950s and 1960s, hit the region, the city itself was able to retain its economic prosperity. However, in the 1970s and 1980s the situation deteriorated. By 1986, the unemployment rate for the region climbed to 10.7% and to 12.7% for the city of Aachen (the state's average was 10.4%).

In the late 1970s the city administration and the business community became aware that something spectacular had to be done in order to improve the economic strength of the region. It was quite obvious then that the residue of the coal industry would not be able to survive longer than two decades at the most, leaving more than 20,000 mine workers at the risk of unemployment. At that time it was also clear that economic relief would not come from attracting new industries from outside the area. Thus the regional economic strategy had to be based on endogenous development potential and the specific economic strengths of the region. The city of Aachen established a 'two-tier' strategy: one dimension was enlargement of the catchment area by installing a close co-operation with the surrounding regions in Belgium and the Netherlands; the other was to combine the local economic actors in order to found and operate a technology park. The idea was to create a sheltered environment for students and scientists from the Technical University if and when they wanted to open up their own enterprises. Hence AGIT was founded - the Association for Innovation and Technology. AGIT is a private institution with participation by local authorities, the chamber of industry and commerce (which has a much stronger legal standing in West Germany than in most other European countries), the trade unions and - of course - the Technical University. The state government granted allowances for the building and operating cost of AGIT. A crucial part of the policy of the government in North-Rhine Westphalia was to give assistance to technology parks if, and only if, they are not run by one local institution alone - for instance, only by a university or only by the local authority. A significant number of local institutions and a significant amount of local money must be raised. Also, the state government preferred these institutions to second members of their staff. AGIT was, therefore, eligible for state grants.

AGIT embodies two more or less separate approaches. One is the building where office, laboratories or production sites and, of course, consulting and management services are offered to new entrepreneurs. This approach proved to be quite successful: 14 new firms were in the building by the end of 1986, so that the building was filled and a new one was under construction. The other part of AGIT is concerned more with the marketing side of technology policy. AGIT offers and runs a special promotion service in the United States for small and new enterprises from the Aachen region. This type of support seems to be crucial for the new 'high-tech' entrepreneurs. Usually, the local and even the national market is too small for their very specialised products so that they have to go international at a comparatively early stage in order to reach their 'break-even' point. Hence in the mid 1980s the state government of North-Rhine Westphalia created a programme to strengthen international economic relations not only covering export promotion but also international technology, patent transfer and joint ventures. By 1986 AGIT was planning to open up a third 'product-line': consultancy and promotion services to all enterprises in the Aachen region and not only to those in the technology park. Also, as part of a more decentralised regional policy, the state government intended to use AGIT and similar institutions as a communication and co-operation network and as an agent and moderator of its policies.

THE CASE OF DORTMUND

A second case study of success is provided by the city of Dortmund. It is part of an old industrialised region - the Ruhr area, which is a polycentric 'agglomeration area'. In this type of area it is to a certain extent more difficult for a city to create its own local economic strategy because interaction and competition amongst the cities within the region are denser and more complex than - by comparison - in the Aachen region, where Aachen is undoubtedly the centre of economic activity. Dortmund has a population of some 600,000 inhabitants. The trend to declining population is more or less due to the economic decline of coal mining and the steel industry. As a very old commercial city Dortmund's industrial development started in the middle of the 19th century. It is a quite typical city of the Ruhr area, still depending on the old industries and still possessing a working-class community. Up to the

1970s the city had hardly any supra-regional service enterprises - except the administration of Hoesch, the leading local steel producer. The foundation of the Dortmund University in 1975 - as part of the 'Development Programme for the Ruhr', when five new universities were created in the Ruhr area - meant a very important impulse for structural change.

At the beginning of the 1980s economic and labour-market developments in Dortmund became more difficult and threatening. The unemployment rate grew by 1986 to 16.0% in the whole Dortmund region and to 16.4% in the city itself. As a consequence unemployment was the third highest in North-Rhine Westphalia. Being a large city meant that Dortmund had as well an impressive absolute figure of unemployment: more than 34,000. It was obvious that - left alone - the economic situation would not recover but get worse. By 1987 North-Rhine Westphalia had not overcome the world-wide steel crisis and the reduction of capacities and jobs. For a long time the business community and the politicians in Dortmund firmly believed that the steel crisis would be a cyclical, short-term affair. Hence in the 1960s and 1970s they actually rejected plans for a car-production plant in Dortmund that might have created some 20,000 new jobs. It was part of the 'mental structure' that 'change' was a foreign word. 150 years of economic success and the common convictions of politicians, administration, business community and trade unions made a new start difficult to envisage, let alone launch and implement.

A great advantage for the Dortmund development was that the 'right people' came in at the 'right time'. Hoesch - the dominant local enterprise - got a new chairman of the board, who came straight from the federal government where he had served as a Secretary of State in the social-liberal coalition of SPD and FDP under Helmut Schmidt. The chamber of commerce elected a new managing director who, surprisingly enough, came from outside the Ruhr area. Meanwhile, the city administration appointed a new head of the economic promotion department. These people - together with the dean of the university - acted as catalysts of local economic development. They founded a technology park, again as a joint venture, but this time excluding the trade unions. Together with the trade unions, the city administration funded in return a so-called 'Development and Training Centre' especially designed to qualify the unemployed. Dortmund managed to establish an R&D institute for transport technology and to attract a well-known German enterprise that produces this kind of goods. In this way the locality managed to create the 'critical mass' for new economic development from both the supply and demand side.

The convincing aspect of the Dortmund approach was the fact that it was able to set up a more or less coherent strategy. Policy instruments were adjusted to what was available in the regional economy. The approach did not concentrate on new technology regardless of whether or not it had any links to the local economic structure. Instead it found a very specialised technology, a technological niche that gave wider impulses to the local economy. With the above-mentioned 'Development and Training Centre' Dortmund also included training for skills into its strategy. By 1987 the Dortmund city administration was preparing a more elaborate strategy. With that strategy discussion it aimed to create a broad political consensus; that consensus in turn would contribute to a new identity and a new motivation.

THE CASE OF DUISBURG

After looking at two case studies of success this chapter will now investigate a story of failure. The last example is the city of Duisburg, which, like Dortmund, is part of the Ruhr area. Duisburg has a population of just less than 550,000 inhabitants with a declining trend, again due to the crisis of the steel industry. As a result of that crisis the Duisburg region has an unemployment rate of 15.7%, more than 31,000 in absolute figures. At first sight the conditions for structural change are not that bad: Duisburg has a university founded in the middle of the 1970s; also, it has the biggest inland port of the world with many shipping and transport companies which could be a good vehicle for export promotion. On the other hand, there are some disadvantages: Duisburg is situated quite near to Düsseldorf, one of the biggest service regions of West Germany. The consequent competition for new firms proved too hard for Duisburg. Also, there is not just one steel company in Duisburg (like Hoesch in Dortmund); trying to convince the four of them to join into a local economic strategy is very much harder. These companies do not normally co-operate, and it is not likely that they will start co-operation within a local strategy.

At the end of the 1970s Duisburg tried the same kind of approach as Dortmund: the aim was to attract an R&D institution, preferably involved in micro-electronics. Economic development was expected to follow automatically. This approach did not work, so Duisburg thought of setting up a technology park. It too did not work because the city found neither the appropriate site nor other institutions to participate. After that failure it took some time to find a new idea. Finally, Duisburg wanted to install a world trade centre in the city: it would have been the first one in West Germany. Once again the plan crumbled; they did not find private local investors who were willing to take the initiative and bear the risk. The very last idea, which was destined to fail again, was to make the inland port into some kind of an enterprise zone. One plan was for a casino, designed not only to improve the image and attraction of the city but also to provide a new source of revenue for the city budget.

CONCLUSIONS

These few examples show that by 1987 Duisburg had not managed to create a concise and convincing strategy for local economic development. This failure is partly due to the fact that the responsible people in the city administration did not work together. Each of them tried to follow his own plans. So all the plans - which were not that bad in themselves - were not supported by all of the administration and city council. The same situation applied in the case of the other economic actors. The Duisburg case illustrates very well the importance of individual commitment and activity. A comparison of Duisburg and Dortmund does not reveal significant 'real' differences of economic structure. In the context of a similar 'hardware' it is the 'software' that is decisive.

At the same time the Duisburg case shows the general importance of a decentralised strategy and commitment. The state government is not able to assume direct rule in Duisburg or to send in some state task force or commissioner. The same kind of programmes and instruments are offered in Duisburg as in Dortmund. In the final analysis, however, whether and how these programmes are used always depends on the local actors themselves.

North-Rhine Westphalia now provides a growing number of examples of approaches to local economic and technological development. In the city of Essen a technology park similar to those in Dortmund and Aachen was founded in 1985 and by the end of 1986 was already fully utilised. Cologne planned to establish a 'media park', hoping to attract television and video-producers and as well as to develop media and information technologies. In the little city of Hamm a project was started in 1986 to encourage local co-operation in the field of information and telecommunication networks. The state government planned to grant allowances to cities or regions when they attempt local co-operation in communication networks. This programme was to begin in the 1988 budget.

In North-Rhine Westphalia the main aim of economic and regional policy had been to reduce unemployment by creating new jobs - not any kind of jobs, but jobs that would have some kind of long-term prospects both for individuals and for society. The state's experiences with technology policy in general, and technology parks in particular, have shown that a positive impact on the labour market cannot be expected in the short term. Hence, by 1987, the success of technology and innovation policies cannot be evaluated by the amount of jobs that they have created. 'Success' here means the capability to create some 'spill-over' effects to the rest of the local or regional economy. Till now these 'spill-over' effects have been directed mostly towards improved competitiveness by rationalisation. Invention and innovation of new products, which will directly create jobs, has been only a part of the results. In this sense technology and innovation policies would be 'overburdened' if the solution of the labour-market problems, especially those in the old industrialised regions, was expected from them. Technology policy at the state, regional and local levels is necessary but not sufficient.

Chapter Eight

TOWARDS SILICONDALE? LESSONS FROM AMERICAN EXPERIENCE FOR THE PENNINE TOWNS AND CITIES

Tony Jowitt

In August 1985 the Financial Times reported:

> Behind the smoked glass of Bradford's successful Listerhills science park, 18 small businesses are trying to make headway in the technology of the 1980s. The sprinkling of BMWs parked alongside the futuristic single-storey office units indicates that many are getting there.
> But sadly, this new venture seems cruelly to underline the daunting problems facing one of the most hard-pressed cities in Britain.
> Fifty yards away from this small enclosure of modems and software, a group of Asian children sits on a rusting slide in the midst of one of Britain's most decaying urban environments. A heap of domestic rubbish burns unsupervised next to a glass-strewn play area. A cleared stretch of grass and weeds, several times larger than a soccer field, is ringed by three-storey stone houses, many derelict, others still providing some form of family home.
> This is but a small part of the pockmarked landscape of empty mills, waste land and unkempt terraced housing which spreads out in several directions from the West Yorkshire city's attractive commercial core.
> Relieved only spasmodically by decent housing and busy factories, Bradford's sprawling inner areas, home for most of its 300,000 inhabitants, convey an unremitting sense of physical decline(1).

This account offers an evocative picture of a West Yorkshire textile city in the last quarter of the twentieth century - a city whose manufacturing base has been cruelly depleted, with high levels of unemployment and set within the context of major social and environmental problems. And yet within the sea of industrial and urban dereliction and decline there seems to be a small-scale flowering of high-technology which might modify the pervading gloom. With minor modifications this description could apply to much of Britain and Western Europe.

During the nineteenth century the West Yorkshire region underwent a spectacular transformation as one of the cradles of the Industrial Revolution. Bradford, the greatest beneficiary in the area, was transformed from an over-blown village into the worsted textile capital of the world in under fifty years. This regional growth was largely built on a single industry - wool textiles. In Bradford the solitary spinning mill in 1800 was increased to 129 by 1850 and 338 by 1889[(2)]. Although in the late Victorian and Edwardian periods there was a diversification in the industrial structure, with the growth of engineering, transport and construction, the area remained heavily dependent on textiles until very recently - essentially a product of the first Industrial Revolution. In 1961, 34.2% of the Bradford labour force was still employed in textiles. Since that time, however, a catastrophic decline has taken place. By 1978 the textile industry employed 14.7% of the working population, and since then the industry has contracted by a further 25%. The decline in mechanical engineering has, if anything, been even greater, with a 50% reduction in the workforce between 1978 and 1984 alone. Unemployment poses specific problems for the region, and for Bradford in particular; unlike other comparable areas, because of its large ethnic-minority population, it will have higher population growth rates than much of the United Kingdom and will, therefore, have to significantly increase employment opportunities. As the Graham Moss report argued in 1986, the greatest single problem facing the area is to increase employment for, at the present time, the city is on an economic 'knife edge'[(3)].

The situation in Bradford and West Yorkshire generally in the 1980s was paralleled in the Massachusetts textile towns, but at a much earlier time. In 1924 the New Republic wrote:

> Today Fall River is a city of misery, want, unemployment, hunger and hopelessness. The cloud that shadows her seems to have no silver lining, and she lies almost dormant, while stark want stalks her streets and her workers wonder what the end is to be.

In 1931 Louis Adamic wrote an article, titled 'The Tragic Towns of New England', in Harpers Monthly Magazine, and describing them as a depressed industrial desert populated by a beaten, discouraged and hungry people. The same picture was provided of Lawrence, the great woollen and worsted centre, sometimes referred to as the 'Bradford of America', in the 1940s and early 1950s. Yet in the 1980s Massachusetts, with Lowell an ex-textile city as a prime example, was recognised as one of the boom states in th United States. In particular, it had become synonymous with the growth of high-technology; the Route 128 and 495 complexes were seen, with Silicon Valley in California, as one of the 'high-tech' centres of the world[(4)].

This chapter seeks to examine the changes in the economic structure of eastern Massachusetts, to look at the criteria that lie at the basis of 'high-tech' location and to attempt to practically apply these criteria to Massachusetts and the West Yorkshire region. Such an analysis needs to be set in a critical context by posing a number of initial questions. Firstly, it is necessary to ask whether it is feasible for the West Yorkshire area to develop an indigenous 'high-tech' sector. This question seems to be particularly important because high-technology is so often perceived as some sort of modern holy grail; local authorities and other agencies are rushing in a great competitive scramble to reach a high-technology shore that will supposedly secure economic welfare. The scramble often seems to lack both an understanding of historical experience and a knowledge of developments elsewhere. Is it reasonable to think that all areas can have a significant 'high-tech' concentration and, therefore, is it worth the time, effort and money of so many localities to try to develop it?

Secondly, even if it is possible to develop a 'high-tech' sector, the question arises of whether it will produce the benefits that are often uncritically attributed to it - that it will increase employment, produce economic growth and enhance the general welfare of the area's inhabitants. There often seems to be an assumption that high-technology is value-free, that it produces economic growth, does not lead to environmental problems and is generally beneficial. However, evidence from such areas as Massachusetts shows that it has major and more problematic economic, social and political implications. For example, it has been shown that 'high-tech' development does not bring in its wake large numbers of jobs and that it leads to a bifurcated employment structure, one that is singularly inappropriate to provide jobs for those displaced from manufacturing industry [5]. Further, high-technology development has had major political implications, leading in Massachusetts to decline in the power of organised labour and the growth of a powerful 'high-tech' pressure group, in bodies such as the Massachusetts High Technology Council, which has pushed through major cuts in state taxation and attempts to modify the school curriculum.

Thirdly, high-technology development poses a major question about the proper functions of local authorities. Should they simply provide the statutory services, or do they have a wider role in economic development and industrial regeneration? The problems of economic decline are such that it would be almost impossible for local authorities to neglect them. Yet, within a context of tight financial constraints, should they pay more attention to, indeed give top priority to, the infrastructure for which they are responsible, notably education and transport? American experience again shows that the local education system and transportation are crucially important elements for economic development. There is the additional question of the extent to which local government should become selectively involved in business development and of the effects on other businesses within the local or regional economy. How far should the local authority intervene in the market and in competition amongst producers? Finally, the question arises of whether the local authority is the appropriate agency for economic development purposes in the United Kingdom. Andreas Schlieper shows in his chapter that the proximity of cities and towns often presents problems for economic development, particularly where communities are located close to regional capitals. A similar situation to that in the Ruhr is to be found in West Yorkshire with Leeds, Bradford, Halifax, Huddersfield and Wakefield, plus a host of smaller communities, all in close proximity to each other. Does it make sense for each of these places to develop individual strategies, which might be in competition: or should we think of a wider regional economic framework, accepting that West Yorkshire, for all its differences, is a regional entity? Separate economic development is often the result of specific political factors rather than based on coherent economic, social and political analysis.

During the nineteenth century New England, and Yorkshire and Lancashire, were the respective textile centres of the United Kingdom and the United States. Even then, however, an increasing divergence between the two industries was taking place. Whereas the New England industry, which was protected by high tariffs, developed an integrated large-scale business structure, the West Yorkshire textile industry, which operated in a free-trade economy, moved towards a disintegrated business structure and to a large extent aimed at supplying foreign competitors with semi-manufactures. The British industry was overwhelmingly concerned with cheapness and retained a classic competitive business structure. By contrast, the American industry shifted towards a modern corporate capitalism, of the kind characterised by Chandler as consisting of industrial oligopoly, hierarchical managerial bureaucracy, vertical integration of production standards, the integration of financial and industrial capital and systematic research and development. Although this theme cannot be developed in this chapter, the early divergence between the two industries is reflected in their twentieth-century history. The West Yorkshire industry became overwhelmingly concerned with survival, whereas its American counterpart dedicated itself to increased profit levels. The continuing large-scale existence of the textile industry in West Yorkshire, particularly in the form that it has taken in the twentieth century, continues to have important ramifications for the contemporary situation. A largely low-wage, low-investment, non-training and reactive industry pervades the industrial and economic environment (6).

Paradoxically however, by 1939 the American textile industry was migrating from New England to the Southern states; by contrast, textiles remained overwhelmingly the most important industry in West Yorkshire. The Second World War led to an even greater divergence between the two regions. The West Yorkshire economy became more heavily dependent on its existing staple industries: in New England a new, largely military-led, manufacturing industry emerged, particularly in the field of aircraft production and electrical products. By the 1960s both economies were experiencing major problems. In the case of West Yorkshire the long inexorable decline of the textile and engineering industries was sharply accelerating, and in New England the developments of the Second World War were running into problems, although, as we shall see, they had acted as a crucial factor in subsequent 'high-tech' development. Both regions had above average levels of unemployment, a declining manufacturing base, wage levels below the average and a heritage of social and environmental problems. Since then Massachusetts, and in particular the Route 128 and Route 495 areas, have become leading centres of 'high-tech' growth, whereas West Yorkshire has continued to decline.

Before we look at the factors involved in 'high-tech' location, two points ought to be made about 'high-tech' development in Massachusetts. The Massachusetts experience is markedly different from that in Silicon Valley, in that it did not emerge from a nurtured situation but was a largely spontaneous phenomenon. Also, although in the 1980s there is a fairly wide spread of 'high-tech' products being developed or manufactured in the region, the industry is overwhelmingly dependent on the mini-computer and its applications. Some commentators have identified the 'high-tech' take-off point in 1967 when Digital Equipment (DEC) introduced its PDP-8, the first computer to sell for under $20,000. Today six of the top nine mini-computer manufacturers (in turnover) are located in the region (DEC, Data General, Wang, Honeywell, Prime, Nixdorf)[(7)]. Indeed, in the regenerated mill city of Lowell, some argue that the city has once again become dependent, as it was in the cotton era, on a single industry and on one employer, Wang.

Research on 'high-tech' location has in recent years become something of an industry in its own right [(8)]. Drawing on this work, it is possible to develop a list of factors that have played a critical role in 'high-tech' location and to apply these to both the Massachusetts and the West Yorkshire areas. Those factors are: (1) association with, and proximity to, high-quality institutions of higher education; (2) an association with military research and development; (3) the availability of venture capital; (4) a pro-business climate emanating from central and local government; (5) a pleasant environment for business premises and employee housing; (6) an area close to good cultural, recreational and retailing facilities; (7) a good communications network; (8) the availability of a pool of well-educated and skilled personnel; (9) the availability of a pool of cheap non-unionised labour; and (10) the existence of advanced manufacturing and research facilities in the area.

ASSOCIATION WITH AND PROXIMITY TO HIGH-QUALITY INSTITUTIONS OF HIGHER EDUCATION

A number of commentators see this as the key factor in 'high-tech' location, and there seems little doubt that both the Route 128 area and Silicon Valley are located close to the outstanding American universities. Massachusetts is the premier educational centre in the United States, with the Massachusetts Institute of Technology (MIT), Harvard, Northeastern, Boston University and the University of Massachusetts. In addition to the massive quantitative concentration, these institutions are of the highest quality, particularly in the field of engineering. They provide the basis of the skilled labour force in the Massachusetts 'high-tech' industry. A survey by the Massachusetts High Technology Council showed that 80% of the college graduates whom they had hired between 1978 and 1980 held degrees from Massachusetts' institutions. In 1981 almost 1000 bachelors' degrees in electrical or computer engineering were awarded in the state, plus 30 masters degrees and 57 doctorates; this figure does not include degrees from Harvard which are not classified under engineering (9). The Massachusetts Institute of Technology is widely rated as the best in the United States in the fields of electrical engineering and computer science. Its influence on 'high-tech' developments in the state has been immense. One commentator estimates that during the 1960s some 175 new Massachusetts' firms had been founded by full-time employees of four of MIT's research facilities. The best 'spin-off' was the work of Kenneth Olsen who developed the mini-computer out of his work at MIT's Lincoln Laboratory (10). American universities and, in particular MIT, have a very different attitude from British universities to the commercial exploitation of research by members of staff, as well as more flexible arrangements to combine an academic and commercial career. They are much more closely involved with on-going business activities, in bodies such as the Enterprise Forum at MIT which allows commercial organisations to bring their problems to academia (11).

Although there are a reasonable number of institutions of higher education in the West Yorkshire area, in Leeds and Bradford Universities, Leeds and Huddersfield Polytechnics and Bradford College, they are not in the same league as Harvard and MIT. In science and technology they do not recruit the best qualified students in the country. The recent cuts in government funding for the universities has been particularly severe on the so-called technological universities, probably consigning them to being, if not second-class universities, different institutions to the elite universities. Starved of resources, the technological universities are in danger of further subsiding in world ranking. This problem is further compounded by a continuing decline in government expenditure on civilian research projects. It is surely significant that the University of Texas has embarked on the biggest single expenditure programme in American higher education in an attempt to rival the east and west coast universities and to remain at the frontiers of research and that the Arizona State University is in the process of developing a $32 million Centre for Excellence in Engineering. British universities have also a very different attitude to the commercial exploitation of research and, for all the government's rhetoric about increased cooperation between the university sector and the commercial sector, this attitude is unlikely to change with the increasing disparity in salaries between the two sectors and the anti-industrial bias that continues to pervade so much of English society, not least the Thatcher government. There will, of course, be spin-offs from British universities. However, except for those of the very highest quality, the amount will be small scale. This situation poses a dilemma for local authorities, as the work of the local university will be a crucial factor in economic growth and mutual assistance in their areas. Relationships to the university sector will need more careful consideration in the future. In Massachusetts, because of the exceptional quality of local institutions, such reflection has not been required. However, in West Yorkshire it may be an essential factor in stemming the tide of industrial decline.

AN ASSOCIATION WITH MILITARY RESEARCH AND DEVELOPMENT

Despite the very great differences between the British and American economies in relation to military-led economic activity, in both countries it is a crucial factor in economic development. During and after the Second World War Massachusetts became a major centre of military research and production. In particular, the latter became associated with MIT which set up a series of laboratories to work at the forefront of research and that were to be a major source of 'high-tech' spin-offs. Also, the defence sector has always been a major customer for 'high-tech' products. In 1977 Markusen estimated that production for the military accounted for 47% of all 'high-tech' manufacturing employment; since then this figure may have risen with increased American defence expenditure(12). Possibly more important than its quantitative impact has been the nature of military production. Unlike private industry it has had liberal budgets and wanted the product irrespective of cost or the time involved. The nature and particularly the length and flexible costings of military contracts seem to have been the crucial gestation factor for a whole series of American firms.

In Britain, military expenditure on research is much smaller. In addition, the defence research bodies, largely established at the time of the Second World War, were located in the area to the south and west of London. The defence research establishments in that area have been of crucial importance to the development of the M4 'high-tech' corridor and will continue to concentrate firms in that area. Much greater academic hostility to military research exists in Britain, and local political hostility could be expected to a number of areas of possible research such as nuclear technology and biological and chemical weapons. Although military expenditure is an important factor in 'high-tech' development, West Yorkshire is unlikely to benefit from it. Of course, the question arises of whether that kind of research is wanted as part of a local strategy of economic growth.

THE AVAILABILITY OF VENTURE CAPITAL

Although the evidence is more difficult to untangle in this area, it is clear that Massachusetts was in the forefront of a series of new financing arrangements for 'high-tech'(13). The First National Bank of Boston began supporting companies emerging from MIT in 1943, and in 1958 it was the first bank to set up a Small Business Corporation. Also, in 1946 Boston was the location of the establishment of American Research and Development (ARD), which was specifically set up to finance 'high-tech' companies and made the crucial investment in DEC. Recent research on the role of venture capital has shown that the financial support is often less important than the overall business package that venture capitalists provide. Recognising that many of the new companies have scientific expertise but little experience of running a company, they can provide the whole range of business support in areas such as personnel and marketing until the company is firmly established.

British banking has an appalling historical record of industrial financing from the nineteenth century. Only recently has it acknowledged the specific needs of 'high-tech' with Barclays offering special services at certain branches to 'high-tech' companies. Interestingly, however, more than 60% of the 62 designated branches lie south of the Wash-Bristol Channel line, and very few are located in the depressed industrial regions (14).

If local government can provide some limited financial assistance, it cannot provide the whole range of ancillary business services. Do local authorities have a right, for example, to take on the marketing of the products of a new firm, and do they have the expertise to do so? Also, there are clear differences of objectives between local authorities and entrepreneurs. Local authorities have neither the necessary amount of capital nor the skills to develop 'high-tech' initiatives. Their role is, as in Massachusetts, more in the supporting fields of education, transportation and facilitation of private initiative.

A PRO-BUSINESS CLIMATE EMANATING FROM BOTH CENTRAL AND LOCAL GOVERNMENT

Between 1945 and the 1980s a remarkable transformation in government/business relations took place in Massachusetts. Whereas Massachusetts had been seen as a bad investment area by businessmen, because of high taxation levels and legislative support for labour interests, in the 1980s it was seen as a good place to invest. This transformation was reflected symbolically in the loss of its old nickname of 'Taxachusetts'. A paper by Frank Keefe, Secretary of Administration and Finance for the State of Massachusetts, reflected the importance that local officials attach to this factor. He argued:

> .... we have come to recognise the perception of our state's business climate is as important as the reality of our proximity to markets and the cost and skill levels of our labour force.

A consequence of this transformation was a major decline in the power of organised labour in the state, particularly its influence on the legislature. Indeed, a number of commentators have argued that this power has been transferred to bodies such as the Massachusetts' High Technology Council which has masterminded tax cuts in the state and pushed Boston into making major work-related changes in the state education curriculum (15).

There are fundamental differences between Massachusetts and West Yorkshire in their systems of local and regional government. Power, and particularly financial power, is far more devolved in the United States, and many of the measures taken by Massachusetts and various American cities are simply not available in the United Kingdom. The disappearance of regional government in England has exacerbated this problem. Abolition of the metropolitan county councils in 1986 destroyed a regional forum at a time when the rest of the EEC is increasingly geared towards a regional structure; also, it will exacerbate competition between local authorities within the same region.

Local authorities in the distressed industrial regions are often caught in a major dilemna. On the one hand, they require high levels of local taxation to tackle the heritage of social and environmental problems and to renew and regenerate the local economy. On the other hand, they are confronted by business interests and property owners who demand low levels of local taxation. Once again the whole question of the role of the local authority in economic development is raised. A real dilemma is posed about the extent of its involvement in restructuring the local economy, in terms of both finance and personnel.

A PLEASANT ENVIRONMENT FOR BUSINESS PREMISES AND EMPLOYEE HOUSING

This factor seems to have been of only marginal importance in the United States, although in Britain it has often been cited as a crucial reason for 'high-tech' location. An article in the Financial Times quoted Peter Ward, personnel director of Hewlett-Packard's UK subsidiary, as saying that they would not locate further north than Worcestershire: 'Any other choice, particularly sites in the cities of Britain's manufacturing heartlands, would be suicidal because of the difficulties of luring bright young people to work in places with bad images'. As Michael Breheny of Reading University put it more succinctly: 'The places with economic problems have no chance whatsoever of attracting mobile high-technology industry' (16).

This powerful locational factor does not seem to have operated in Massachusetts, for the mill city of Lowell differs little from the West Yorkshire towns. The latter have, of course, to live with the perceptions of outsiders of the Bradfords and Barnsleys of this world. Publicity and promotion may help to change the situation, but the campaign remains long-term. Part of the answer may lie in a changed self-perception of the area, involving a shift away from the traditional concept of inner-city regeneration to the idea of the 'greening' of the city and of promoting industrial development in areas such as the Wharfe valley. The logic of inner-city industrial regeneration involves huge capital expenditure, in the opposite direction to the functioning of the market.

AN AREA CLOSE TO GOOD CULTURAL, RECREATIONAL AND RETAILING FACILITIES

Boston possessed an immense advantage in relation to this factor for it has always been recognised as a major cultural centre in the United States. In addition, New England has been a pioneering area in recreational and retailing developments over the last quarter of a century. Although the West Yorkshire region has good credentials in this respect, it cannot compete with the prestige of London, which is within easy reach of the existing 'high-tech' centres. Even so, as a factor in 'high-tech' location, cultural, recreational and retailing facilities seem to have been of less importance in the United States than in the United Kingdom.

A GOOD COMMUNICATIONS NETWORK

The critical areas are road and air transportation. In both, West Yorkshire comes out badly. Their importance is reflected in the fact that the New England 'high-tech' complex is named after Route 128, the highway that acts as the western ring road round Boston. Although West Yorkshire is served by a reasonable motorway network, it suffers from chronic traffic congestion which is compounded by the difficult topography of the region. The local airport cannot compete with a major international airport like Logan in Boston. When an American manager can complain about the paucity of trans-Atlantic flights into Manchester airport, there seems little hope that the Leeds-Bradford airport can act as a catalyst for 'high-tech' growth [17]. Local transport problems have been further exacerbated by government policy, particularly in relation to the third London airport and to road building. Between 1978 and 1981 half of all expenditure on new trunk roads was spent in the South-East region [18]. The chapter by Howells and Charles emphasises the regional disparities in the development of the new telecommunications services. These disparities compound the problems of West Yorkshire.

THE AVAILABILITY OF A POOL OF WELL-EDUCATED AND SKILLED PERSONNEL

In Massachusetts the concentration of higher education facilities provided a ready source of high-quality personnel. In the United States as a whole this concentration was to be found in only about five areas; in Britain it is probably confined to the golden circle around London. At sub-degree level Britain simply does not provide enough high-quality educational training on either a full- or part-time basis. Indeed, the Yorkshire and Humberside region lags behind most other areas in the United Kingdom. It has the second-lowest proportion of school leavers entering full-time education amongst the UK regions [19]. Major initiatives are needed throughout the educational system, building on such initiatives as Pittsburg University's requirement that every graduate be computer literate and Boston's in the schooling system.

THE AVAILABILITY OF A POOL OF CHEAP LABOUR

The development of high-technology manufacturing produces a sharply bifurcated labour force: a small number of highly skilled, highly paid designers and managers is accompanied by a much larger number of semi-skilled or unskilled workers. As one commentator has written: '... whom do New England's 'high-tech' firms employ? They tend to recruit young, inexperienced people out of school or out of the home, especially women' [20]. A pool of labour is available in the depressed industrial regions of the North. However, it ought to be recognised that the long-term unemployed and those made redundant from the older manufacturing industries are unlikely to find work in 'high-tech' industry, even if it were available. Analysis of employment in New England found that:

> ... of some 833,000 people whose principal activity in 1958 was to work in the mill industries in New England. Sometime after 1958, 674,000 of these workers left the mills. By 1975 only 18,000 of them - fewer than 3% - were employed in the 'high-tech' industries in the region. (Another 2000 had migrated to 'high-tech' jobs outside New England)... This picture is almost identical for the youngest cohort taken by itself: the roughly 158,000 mill workers in 1958 who were then under the age of twenty five. By 1975, eighteen years later, only about 3.8% had been hired by the region's 'high-tech' companies and fewer than 1% had found 'high-tech' jobs elsewhere (21).

The real problem in the distressed industrial regions is to rapidly find a large number of jobs. On past evidence 'high-tech' industry does not create large numbers of jobs directly and will not soak up the skilled and semi-skilled workers recently made redundant. It will tend to compete for labour with existing mail-order and textile firms, particularly for women workers and young workers.

The time scale of industrial decline in New England has produced a different situation from that in the United Kingdom. Long-term decline and unemployment transformed Massachusetts from a centre of labour militancy pre-1930 into a state that in the 1950s and 1960s had a lower number of days lost due to work stoppages than the national average. Indeed the figure was lower than in the so-called docile anti-labour states such as Alabama. By the late 1960s there had emerged:

> ... a substantially new labour force... more multi-racial, more female, younger, disciplined by the experience of long-term employment in the immediate family or among neighbours, not particularly interested in unions (if not actively anti-union), and 'flexible' in terms of the number of hours of work, days of the week, work rules, and wages it was prepared to accept (22).

This situation was reflected in a sharp decline in wages, which by the 1970s were significantly lower in New England than in the United States generally, a factor that was particularly notable because the cost of living in New England was above the national average.

THE EXISTENCE OF ADVANCED MANUFACTURING OR RESEARCH FACILITIES IN THE AREA

In addition to 'spin-offs' from higher education 'high-tech' companies have emerged from research centres and from private-sector advanced manufacturing companies. Two of the major centres of 'high-tech' location in Britain have derived from these sources - the M4 corridor from defence research establishments and the Poole area from Plessey.

The North is unlikely to benefit from this source because of the concentration of both types of facility outside the area (see Howells and Charles). To a certain extent this situation reflects an almost incomprehensible duality in government policy. On the one hand, in its role in economic planning and employment generation, central government policies are geared towards regenerating the distressed regions; on the other hand, in the crucially important sectors of education, defence and transportation, its policies do not take into account the plight of the distressed regions. Indeed over the last quarter of a century these policies have favoured the southern half of Britain.

CONCLUSIONS

Virtually none of the criteria of importance for 'high-tech' location favour the West Yorkshire region; the overall picture seems to be an exceptionally gloomy one. It has been argued that there have been successes. The Graham Moss Report cited the Listerhills Science Park at the University of Bradford as an example: 'The Listerhills Science Park developed on City Council-owned land to the north of Bradford University by English Estates, has been in general estimation second only to Cambridge in its successful attraction of high-technology industry' (23). However, this generous analysis needs to be seen in context. Science parks have had only a limited impact on high-technology location particularly in the United States but also in Britain. As a recent commentator remarked:

> ... the symptoms of panic ... in the present scramble by local authorities, by quasi-public agencies and by the public sector to make a Disraelian leap in the dark for the science and technological shore. Indeed, those parts of the UK most affected by economic decline . . are . . . clutching at high technology, more particularly science and technology parks, as their sole panacea for future survival . . . The point is lost that without the support of a genuine regional economic planning framework they have no future - the market is working too strongly against them (24).

A competitive scramble for science parks in different places in the same region seems doomed from the outset, will prove a drain on limited local resources and, in the long run, might only have a very limited effect on the future economy of the area.

'High-tech' centres have developed in three basic ways. Firstly, they have emerged as a largely spontaneous spin-off from existing firms, research establishments and higher education. As already indicated, this process is unlikely to occur in the West Yorkshire area, except on a limited scale. The second way is by means of the location of branch manufacturing plants from the major 'high-tech' firms. Although a short-term stimulus to employment might be provided in this way, in the United States it has rarely been fruitful in the long term because it does not bring in top management. Hence branch plants are susceptible to decisions made elsewhere. Furthermore, many branch plants do not have a high-technological or research component and are, therefore, unlikely themselves to produce spin-offs that will generate further employment. In any case the Third World is seen as a more viable alternative for manufacturing purposes. The third way is by a deliberate planning process. In the United States this approach has only rarely been attempted; the only important example regularly cited is the Research Triangle in North Carolina. The latter involved huge amounts of capital expenditure on the local infrastructure, for example in the educational sector a £15 million expenditure on customised job training in Community Colleges, a number of initiatives in technical training, and the provision of close to 10% of all research funding at the University of North Carolina. This scale of investment is beyond the reach of local communities in the United Kingdom, particularly without a regional body. Moreover, the validity of the exercise in North Carolina has been called increasingly into question, particularly whether the return has justified the huge investment [25].

For all these reasons the prospect of the development of a large 'high-tech' sector in West Yorkshire must seem remote. The logic of industrial location is simply working too strongly against the area. One must also not forget that 'high-tech' industry does not provide a large amount of jobs, although of course it has a multiplier effect. It is, accordingly, necessary to reconsider the economic position of its localities, pushing to one side the panacea of 'high-tech' and reassessing future economic growth in a more realistic framework. The chasing of 'high-tech' investment by local authorities is a mad competitive scramble in which the West Yorkshire region has little chance of achieving significant results. American experience shows clearly that only a few areas have succeeded. The reasons for industrial success are varied but, in the major examples of 'high-tech' development, have related to the large-scale growth of particular products. Both California, with semi-conductors, and Massachusetts, with mini-computers, illustrate this process. Generally only on a basis of this type can there be a process of 'high-tech' diversification. In Northern England possibly only the Manchester area has the potential to develop as a 'high-tech' centre. Interestingly, like the Greater Boston area, Manchester participated in new manufacturing developments in the 1940s and 1950s, in the electrical and aerospace areas, which provided it with a number of advanced manufacturing establishments, and has subsequently built on this basis with a number of 'high-tech' branch plants.

A general attempt to develop 'high-tech' industry across the technological spectrum in West Yorkshire offers little prospect of success. Possibly a concentration on one specific area, in a field such as health that has high projected levels of growth, might offer some chance of success. However, for this purpose it would be necessary to integrate all the local authorities in the area, the higher education institutions, health authorities and other public and private agencies in some sort of planning forum. Some difficult decisions would also have to be taken about technological health care and private medicine. The picture is not totally gloomy. West Yorkshire may be unlikely to develop as an indigenous 'high-tech' centre; although unlike older industries 'high-tech' is mobile in terms of location, like older industries it is gravitating towards concentrations in the South. Nevertheless, 'high-tech' has an absolutely crucial role to play in the area's future economic development, particularly in regenerating and restructuring existing manufacturing and service industries. It has also a role in the wider community and societal context, as Bradford Metropolitan Council has shown in a number of exciting community initiatives with the elderly, housebound, disabled, women and the unemployed (see the chapter by Blackburn and Kennedy). The older manufacturing industries, which still provide important amounts of employment, must receive large-scale assistance to modernise. Thus a recent American symposium on Technology, Planning and Economic Growth had a general chorus of approval for suggestions that, in most instances, helping existing industry to adapt to new technologies instead of going all out to attract new high-technology industries might prove more beneficial and also avoid the problems of a bifurcated labour force.

A local authority needs not only to fully integrate the whole range of its activities if it is to engage in economic development. It must also think more deeply about its role in provision of the economic infrastructure, particularly education and training. Local authorities need, in addition, to place higher education at the centre of their thinking and to look at ways of increasing cooperation with local educational institutions. The existence and prestige of such bodies often seems to be the key to future economic growth and development. Not least, a local authority must recognise the historical reality of the area, that the West Yorkshire economy was largely the product of a particular period and that its future economic development can combine a judicious mixture of past, present and future. In that perspective its industrial heritage of mills and warehouses, chapels and chimneys, may be as important as its science parks. For social and political reasons, as well as economic ones, economic development should be premised on the idea of a mixed economy, based on a slimmed-down and technologically assisted manufacturing base, the continued development of the service sector, expanding tourist and leisure services, and lastly a small dash of high-technology.

NOTES

1. Financial Times 21 August 1985.

2. For the spectacular growth of Bradford and the West Yorkshire textile industry see E. Sigsworth, Black Dyke Mills (Liverpool, 1958) and D.T. Jenkins and K.G. Ponting, The British Wool Textile Industry 1770-1914 (London, 1982).

3. For details about changes in the local economy since the 1960s see Bradford MDC, The Changing Face of Bradford: District Trends (Bradford, 1984); Bradford MDC, Bradford in Figures (Bradford, 1984); Graham Moss Associates, Bradford Integrated Operations Study. The Final Report Of a Study Commissioned by Bradford City Council with Support from the European Commission (1986).

4. For the changes in the New England economy see R.C. Estall, New England. A Study in Industrial Adjustment (New York, 1966); B. Harrison, 'Regional Restructuring and 'Good Business Climates': The Economic Transformation of New England since World War II' in L. Sawers and W.K. Tabb (eds.), Sunbelt/Snowbelt: Urban Development and Regional Restructuring (New York, 1984). For the development of the Route 128 'high-tech' area see N.S. Dorfman, 'Route 128. The Development of a Regional High Technology Economy', Research Policy, 12, 1983 pp. 299-316; and A. Saxelman, 'Silicon Valley and Route 128: Regional Prototypes or Historic Exceptions?' in M. Castells (ed), High Technology, Space and Society (London, 1985).

5. B. Harrison, op.cit.

6. For the divergence between the New England and West Yorkshire textile industries see J.A. Jowitt, 'Textile Workers, Trade Unions and Politics in Bradford and Lawrence 1880-1920' in The World and the Industrial Revolution: Comparative and International Aspects of Industrialisation (Proceedings of the Lowell Conference on Industrial History, Boston, 1987).

7. N.S. Dorfman, op.cit., pp. 301-303.

8. See P. Hall and A. Markusen (eds.), Silicon Landscapes (Boston, 1985); R.P. Oakey, A.T. Thwaites and P.A. Nash, 'The Regional Distribution of Innovative Manufacturing Establishments in Great Britain', Regional Studies, 14,1980, pp. 235-253; R.P. Oakey, High Technology Small Firms: Regional Development in Britain and the United States (London, 1984): E.Malecki, 'Technology and Regional Development: A Survey', International Regional Science Review, March/April 1980, pp. 5-17; M.Peltz and M.Weiss, 'State and Local Government Roles in Industrial Innovation', Journal of the American Planning Association, 50,3,1984, pp. 270-280; E.Malecki, 'High Technology and Local Economic Development', Journal of the American Planning Association, 50,3,1984, pp. 262-269; P.Hall, 'Technology, Space and Society in Contemporary Britain' in M.Castels (ed), op.cit, pp.41-54; and J.R.L.Howells, 'The Location of Research and Development:Some Observations and Evidence from Britain', Regional Studies, 18,1984, pp. 13-29.

9. N.S.Dorfman, op.cit., pp. 302-303, 305.

10. E.B.Roberts and H.A.Wainer, 'New Enterprises Along Route 128', Science Journal, December 1968,2,pp. 79-83; and E.B.Roberts, 'A Basic Study of Innovations', Research Management, July 1968.

11. M.Bullock, Academic Enterprise, Industrial Innovation, and the Development of High Technology Financing in the United States (London, 1983), pp. 7-13.

12. M.Castells, op.cit., p. 26.

13. See M. Bullock, op.cit.

14. Financial Times, 12 November 1986.

15. F.T.Keefe, 'The Massachusetts Success Story', privately printed conference paper presented at the RETI Conference, Leeds, September 1985.

16. Financial Times, 12 November 1986.

17. Ibid.

18. Regional Trends (1982).

19. Ibid.

20. B.Harrison, op.cit., p. 78.

21. Ibid, pp. 77-78.

22. Ibid, p. 68.

23. Graham Moss Associates, op.cit., p. 4.

24. T. Taylor, 'High Technology Industry and the Development of Science Parks' in P. Hall and A. Markusen (eds.), Silicon Landscapes (Boston 1985), p. 135.

25. M.I. Luger, 'Does North Carolina's High Tech Development Programme Work?', Journal of the American Planning Association, 50,pp. 280-289.

Chapter Nine

STIMULATING INNOVATION AND NEW TECHNOLOGY DEVELOPMENT AT THE LOCAL LEVEL: TWO CASE STUDIES

John Blackburn and David Kennedy

In the previous chapter Tony Jowitt investigated the factors that have played a key role in the location of 'high-tech' activities and applied them to the Massachusetts and West Yorkshire areas. His conclusions stressed not only the decline in the economy and the environment of West Yorkshire but also the scale of the problems of rejuvenation facing the area. Bradford and Calderdale exemplify this picture. Both are textile areas; both have experienced a similar economic history. Although their geography is different, and they differ in size (Bradford's population is 462,000 as against Calderdale's 193,000), their economic and social structures are largely the same. At the same time these two metropolitan district councils have taken different approaches to the development of new technology policies for their local economies. They have also come to rely heavily on the European Community in implementing these approaches. This chapter analyses these new technology policies and the role that the EEC has come to play in their implementation. Examples are given of the policies in practice, and there is a discussion of how each local authority is developing its links with other West European countries in this field. Bradford and Calderdale offer contrasting models of local policy responses to the challenge of new technologies.

THE BRADFORD MODEL

Bradford MDC is England's fifth largest local authority. Geographically, it is centred on the old City of Bradford but includes a number of towns up to fifteen miles away from the city centre. Demographically, with an unemployment rate of 14%, it has 30,000 people out of work. The local authority itself is a major employer in the district, with 27,000 staff. Despite the sharp decline of the textile industry there are still more people employed in textiles than any other industry. However, the largest private companies are now in the service sector, such as mail-order companies, supermarkets and building societies.

For many years Bradford Council has taken the view that unemployment is a structural, long-term problem. It regularly produced forecasts which, when published, were considered to be exaggerated but have now sadly proved to be correct. The Council believed that unemployment would become even higher if developments in new technology were not positively encouraged. Consequently, it took a very positive approach to the use of new technology, both within the Council and within the local economy. Tony Jowitt has pointed out that a high-technology policy is not value-free, and it is here that Bradford's policy is of interest. The Bradford Council recognised that the development of new technology was an important aspect of the local economy. At the same time its policy gave prominence to the social aspects of new technology. Bradford's policy was explicitly designed to ensure that developments in new technology did not further disadvantage the poor, the handicapped and the elderly in society. Instead, the policy was designed to ensure that new technology was used to help those very groups. In short, the new technology policy 'puts people first'.

The second major factor in the new technology policy was the recognition of the need for the Council to take the lead in preparing Bradford's economy for the twenty-first century. Because of its size the Council has a major impact on the local economy. For example, the Council was the first major employer to instal word processing; in fact the officer who set up the Council's systems left to establish a very successful 'hi-tech' business in the science park at the University. Taking a second step, the Council recognised the importance of developing a high-technology infrastructure. In the last century the canals and then the railways had served as the arteries of the economy: by the late twentieth century 'broadband' cable and direct broadcasting by satellite(DBS) would be the means of communication central to the local economy. The golden age of nineteenth-century free enterprise had also been the golden age of municipalisation; it was the infrastructure installed by the Victorians that enabled Bradford to become the woollen capital of the world. By developing modern means of communication the Council hoped to lead the way for local businesses which could benefit from the Council's experience and equipment.

Finally, the Council recognised that, if Bradford was to take a full and active role in Europe, it was essential that the city should be linked to the main European centres and consider itself as a European city. In the nineteenth century Bradford had been a truly European city. Wool merchants from across France and Germany had established companies in Bradford, while the Bradford merchants were equally at home in the majority of European capitals. Going even further back, Jean-Jacques Rousseau had written in the eighteenth century: 'there is no longer a France, a Germany, a Spain, not even English, there are only Europeans. All have the same tastes, the same passions, the same way of life.' At the same time, Voltaire could describe Europe as 'a great republic divided between several states'[1]. It is a sad reflection that despite the revolutions in communications since then Bradfordians are, in some respects, less European than their ancestors of the previous century.

The Bradford Council had then two clear aims: to stimulate the development of new technology for social as well as economic purposes; and to link Bradford more actively into the Europe of the 1990s. How, though, was this high-sounding policy to be translated into practice? Implementation focused on four projects which were all aimed at helping disadvantaged groups and, in three cases, at promoting better links with Europe.

The teleshopping experiment involved the use of viewdata to provide a 'home-shopping' service for the elderly and the housebound. With the help of Council staff and a computerised system an elderly person could bring up a shopping list from the local supermarket on his or her television screen. When they pressed certain buttons on a small panel, their requirements were printed out on a printer in the supermarket. Council staff, previously unemployed for over twelve months, and on the government's Community Programme scheme, then collected the goods and delivered them to the elderly person's home. This project used new technology to give a social role and purpose to people who were previously unemployed, helped the elderly and boosted a local Bradford business. In addition, the scheme employed a large number of people who were handicapped.

The tele-shopping system was also used to develop viewdata links with an ITEC in Paris for the purpose of swapping training modules in French and English, as well as with a training centre in Roubaix, Bradford's twin town. The second stage of this viewdata project was to involve businesses in Bradford and in France so that eventually anyone in France with a television and a telephone could bring up on their screen a mail-order catalogue and, using a Eurocard, order goods from Bradford instantaneously. This proposal expanded Bradford companies' market from 50 million to over 100 million at the press of a button.

The potential of this system for small and large businesses in opening a European market was enormous. In addition, it provided training for unemployed people who would then be better placed to obtain jobs in areas of new technology. Finally, the same system was used to enable deaf people to communicate with each other, thus providing another use of new technology to help people who were disadvantaged.

Two other projects illustrated how the Bradford Council was enabling disadvantaged groups, in this case women and people with disabilities, to benefit from new technology. The Women's Technology Centre provided training for women in computing and electronics: it also provided a creche so that no one would be prevented from attending the Centre. The impact on women who had been denied education or training was particularly striking. Their gain in self-confidence was tremendous. Interestingly this project developed links with similar projects in Europe. In 1986 a group of women from the centre in Bradford went to France to discuss developments with their colleagues in similar centres. The third project, the Disabled Access to Technology Association (DATA) was a voluntary group, funded by the Council, which provided training courses in computing and electronics that were specially designed for people with disabilities. DATA also helped trainees to find jobs in local companies once they had the necessary qualifications and experience.

Finally, in 1986, the Council launched a new project involving Direct Broadcasting by Satellite (DBS). With predictions that 75% of British households will have satellite receiving dishes by 1990 the

Council thought that it made sense to train young people in this new technology. Accordingly, it established a programme to instal satellite dishes in schools. This programme was a joint project with a local company and was to enable Bradford's schools to receive foreign-language broadcasts direct from Europe for language training and also to enable young people on the Youth Training Scheme, or other older unemployed people, to receive training in installing and maintaining satellite dishes - an area where jobs for the future could be safely predicted.

These four projects illustrated how Bradford sought to use not only EEC grants but also EEC support and encouragement to enable the Council to stimulate the use of new technology for everyone and to make people more aware of opportunities within Europe. They also showed how the Council was using new technology to 'put people first'.

At the same time the need to develop new technology in local companies was recognised; indeed, as Tony Jowitt has stated, the University of Bradford has one of Britain's most successful science parks. The Council had a major programme of assistance to local companies to enable them to benefit from EEC grants to retrain workers in the use of new technology. The important point to recognise is that new technology was not seen as 'value-free'; local political action was needed to ensure that it was used to help the disadvantaged in society and not to merely reinforce the present gaps between 'the haves' and 'the have nots'.

Policy development in Bradford involved not just a new conception of the communications infrastructure and services but also a reassessment of the potential for public-private partnerships. Here it was recognised that the most common relationship is one in which local companies rely on local authority contracts for much of their work. In Britain successive central governments as well as local authorities have failed to make effective use of their position as major buyers. The considerable benefits of an aggressive procurement policy of 'leading the market' were already apparent from American experience and from the massive investment in Minitel by the French government (producing a French lead in viewdata). At the local level very few councils have used their buying power to help local companies to survive in their difficult first years. A small contract by local government standards can be a life preserver for a small company. Bradford recognised the need to develop a much clearer strategy to make full use of its buying power to help local IT companies and also to use links with the EEC and Europe more generally to assist entry of local companies into the European market.

From a Bradford perspective, where are these policy developments heading: how will they look in the year 2000? Will Bradford become Silicondale? The following table shows projected employment in the information technology industry.

Table 9.1: Employment in IT (millions)

	Japan	United States	Western Europe
1983	0.99	1.66	1.85
1995	2.30	3.13	1.73
2000	3.25	4.08	1.65

Source: Figures from I. Mackintosh, Sunrise Europe: The Dynamics of Information Technology (Blackwell, Oxford, 1986)

Both Japan and America will experience an increase in IT employment, while Europe will have a decrease. If projection of employment is merely one indicator, all the others are equally depressing. IT productivity and capital spending on IT also show Japan and America racing ahead as Europe falls behind. These figures are based on current projections: this is what will happen if Western Europe does nothing.

An alternative scenario can be based on two key factors: firstly, the implementation and development of new technology, and in particular telecommunications; and, secondly, exploitation of the large market that Europe represents. In a recent book Ian Mackintosh put forward the proposal that the only way to prevent Europe from sinking into a poor third place behind Japan and America was to develop a European Communications Network based on 'broadband' cable[2]. In other words, it will be necessary to wire up every home, office and factory in Europe and so create a 'Eurogrid'. Similarly, the report of the IT 86 Committee highlighted the limitations imposed by the size of the UK market and the need for Britain to become actively involved in European programmes such as Esprit, Race and Eureka[3]. As the United States turns its attention increasingly to the Pacific Basin, and Western Europe enters a 'hi-tech' cold war, so it becomes increasingly important that the member states of the EEC work more closely together.

Whilst creation of a 'Eurogrid' may sound ambitious, Japan has already started to work on an integrated network system that by the year 2000 will wire up the whole of Japan from offices to shops, from houses to hotels, from factories to fish-farms. Japan will then be able to export its expertise throughout the world. A similar system for Europe would cost £560 billion over twenty years. Such a sum is so large that it is difficult to grasp. However, when shared out within the European Community, it works out at less than £1.40 a week per household. When this sum is set alongside the annual cost of unemployment in Britain (£20 billion) and the estimate that seven million jobs will be created by such a network, the economics begin to make sense. By investing in a new European communication network reaching a market of over 300 million customers it might be possible for Europe to keep up with Japan and America.

By 1987 Bradford was beginning to examine how to cable the District so that it could be ready for the year 2000. Its old people were already ordering their shopping by cable, and its young people were installing satellite receiving dishes. Bradford Metropolitan District saw IT as not just another means of control and data management but as a tool to liberate people who are handicapped by age or disadvantage. By working with other European countries and the European Commission it was hoped that Bradford in the year 2000 could become as prosperous as Bradford was in the year 1900.

THE CALDERDALE MODEL

Calderdale is the fifth smallest metropolitan district in terms of population and the sixth largest in terms of area. It is historically an area of highly-skilled manufacturing industry; by 1987 still more than half the district's employment was in manufacturing. The local economy survived the massive long-term rundown in the textile industry reasonably well but was seriously affected by the recession of the 1980s which devastated in particular the local engineering industry. Unemployment rates went from their typically low figures in the 1960s and 1970s (1-2%) to 1980s levels which were at or about the national rate. The district had Assisted Area status withdrawn in 1979 and, with it, access to mainstream external funding including the European Regional Development Fund. It had no inner-city status, was no longer eligible for Urban Programme aid, and had no Enterprise Zone. In a nutshell, it had been thrown back on to its own resources when recognition of the need to stimulate economic regeneration had suddenly increased. Other facts of practical relevance for local policy-makers included: a small budget (in 1986 some £100 million per annum for the whole range of Council activities); uniquely high demands on the budgets in such areas as care for the elderly, road maintenance and replacement of a decrepit infrastructure; and a hung Council since 1979 (23 Labour, 16 Conservative, 15 Liberal in 1986).

The main themes of the Council's economic development policy were inevitably determined by this background. They were also directed by the Council's unanimous rejection of the 'commuter-zone' or 'playground' option; by its belief that it could and should play an active role; and by its pragmatic acceptance that it must 'cut the coat to suit the cloth'. The main themes were:

1. To try and obtain the maximum impact of Council action by attracting external funds.
2. To pursue policies with the widest possible application (i.e. to be of value to as many firms and individuals as possible).
3. To concentrate efforts where the marginal impact is greatest.
4. To sow the seeds of long-term improvement in the local economy.

The stimulation of innovation was just one arm of the Council's economic development policy. It was aimed at both start-ups and existing businesses, though the latter category was most important. Out of nearly 2,000 firms in Calderdale, 1,859 employed less than 50 people. Small firms have great problems with new technology, as can be illustrated by reference to the Calderdale Microprocessor Applications Project. This project started in a fairly ad hoc way in 1980 when the miracle 'chip' first became high fashion, as panacea or bogeyman depending on one's perspective. The Council developed an increasing awareness that, although local industry desperately needed to innovate, the existing channels of advice and assistance (mainly from the Department of Trade and Industry) were inadequate and that the local authority had a useful and legitimate role as facilitator.

A detailed investigation was carried out in 1981 by Professor Michael Hampshire of Salford University (funded jointly by Calderdale Council, the DTI and the University). It aimed to: identify constraints on the take-up of micro-electronics; investigate the attitude of small firms to micro-electronics; identify how their needs might be met; help firms integrate micro-electronics into existing products; identify products that might be rendered obsolete by micro-electronic technology; improve production efficiency and quality by using micro-electronics; and identify areas that might benefit from micro-electronics. In visits to almost 100 local manufacturing companies two fundamental problems emerged. Although the general awareness of micro-electronics at board and senior managerial level was good, there was not enough detailed understanding to make sensible decisions. Moreover, there was a critical shortage of 'in-house' expertise, of both professional engineers and technicians. The study found only six people with design and programming expertise and a further four with technician-level experience of micro-electronics. The report made recommendations to both central government and the local authority. It presented the Council with a classic problem: the cause of the problems was seen as very deep-rooted and the solution needed far-reaching and long-term attention; and most recommendations were beyond the Council's resources. For example, it was recommended that graduate design, management and supervisory skills be provided to firms and that an attempt be made to stimulate, through preferred curricula and differential grants, the availability of more technically-qualified young people. Another recommendation was that the Council should start a promotional campaign in Japan aimed at attracting Japanese industry to Calderdale. The Council's promotional budget was less than £1,000 per annum. In the face of impending impotence the Council took a positive approach and concentrated its attention upon what it could do. This approach involved continuation of the consultancy visitation service as a 'front-line' tool to help firms and to generate a more articulated demand for services provided by other agencies, such as technician training, which is difficult to supply in advance of demand, and the injection of graduate engineering skills into small firms through something like the Teaching Company Scheme.

After a great deal of persuasion of, and negotiation with, potential funding partners, the microprocessor applications project became reality in 1985 as the Calderdale Industrial Microelectronics Centre (CIMEC), a joint venture between the Council, the DTI, the Engineering Industry Training Board and the University of Bradford, the latter of which provided the essential technical base and support for the Centre. CIMEC had a complex and short-term resource base and was a fairly small-scale operation comprising a manager and a project engineer. However, in its first year of operation it generated project income of £25,000 on a revenue budget of £50,000. This situation was more important for what it said about the need for its services than its welcome move away from dependence upon the Council's support. Also, it attracted assistance as an innovatory project from the European Social Fund. 120 local firms were visited; less than five per cent were not interested. Ten projects were completed, and most firms were helped in some way. The work included the design and development of a magnetic therapy unit for use in sports injury clinics; the development of software for data analysis in hen breeding; an electronic device to replace an acupuncture system; the development of a C.N.C. lathe; an AMT (Advanced Manufacturing Technology) feasibility study; and several MAPCON feasibility studies. The most common enquiry was about automation and, later on, computer-aided design. This situation obviously limited the job creation potential and reawakened the fear that the Council might be supporting an initiative that reduced the number of jobs locally. It was a situation to which all politicians became sensitive. At the same time an ironic consequence of the devastation caused to local industry was that the implications of not introducing new technology became so difficult to ignore. The bedrock of the Council's action was to keep the district's firms alive.

The Calderdale Industrial Microelectronics Centre was just one of several projects aimed at stimulating innovation and new technology development at the local level. Others included the Calderdale Innovation Centre, established in 1981, which was to help inventors and innovators develop their ideas to the stage where they could be used as the basis for new businesses or taken up by established local firms. The Microsystems Advice and Training Centre, established in 1985, helped small companies to choose hardware and software appropriate to the needs of the 'administration' of their business and trained the users of the systems. All three centres work in close collaboration with the local College of Further Education, which itself has adopted a very positive stance, pioneering efforts to provide business and technical information to local firms (through the Calderdale Information Service - CALDIS) and the development of enterprise training for new and growing entrepreneurs. Each contributed to the other in a mutually supportive fashion. They have been developed in a piecemeal way as resources have been found. Since 1985 thoughts moved away from the simple proliferation of projects towards trying to generate a more co-ordinated, more integrated, more stable and more commercial approach. The Council learned from its experience of experimental projects that it had a legitimate and central role in bringing agencies together. Central government, the European Commission, training agencies and the universities and polytechnics, all have a role to play; also, elements of the private sector have also shown themselves willing partners in an increasingly collective effort to maximise the impact of their action upon economic regeneration.

Of the projects mentioned, the European Commission helped fund the Calderdale Industrial Microelectronics Centre (CIMEC), the Microsystems Advice and Training Centre and the Calderdale Innovation Centre and, through its COMETT programme, was considering an application from Calderdale to extend the experiences of enterprise training into the Netherlands, Belgium, France, Greece and Spain. Bradford University assisted CIMEC which also received some of its funding from seventeen local engineering firms. The Dean Clough Industrial Park was the host and motivating spirit of the Council's Enterprise Training Services.

The culmination of these efforts was the development of the Calderdale Business and Innovation Centre as the vehicle for implementing the above aims. The advantages of having already initiated projects and policies in partnership with other agencies and private-sector interests were revealed clearly in the development of the Business and Innovation Centre. Although many technical and organisational complexities were involved in this development, previous experience of collaboration had established the mutual trust required to contemplate the setting up of a company, limited by guarantee, which was literally half-owned by the Council and half by the local private sector. Council staff were to be seconded to the company, Council equipment was to be loaned, and line management was to pass from the Chief Executive to the Director and Board of the company. The principle was simple enough: in order to stimulate non-Council agents to participate actively in such projects, the organisational structure must allow authority and responsibility to be shared. Similarly, pulling the existing support matrix together into a single organisation was proposed for simple enough reasons - to strengthen the corporate identity, to generate economies of scale, to eliminate top heavy and over-complex management and to concentrate upon prime objectives.

Above all, the European Commission had come to play an ever more important role in local economic strategy. In particular, its importance transcended its role as a source of funding. The Commission had well-developed policies (and the systems to evaluate and review them) that put the national government to shame. It invited participation and discussion; it experimented broadly. The Commission used its financial influence positively and, thus, had a 'pump-priming' role. However, it also gave weight and credibility to the proposals made by sponsoring authorities which could then lever out further funding. More than anything, the Commission worked to erode the isolationism and inward-lookingness that more and more seemed to be a fundamental problem at the root of the decline of British manufacturing industry and was painfully apparent in regions like West Yorkshire. Another recent initiative illustrates this point. Through its Business and Innovation Centre activities (and specifically working through the European Business and Innovation Centre Network - EBN) Calderdale has been participating since 1986 in the 'Transfer of European Enterprise' Scheme.

With partner BICs in Liege (Belgium), Enschede (Holland), Nancy (France) and, more recently, Madrid (Spain), the Council attempted to help small and medium-sized firms in Calderdale to export or import technology. Again, while there are serious 'technical' difficulties to overcome (language, legal differences, etc), the main problems are more intangible - there is no tradition of such exchange. Technology transfer is a notoriously difficult and lengthy process, and no definite transfer has yet been made. However, by early 1987 130 offers and requests had been tabled, 12 of which included Calderdale firms. Already four of these firms had met and held discussions with European companies. The Commission helped authorities like Calderdale with its projects; in turn, those projects encouraged local firms to see the European market. Calderdale, like Bradford, had come to see that penetration of the European market was the key for local economic strategy. Small beginnings had been made; there was often little to show as a result; but a critical step had been taken towards Europe.

CONCLUSIONS

Perhaps the clearest contrast to emerge from these two case studies relates to the different conceptions of the purposes of new technology policies in Bradford and Calderdale. In Bradford social issues have been more central; the new technology slogan is 'putting people first'. In the case of Calderdale new technology policies have grown directly out of economic development strategy. At the heart of this difference is a contrast in the structural origins and complexity of policy formation in the two metropolitan districts. The Unemployment Unit was notable in the Bradford case. It identified new technology as a social and political as well as economic issue whose implications and management were not 'value-free'. Calderdale's initiatives had their basis in the economic development interests of the Chief Executive's Department. Also, as a bigger local authority Bradford was able to generate the structural complexity to think in more detail about local economic strategy. Together the Chief Executive's Office, the Economic Development Unit and the Unemployment Unit were able to devote a much larger body of staff to policy development. Calderdale operated in a more pragmatic, even opportunistic fashion, painfully aware that the availability of resources for non-statutory activities was extremely limited. Bradford's problems were in many respects the consequence of having to manage such structural complexity; Calderdale gained in terms of simplicity and ease of internal coordination. At the same time structural complexity had its own advantages; greater specialisation could be achieved, with a more developed analysis or strategy on the wider implications of new technologies.

A comparison of the experiences of Bradford and Calderdale in promotion of new technologies and EEC liaison reveals also the nature of changes in internal organisation and in external relations. As both local authorities have become more involved within European issues, they have recognised the need to have a clear organisational approach to Europe. The consequence has been a measure of centralisation but one that reflects local practical realities rather than abstract strategic planning. Once again, Calderdale was conscious of the need to maximise the use of its limited resources as a small authority. One full-time EEC Liaison Officer was appointed in the strategy section of the Chief Executive's Department. Although the Council discussed the option of having someone permanently in Brussels, it decided that the best use of the available resources was to have one person thoroughly familiar with the projects being proposed and also responsible for maintaining contacts and keeping up-to-date with EEC policy developments. This arrangement was most easily accomplished in a small authority. In addition, in association with other local authorities in the region, Calderdale engaged the services of a consultant/fixer in Brussels. The central function of the EEC liaison officer was to prevent uncoordinated and potentially confusing and damaging contacts with the European Commission. In this task he had the strong and unambiguous support of the Policy and Resources Committee. Local authority departments and agencies accepted these constraints reasonably well. In any case, the evident success of Calderdale's applications to the EEC reinforced the practical benefits of the arrangement to all parties. The arrangement was at the same time handled fairly flexibly. Once the relevant specialists had been briefed on the 'dos and don'ts' of EEC liaison, they were given substantial autonomy. In addition to having a central EEC section in the Chief Executive's Office, Bradford benefited from having an officer seconded to the EEC. Here the stress was on information dissemination to the directorates and divisions and, more generally, on raising European consciousness. Flexibility was encouraged. Indeed, the growing number of links outside the formal EEC liaison process within the authority was seen as helpful in developing a 'Europeanism'.

External relations involved a new attention to relations with local industry and higher education. In the past the relationships between the two councils and local industry and higher education have been tenuous. This situation has been replaced by a new debate about the roles of local universities and colleges of further education and the need to develop a more cosmopolitan and 'training-conscious' role for local industry. On the one hand, both local authorities have recognised the University Grant Committee's greater stress on 'relevance' and the entry of the Manpower Services Commission as a major funder of the local colleges. These interventions have claimed to establish a more realistic relationship between industry and education. On the other hand, new problems have arisen as a consequence. The UGC's financial cuts have had a disproportionately worse effect on the technological universities; whilst the White Paper Higher Education: Meeting the Challenge of 1987 planned to take control of many colleges from the local authorities(4). Against this background it was difficult for Bradford and Calderdale to envisage the development of a network of contacts of the kind to be found in Nord-Pas-de-Calais (see the chapter by Dormard). Both local authorities recognised just how important were their relationships with higher education for local economic strategy. Bradford started with the advantage of a local university. In this latter respect Calderdale was disadvantaged in, for example, marketing and promoting its area as a tion for new technology-based business. On the other hand, this situation forced a pragmatic and open attitude to those institutions of higher education outside the district, particularly the University of Bradford and Huddersfield Polytechnic. Several initiatives involved these institutions directly (as we have seen); future planning sought to increase these linkages both formally and informally. Despite this impression of pragmatism Calderdale had succeeded in developing a new conception of public-private partnership with its business and innovation centre. Authority and responsibility were being shared with private enterprise in a new fashion. Bradford gave particular attention to a more active procurement and training policy. In these often different ways both local authorities were trying, with their limited resources, to use the combination of new technology and European collaboration and markets to force overdue change in the local economic structure. The limitations of their success reflected more than just the scale of the economic and cultural problems. The prevailing structures of institutional power made for enormous difficulties in developing the networks of external relations on which their positive role in local economic development depended.

NOTES

1. Norman Hampson, The Enlightenment (Pelican, London, 1986).
2. Ian Mackintosh, Sunrise Europe: The Dynamics of Information Technology (Blackwell, Oxford, 1986).
3. Information Technology: A Plan for Concerted Action: The Report of the IT 86 Committee (HMSO, 1986).
4. White Paper, Higher Education: Meeting the Challenge (Cm. 114, HMSO, 1987).

Chapter Ten

CONCLUSIONS

Kenneth Dyson

Some of the conclusions of this volume have been sufficiently clearly stated in the individual chapters for detailed repetition here to be unnecessary. In particular, the following points need emphasis:

1. A broad cross-national consensus seems to have emerged about what constitutes 'the state of the art' in new technology and innovation policy instruments, not least about the need for a 'multi-dimensional' strategy to encompass the complex activities and linkages in regional and local economies. Enterprise has emerged as a driving concept at the regional and local levels. At the same time, as the chapters on France and West Germany reveal, there are interesting and important differences of detail that are the product of legal, institutional and political factors.
2. The Bradford/Calderdale comparison illustrates the relationship between local authority size and technology and innovation policies. With smaller size problems of internal coordination tend to be eased but at the expense of refinement of strategy; with larger size advantages of internal complexity and specialisation of strategy are more readily realised.
3. Local and regional economic strategy needs to take greater account of the role of higher education, of the venture capital market and of modern 'broadband' telecommunications as central elements of the infrastructure. Not least, European Commission policies are pushing in these directions: for instance, COMETT in education and training infrastructure, RACE and STAR in telecommunications, and the Venture Consort Scheme (in collaboration with the European Venture Capital Association) and New Community Instruments (NCI) as a financing mechanism. Here some European regions and localities start with advantages. Thus in North-Rhine Westphalia local savings banks are backing technology centres, providing special credits for 'high-tech' ventures promoted by colleges of technology, and forming venture

capital funds. One of the traditional strengths of small businesses in West Germany has been the presence of thousands of these banks whose managers have close knowledge of the locality.

4. Serious problems of complexity and coordination have emerged as policy initiatives have proliferated at the EC, national, regional and local levels. The consequence has often been confusion for businesses. Notably, the European Commission has attempted to tackle some of these problems with the idea of 'task forces' (e.g. for small firms) and of 'integrated operations'. However, much needs to be done at the EC level, and especially at the regional and local level, in coordinating the dissemination of information and business support services. North-Rhine Westphalia has, for instance, a separate Ministry for Small and Medium-Sized Enterprises and has created at Muelheim a powerful technology transfer centre (ZENIT, the Centre for Innovation and Technology).
5. There is a clear need for local authorities to do more to coordinate the impact of their demand on the local economy in order to encourage innovation and the use of new technologies. They are often the major single employer and user of technology and the organisation with the largest budget. Measures of positive discrimination can be considered e.g. by ensuring that a certain proportion of public contracts go to small firms employing new technologies.
6. The importance of the regionalisation of RTD policy is revealed in the development of 'technopoles' and the priority to industrial R&D in France (notably after the 1982 research law), in the 'high-tech' role of the West German federal states, and in the more active and innovative role of many US states in science and technology development (eg. California, Massachusetts, North Carolina, Texas).
7. The EC's impact is as much non-financial as financial, giving new confidence to local authority actors and greater credibility to local proposals and helping to erode isolationism.
8. New technology policies are not 'value-free'. They raise issues of priorities, with local authorities having a special role in adapting new technologies to social purposes (as, for instance, in Bradford). At the same time local authorities must take an active lead in encouraging enterprise, in pushing for private-sector involvement to complement or even substitute for public action (here note the case of Calderdale).
9. Local authorities must not just combat the fallacy of thinking that home-grown technology is superior to imported technology; also, they must endeavour to use the breadth of the European market to build up competitiveness. Their

function is, in other words, to combat parochialism at all levels. The primary duty of local authorities is to encourage best practices (eg. on design and quality of delivery) and 'up-market' specialisation.

Above all, returning to a theme in the introduction, it is apparent that British local authorities face a distinctively difficult problem that can only be mitigated by national political action. On the one hand, like local authorities throughout Western Europe, they cannot ignore the pressures to act in local economic development. On the other hand, they face two particular difficulties:

1. In Britain in the 1980s centralising pressures have been especially sharp, reducing the role, status and power of local authorities in key policy areas. Not least, the abolition of the metropolitan county councils in 1986 removed actors that had been important pioneers in economic development policies (eg. enterprise boards, EC liaison) - at a time when Belgian and French regions were receiving new powers and authority. Britain appeared not to be participating in a general West European learning process about the importance of decentralising economic and industrial powers.
2. British local authorities must act against the background of the notable structural weaknesses within British capitalism. These weaknesses have deep roots in Britain's pattern of political and economic development and are most obviously apparent in a lack of solidarity within capitalism (eg. the relative weaknesses of industrial associations and chambers of commerce, the relative lack of engagement of employers in vocational training, and the relative distance between banks and industry)[1]. Notably absent are: (1) an effectively organised, well-established system of vocational education qualifications, making available a highly skilled and competent workforce and management, and actively supported by employers; (2) a system of well-organised chambers of commerce, at local, national and international levels, integrating the local business community, playing a key role in apprenticeship training and in technology transfer and, not least, keeping local business and SMEs aware of the overriding importance of international competition and providing a facilitative role in entering and penetrating foreign markets; (3) a highly developed and decentralised system of exhibitions, particularly of a specialised character, providing marketing 'know-how' to traders; and (4) a system of close, collaborative links between banks and industry, at local level (eg. the role of the savings banks sector in West Germany and the *Caisse des Dépots et Consignations* in France) as well as the national level, providing medium- to long-term finance and

focusing entrepreneurial minds on the priority to market research(2). In each of these four instances the illuminating contrasts are most clearly with West Germany and (increasingly) with France.

British local authorities find themselves in a rather paradoxical situation. On the one hand, the best are keen to provide leadership and catalyst roles in breaking out of the 'low-tech, low-innovation' syndrome in Britain. They have in fact been pushed into this role by the failures of the private sector. On the other hand, the role, status and power of British local authorities is simultaneously under threat, and, in the absence of a regional tier of government, they are over-extending their activities and spreading them too thinly. This situation contrasts with the upsurge of regional dynamism in France, enabling that country to capitalise on the richness of its diversity (as Dormard's chapter shows). What is perhaps most clear is the lack of realism of proposals for local authorities to withdraw from a role in local economic development. At the end of the day the involvement of local authorities in new technology and innovation policies is not just a product of 'external' economic and political pressures. It is more deeply rooted in the role of 'high-tech' infrastructure as a symbol of regional and local status and power, offering the promise of future negotiating strength to local politicians and officials.

The remainder of the conclusions will concentrate on the emerging key features of local authorities' role in new technology and innovation. It will in particular identify the major requirements and limitations of a strategy of indigenous development, as outlined in the introduction.

PUBLIC-SECTOR/PRIVATE-SECTOR COLLABORATION

The combination of expenditure constraints (at national and local levels) with recognition of the enormous scale of the problems of local economic rejuvenation in regions of industrial decline has induced a new pragmatism (evident, for instance, in the case study of Calderdale). Responding also to a new government-induced mood of economic 'self-help' in the regions local actors have increasingly identified the importance of public sector/private-sector collaboration, the need for new alliances (embracing universities, polytechnics, colleges of further education, chambers of commerce, trade unions, and local authorities), and the contribution of the voluntary sector and community groups to local economic development (for example, Joint Action in Salford).

Indicative of this process was the formation (in 1986) of the Northern Development Company for the North-East of England and Cumbria, based on the collaboration of the local authorities, trade unions and some 160 private-sector companies, and working closely with English Estates. The new body was seen as a 'model' joint venture between public and private sectors by the Conservative government: in 1987 the EC designated it as the base for one of the first three European Business Information Centres in Britain. Earlier the Merseyside Enterprise

Forum, which brought together representatives of industry, commerce, the churches and trade unions, and was inspired by the (now defunct) Merseyside County Council, had shown what could be done. Ideas of economic 'self-help' and public/private collaboration were notably pursued by English Estates which, once it ceased to be a closely-controlled agency of the Department of Trade and Industry in property development, adopted a high-profile role in 'high-tech' office and science park development (for instance, in Leeds and Bradford). Under the 1980 Industry Act English Estates was given a wider role in stimulating private-sector involvement in regional and industrial regeneration. Increasingly it began to sell itself as a 'developing agency', ideally equipped for coordinating urban regeneration projects.

At the same time the question of the role of local authorities in public/private collaboration remained open and controversial. In the first instance, the Conservative government gave its support to the concept of enterprise agencies. By 1986 over two hundred and fifty enterprise agencies had been established under the umbrella organisation Business in the Community (BIC). A notable concentration was to be found along the M6 and M62 corridors linking Leeds, Liverpool and Lancashire, perhaps spurred by the St. Helens' model. They benefitted in particular from the tax incentives for private-sector sponsors that were introduced in the 1982 budget and from the renamed Business Expansion Scheme (earlier the Business Start-Up Scheme of 1981) which aimed to encourage private investors to own shares in small and unlisted companies. Based on the pioneering enterprise agency, the Community of St. Helens Trust, which had been strongly backed by Pilkington, and on the London Enterprise Agency, enterprise agencies provide the major vehicle for the private sector to take an active role in helping to develop the local economy by promoting and assisting small and medium-sized businesses (for example, with training workshops and by secondment of experienced staff from large companies). Emphasis was given to constructing networks for identifying sources of venture capital and making them more accessible to SMEs. The 'marriage-bureau' concept of linking individual investors with companies looking for funds was developed by the London Enterprise Agency even before the BES. By 1987 five agencies were collaborating to establish the Local Investment Networking Company in order to take the concept nationwide.

Secondly, and more controversially, Conservative government policy gave increasing priority to urban development corporations. They were given extensive powers (to acquire land, own it, build factories, and invest in infrastructure and environment), with planning powers for all the land in their area (not just that which they own), but also with dependence on Whitehall (because of annual funding). Particularly notable was the ability of the urban development corporation to assemble and prepare land for development. In 1981 two urban development corporations were established (London Docklands and Liverpool); in 1987 they were increased to seven (with the addition of the Black Country, Trafford Park in Manchester, Tyneside, Teeside and Cardiff Bay). After the 1987 election it was planned to increase their number to twelve. Their purpose was clear: to use public money as leverage for private-sector financial participation. London Docklands UDC was a notably successful case of such leverage, whereas Merseyside UDC faced much greater difficulties. In practice, however, the policy functioned as a political weapon to remove power, albeit temporarily, from left-wing councils. Direct links were being forged between central government and the private sector in local economic regeneration, bypassing local government. Local authorities showed little enthusiasm, sometimes even outright hostility to this policy concept. Urban development corporations, as developed in Britain, were not an effective substitute for strengthened local authorities as controlling instruments for such policies or for elected regional authorities.

THE 'AWARENESS' FUNCTION OF LOCAL AUTHORITIES

If disagreements abound about the precise forms of public-sector/private-sector collaboration, signs of consensus are much more evident when it comes to recognising the central importance of the 'awareness' function of local authorities. Two major factors make this function critical:

1. Effective new technology and innovation policies must overcome the information deficit, parochialism, weak professional skills and limited managerial ability at the local level. In this sense local policy makers face a 'chicken-and-egg' situation. Lack of management skills is a key factor in industrial decline, with management education failing to keep pace with the revolutions in business techniques and markets(3). In particular, the marketing skills of SMEs need to be developed if an area is not to be trapped in a pattern of low-risk, low-profit activities. Hence local authorities need to assist in the evolution of mechanisms to offer professional consultancy (eg. the BICs outlined in Malan's chapter). They must spearhead recognition of the importance of European networks and collaboration in helping companies to shed some of their blinkered insularity and to recognise the challenge of competing in large markets. European networks and collaboration are important as: (1) a learning experience for local actors about how best to tackle local and regional problems; and (2) an entree to larger European markets, alerting local companies to the advantages of a more open internal EC market and creating a local industrial constituency which has experienced the benefits of working and thinking at a European level. Seen from a national perspective, European collaboration appears as a necessary 'insurance policy' against the threat of technological domination by American and Japanese companies. At a local and regional level its advantages in fostering an international orientation in the corporate sector are more apparent. The need to think internationally must penetrate more deeply into corporate

and political structures. Local authorities can help to spearhead this process, in collaboration with the private sector. An example was provided in 1987 when the Northern Development Company, along with the Birmingham Chamber of Commerce and the Scottish Development Agency, were chosen to operate European Business Information Centres as part of the new European regional network.

2. Local authorities have to recognise the ignorance and confusion that is rife at the local level about programmes, timetables and requirements of public-sector support. New technology and innovation is a field characterised by excessive policy output (as this volume reveals), with a complexity of initiatives at local, regional, national and EC levels. Consequently, smaller companies have some difficulties in presenting their case for assistance. Indeed, guidance through 'the policy jungle' is required not just for them but also for local government officers; hence the growing number of EC liaison officers appointed by local authorities.

Four types of role can be identified for local authorities in this field: (1) to provide a single focus where the many affected interests can be brought together, particularly links to industry and education; (2) to act as a catalyst for change by promoting and giving publicity to models of 'best practice'; (3) to establish basic infrastructure and systems (eg. using the colleges of further education); and (4) to ensure more transparency and greater efficiency in the delivery and implementation of programmes. With business faced by a new world of hundreds of EC acronyms, BICs or the new European Business Information Centres can have a key role in demystifying programmes and acting as a focal point for all EC activities of business interest. There is a clear need for a 'single-door' approach. At the same time the political question of 'whose door' remains controversial, including the economic issue of who pays for costly information services.

A key theme of this volume is the need to subscribe to the long-term importance of 'diffusion-oriented' technology policies and not just to 'mission-oriented' technology policies. The latter policies are targeted to specific big projects (for instance, in aerospace and defence); the former emphasise the broad dissemination and application of new technologies across the existing range of industries (for example, the introduction of microelectronics into mechanical engineering). If Britain and France (and, of course, the United States) are typical examples of the 'mission-oriented' approach, West Germany exemplifies above all a 'diffusion-oriented' system[4]. The EC has also adopted major 'mission-oriented' policies, notably ESPRIT and RACE. However, its growing recognition of the importance of a 'bottom-up' orientation has - as the chapters by Aitken and Wäldchen reveal - pushed it towards a 'diffusion-oriented' approach: note, for instance, BRITE, COMETT and SPRINT. Decentralised measures are best designed to facilitate the latter approach. Accordingly, regional and local authorities have identified two basic requirements for effective diffusion:

1. A need for new mechanisms to transfer technology to industry (eg. the CRITT and 'technopoles' in France) and for policies that encourage the updating of equipment and techniques across the board.
2. A broad base of skilled labour, involving in particular a more direct involvement by industry in vocational training (as in West Germany and Switzerland). Low skill levels lock industry into outdated, simple technologies, with 'low-tech', poorly trained managers themselves a key part of the problem[(5)]. By 1986 the proportion of managers with degrees was 85% in the United States, 63% in West Germany and 21% in Britain (the British figure includes degree or professional qualification). The proportion of seventeen-year old people in some form of education and training was more than 85% in West Germany and Switzerland and 60% in Britain; whilst the proportion of school leavers without any form of qualification was 40% in Britain compared to 10-15% in West Germany and Switzerland[(6)]. These figures illustrate the generally low levels of skill, education and competence in Britain, which has a lower percentage of sixteen-year old people in education and training than any other developed economy except Spain and Portugal.

Local authorities cannot bear the principal blame for the absence of effective technology-transfer mechanisms and of adequate supplies of skilled labour. At the same time they cannot realistically expect or be expected to resolve these problems on their own. The important point is that local authorities have a key role to perform in 'diffusion-oriented' technology policies, not least because of their depth of local community knowledge. In particular, in the short term, and on their own resources, they can monitor specific local skill shortages and the problems of their own local labour markets, shortages of industrial land and buildings for development, and the individual research and training strengths in higher and further education in the locality. At the end of the day, however, the 'awareness' function of local authorities extends beyond local industry, commerce and education to external bodies like the Manpower Services Commission; such bodies must also be 'educated' about the realities of local economic development.

NATIONAL AND REGIONAL STRUCTURES AND STRATEGIES

Local initiatives to mobilise indigenous development potential require the support of appropriate national and regional structures and strategies, both because of the inherent spatial and resource constraints on local action and in order to achieve greater coherence of local action and to reduce wasteful policy competition. A strategy of indigenous development raises complex issues of the organisation of policy that transcend the local level. In tackling these issues Britain can at least learn something from the experience of regionalisation of power in the West German Länder (see the chapter by Schlieper) and, more recently, in France (see Dormard's chapter). Both cases underline the importance of a fresh approach to regional problems by strengthening regional institutions and by allying regional policy to a 'positive' industrial strategy that embraces in particular R&D and training. Six dimensions of public policy need special emphasis.

Decentralisation

More economic powers must be devolved from central government to the regions and localities so that Britain acquires a structure of government better adapted to a more broadly dispersed economic development, as in France and West Germany. Two measures could be introduced relatively speedily: (1) the creation of regional development agencies outside Scotland and Wales, perhaps building on the experience of English Estates and of the enterprise boards; and (2) the removal of the statutory limitation on the amount of rate income that can be spent by local authorities on local economic development.

These two measures cannot, however, be a substitute for the creation of an elected regional level. A major function of the regional tier would be to 'rationalise' local rivalries that are apparent in the proliferation of initiatives. For instance, there is a danger that too many science parks will dilute their individual impact. As in North-Rhine Westphalia, a regional tier can consider quality 'thematic' parks, based on developing the individual strengths of local areas rather than slavish imitation: for example, the 'media park' in Cologne and the 'fashion park' in Düsseldorf. English regions, like the North East, have been too long bogged down in petty parochial rivalries, without any coherent strategy, let alone identity. Regional industrial strategy must be a key priority. At the same time it will require much more 'authoritative' and better financed mechanisms for this purpose than the Northern Development Company.

The French decentralisation reform of 1982 reinforced an interpenetration of central and local politics that has been a long-standing feature of government there. This interpenetration was symbolised in the figures of Mauroy and Defferre in the Socialist government in Paris; it was given more concrete form in the state-region planning contracts and in the extent to which, compared to Britain, new technology and innovation policies embraced a role for regional decentralisation of national research activities. Indeed, many of the differences in the new technology and innovation policies of Britain and France are to be understood against the background of two factors: (1) the voluntarism of French policy, with new technology and innovation policies manifesting the ambition and will of the state; and (2) the more pragmatic, subtle and mutually accommodating character of central-local relations in France.

National Infrastructure and Training Programmes

As we shall see later in this chapter, 'high-tech' and innovation policies are likely to yield long-term results. Meanwhile, national infrastructure and training programmes have two key roles: (1) for job creation in the short to medium term; and (2) to make present regions of industrial decline more attractive to future investors. The regionalisation of infrastructural expenditures on education, health, housing and transport and of training programmes is essential. It is also necessary to broaden the definition of infrastructure programmes to incorporate advanced telecommunications links. In practice, infrastructural projects seemed to favour the South: for instance, the M25, the Channel tunnel, and the major expansions of Stansted and Gatwick airports. Training policies were pursued against the background of an ignorance of local labour market conditions. Also, as Howells and Charles suggest in their chapter, defence expenditure is heavily biased towards the South. In Britain defence procurement remains an underutilised tool to foster 'high-tech' industry in the 'less-favoured' regions. Many of these deficiencies in infrastructure, defence and training programmes reflected inadequate structures of government and instruments of policy: linked to these inadequacies in a 'chicken-and-egg' fashion was an absence of political will to tackle regional problems.

Regionalisation and Coherence of Central Government Policies

The importance of regionalisation of central government policies extends beyond expenditure programmes to incorporate taxation and the location of government offices. New fiscal incentives need to be considered, for instance the reduction of employers' National Insurance Contributions in 'less-favoured' regions. Also, on the models of Cardiff and Newcastle, new efforts are needed to move government offices out of London. Relocation can be expected to have catalytic effects, on employment and the 'quality' of demand, and to alleviate some of the problems caused by the 'overheated' housing market in the South East. Equally pressing is the need for a greater degree of coherence in government's regional policies. For instance, unless serious risks are to be taken with unemployment, the pursuit of greater pay differentials at the regional level requires huge injections of regional aid to sustain purchasing power in the depressed regions. As we shall see below, similar problems of coherence face SME and labour mobility policies.

Labour Mobility

The problems of reliance on labour mobility as a natural equilibrating mechanism for regional imbalances were outlined in the introduction to this volume. Labour mobility can only make an effective contribution to resolving problems of regional imbalance if four conditions are met: (1) a very substantial increase in aggregate demand to offset the problems facing job migrants; (2) better information about employment opportunities at a distance; (3) major changes in housing policy, given that growing regional variations in house prices are a tremendous obstacle to mobility; and (4) measures to cut the costs of moving to more prosperous regions[7]. In so far as these conditions are difficult to meet, reliance on labour mobility as a 'policy instrument' would seem inappropriate.

Research and Development Policy

The infrastructure for research and technology development at the regional level is immensely important if new technology and innovation ambitions are to be translated into practical results. For that situation to be realised three elements are essential: (1) an unequivocal commitment by central government to expand industrial R&D; (2) coordination of central government's policies as they affect R&D; and (3) the political will to decentralise R&D and training institutions in order to create new opportunities for local and regional authorities. These elements have been notably visible in France (see Dormard's chapter): witness, for instance, the move of the national computer school to Brittany. They have been absent in Britain. Industrial R&D has failed by a long way to keep pace with our competitors (see the introduction); R&D policy has been characterised by fragmentation, lack of coordination and poor public visibility; whilst, as Howells and Charles show, R&D infrastructure has been heavily concentrated in the South[8].

The West German Länder and the French regions show that the roles of the regions in developing RTD infrastructure, in awakening public interest and in coordinating efforts in R&D operate at two levels: (1) in the identification of areas of 'strategic' research for regional development (eg. in the state-region planning contracts in France); and (2) in diffusion of new technologies. They have at the same time depended on a supportive national context. Here it is worth noting how in West Germany, since the end of the 1970s, the federal government's technology support programme has been refocused away from support for the big companies (which, like Siemens, are typically very profitable anyway) to the SME sector. By 1987 the federal government programme to stimulate R&D work in SMEs was costing £341 million annually, involving in particular subsidies for the payroll costs of employing researchers (to the tune of 40-55%), encouragement of the venture capital sector and aid to improve cooperation with academic institutions. This programme was in turn matched by individual Länder programmes, creating an impressive 'critical mass' of effort in R&D support for SMEs. In both France and West Germany scope for regional priority setting in R&D was accompanied by a spirit of pragmatism in central-local relations. This spirit was apparent in the interlocking efforts of state and regions in France and in West Germany's system of 'cooperative' federalism. It was absent in Britain where the idea of a role for regions in 'strategic' research was completely undeveloped. In fact the idea of 'strategic' research was underdeveloped within central government itself.

SME Policy

Central government's support for the role of SMEs as the major engines of indigenous development in Britain has not been matched by improvements in the quality of small businesses. Improvements have taken place in the tax regime and in financial facilities (eg. the Business Expansion Scheme and the Loan Guarantee Scheme), enterprise agencies have been encouraged, and an increase of new business formation has taken place. Even so, Britain's small businesses have the lowest share of output and employment to be found in an EC country. They are also less profitable and less interested in training and other organisational changes[9]. Central government has failed to develop a comprehensive and explicit policy framework for small businesses, of the kind that can be found in West Germany. Particular attention needs to be given to changes in capital markets that will encourage a greater flow of subsidised loan capital (witness the role of the Kreditanstalt für Wiederaufbau, the Reconstruction Loan Corporation, in West Germany); to measures of support for R&D work in SMEs (see above); and to fostering the role of 'intensive-care' or 'incubation' centres. Malan's chapter has outlined the potential of Business and Innovation Centres, whilst Aitken's chapter focuses also on colleges of further education. Together or separately, they can provide regular investment, technical and business advice for young companies and assurance to both funders and recipient companies. There is a particular need for public policy to address the problems of companies needing smaller funding (eg. less than £200,000), especially when nearly half of the Business Expansion Scheme's investments up to 1986 went to just 29 companies.

Once again, there are failures of central-local collaboration in the promotion of 'incubation' centres. Thus the Department of Education and Science's proposed national network of new technology centres, which are designed to provide consultancy, training and technology transfer, involve the collaboration of higher education and industry and bypass the local authorities. Despite these problems there are two types of development that can be usefully pursued by local authorities: (1) an animateur role in a BIC, as in Calderdale (see the chapter by Blackburn and Kennedy) and Strathclyde (see Aitken's chapter); and (2), more modestly, a role in managed workshops, often with an enterprise agency, with the aim of providing 'start ups' with workshops of convenient size, attractive premises, shared facilities, a community environment and an economical rent, either in purpose-built or, more commonly, in refurbished factory or office buildings. In the last analysis, however, an effective SME policy at the local level requires measures of national political support.

THE LIMITATIONS OF NEW TECHNOLOGY AND INNOVATION POLICIES

Both the policy maker and the policy analyst find it difficult to avoid two temptations: a 'tunnel-vision' approach to policy that comes from being heavily engaged in a particular policy field; and 'fashion' in public policy, associated with the excitement of new ideas. In the one case, there are heavy 'sunk costs' of time, energy and reputation; in the other, a clearer idea of the inadequacies of the old than the limitations of the new. The outcome of these temptations is in any case the same: excessive expectations and eventually disappointment and frustration. Exogenous regional policies went through this policy cycle. Indigenous development policies can, for reasons outlined below, expect to undergo the same experience. The process is not, of course, mechanistic and inflexible. Synthesis of the two approaches can be attempted, as in France. Above all, governments can learn from experience and, as was suggested in the preface, from comparison. If comparison suggests lessons of the kind outlined above, experience suggests major limitations of an economic rejuvenation strategy that places too much faith in new technologies alone.

1. Much of the activity associated with technology and innovation policies is irrelevant to one of the most dramatic and tragic developments in modern industrialised societies - the emergence of a growing, minority 'underclass' of the unemployed. This development reflects a new pattern of inequality that escapes the bounds of traditional class analysis(10). The mounting private affluence of the majority, the expansion of middle-class opportunities and a rise in absolute rates of social mobility contrast starkly with the condition of the 'underclass'(11). This condition is exemplified by the increase of 'street poverty' in the old industrial cities and peripheral council house estates. The new 'underclass' is defined by a mixture of lack of work, lack of education, lack of literacy, lack of stable domestic circumstances, lack of money and lack of coping ability - in short, by what they have not, by an absence of any purpose other than survival and dependence. It is without real leverage over, or interest in, political life and is largely ignored by 'official' politics (except those radical urban politicians who seek to mediate between it and the 'official' world). Political 'insiders' can simply see no way to build a successful coalition based on the 'underclass'. They can only appeal to fairness and to fear. The number of those living at or below the supplementary benefit level was approximately 6.1 million in 1979; by 1986 the figure had risen to some 12 million, almost one-fifth of the entire population.

   Once again, the 'underclass' was unevenly distributed in spatial terms, and the North could claim a good deal more than its fair share. However, it was within the Greater London area that the new pattern of inequality was revealed most sharply. A middle-class wealth explosion in the Greater London area, based in particular on soaring house values, was producing a geographical concentration of the new 'super rich', living uncomfortably beside the growing 'underclass'[12]. The next volume Local Authorities and Long-Term Unemployment: The European Dimension will be exploring some of the implications of this new phenomenon for public policy, for local political initiatives and for EC initiatives. For the purpose of this analysis it is simply important to note that technology and innovation policies offer little immediate alleviation to the problems of a society in which the division between employed and unemployed has become more important than that between the working and the middle classes.

2. One needs to beware of simple answers that see new technology as offering a messianic solution or the 'post-industrial' service economy and small businesses as a panacea. Whilst new technology in the form of products and processes is vitally important, there is a danger that policy makers can become trapped within a whole mythology associated with it[13]. It is not simply a matter of new technology being 'value-laden', in the way outlined in Blackburn and Kennedy's chapter. Automation of manufacturing processes and development of new technology products per se are in any case only part of the answer to the 'high-tech' challenge. Three additional factors need to be borne in mind: (1) the availability of manufacturing expertise and a corporate willingness to invest in training staff with new skills are critical, especially in production engineering and management. Once a region or locality (or country) goes off the 'learning curve' of technological competence in this area, it will probably be impossible to rejoin that curve; (2) the depletion of the infrastructure of industrial support at the local and regional levels can reach a critical point under the combined impact of protracted recession, an 'over-valued' currency and fiercer international competition. Britain endured all three together in the early 1980s. The capacity to compete is lost once the design and production capacity is no longer available. At the regional and local levels in Britain devastating, rapid effects have been experienced on engineering subcontractors and suppliers of factory equipment (notably machine tools and textile machinery); and (3) Japan has illustrated that success comes not just from having new technology but from a new concept of quality production as one continuous stream, each part of which interacts with the others. The emphasis is on 'integrated approaches' and 'total solutions' to production engineering problems, with the aim of maximising cost reduction with new technology. This aim requires simultaneous improvements in labour relations (involving in particular more flexible working practices), in factory lay-out (eg. changing work-flow patterns), in product design and quality, and in sub-contracting arrangements (with longer-

term contracts with subcontractors in return for greater responsibility for quality standards). Such an analysis suggests that the 'awareness' function of local authorities in the fields of new technology and innovation is more complex and multi-dimensional than many of them recognise; and that, in the final analysis, even with the most refined and sophisticated policy instruments in these fields, the game will be won or lost in the corporate sector and determined by the latter's capability of managing industrial change on a broad scale.

New technology has also been presented as an engine of change from an industrial society, based on manufacturing and large hierarchical structures, to a 'post-industrial' society that is decentralised and based on services and the emergence of the more sophisticated 'information operative'. This model of 'post-industrial' society has been presented as the logical structure of a society wedded to the new information and communications technologies. In practical terms the service sector has proved to be the major source of job creation in the 1980s[14]. However, as American experience reveals, the overwhelming majority of new jobs in the service sector have been created in the 'humdrum', 'no-tech' category, in particular in restaurants and the retail trade. The 'high-value-added' service jobs, like software engineers, have been of much less importance in job-creation terms. In fact the American transition from manufacturing employment to service employment (the latter expanded from 59% of non-agricultural employment to 75% in 1986) has been associated with low wages, very low productivity growth and a long-term stagnation of income levels. As can be seen in Massachusetts (see Jowitt's chapter), the health of the service sector - including the 'high-tech' quality of its employment eg. in business services - is shaped in practice by its ties to manufacturing industry. If the latter declines or moves out, the service jobs will follow. Consequently, localities and regions cannot expect 'high-tech' and 'high-growth' service employment to substitute for a successful manufacturing base[15].

American experience suggests also a more sceptical view of the job-creating effects of new 'start ups'. In the field of 'high-tech' they are more apparent in software and design than in manufacturing (the jobs are in the latter rather than the former); also, they tend to prefer to subcontract production to low-cost offshore suppliers, with little positive effect therefore on the local, regional or national manufacturing base[16]. One can also be sceptical about the role of small firms in helping to absorb the unskilled and semi-skilled male workers who dominate the unemployment registers of Western Europe. Small firms employ a relatively high proportion of female and part-time labour and, in manufacturing firms, skilled workers[17]. A UK study showed that on the whole they were relatively unstable, paid lower wages and offered inferior conditions; less than 1% grew over a twelve-year period to employ more than 100 people each. In other words, in terms of job creation only a very few small firms matter. As David Storey has argued, the policy problem is to identify and back them rather than scatter help[18].

TIMESCALE AND ITS IMPLICATIONS FOR POLICY

The problems of regional imbalance in Britain are so complex, deep-seated and substantial that, even with a judicious mix of exogenous regional policies and policies to mobilise indigenous development potential, a medium- to long-term timescale would be required in order to ameliorate them significantly. Such a conclusion - that there are no 'quick fixes' - is not politically attractive. Also, given the balance of political forces in Britain during the 1980s, the political conditions for a long-term majority behind the ideas sketched in this conclusion may seem somewhat unpromising. In the meantime the prospects are bleak. The growth of small businesses in Britain may seem a consequence of a newly resurgent 'enterprise culture'. In reality, it is more a product of 'forced' entrepreneurship as a consequence of the competitive failure of large firms. The gap left by uncompetitive large firms is not, in other words, simply being filled by new competitive small businesses[19].

The painful fact is that though 'high-tech' is crucial, it will provide tomorrow's jobs, not today's. As Leontief has demonstrated, with the gradual adoption of new technologies there will be an expansion of demand for labour - for professionals with computer skills and for production workers rehired in growing industries required to produce new equipment for the technological revolution[20]. Meanwhile, a generation is being wasted at appalling human and social cost, and spatial imbalances in 'high-tech' employment remain acute. Devices like science parks and BICs are simply not an answer to today's unemployment and regional problems. Their gestation period is in any case a decade and longer. Against this background unemployment has to be fought in the short term by accepting the role of 'low-tech' and even 'no-tech' jobs in the service sector, even if part-time (eg. retail and wholesale distribution, hotels and catering). Already market forces are producing an expansion of the 'flexible' work force, with more part-timers, temporary workers, home workers and self-employed[21]. Local authorities have in some respects actively encouraged this process, for instance by policies to encourage tourism in areas of industrial decline (eg. Bradford) and by efforts to attract large retail developers (eg. Oldham). It is, however, notable that across Western Europe this change in the occupational structure is embraced with reluctance, sometimes even rejected as an option.

At the same time local authorities have a more positive role to play in local economic development by: (1) fostering new financing mechanisms (eg. a revolving loan fund on the Massachusetts model); (2) engaging in clean-up programmes, so that renovated architecture and smart shop and factory fronts can help to improve the civic image and to lift civic spirit; (3) actively marketing a positive image of a city or region (eg. the slogans 'Bradford's Bouncing Back' and 'Glasgow's Miles Better'), emphasising scenic, cultural and architectural strengths; (4) encouraging a higher level of vocational skills at all levels; and (5) involving themselves in the expansion of community services, especially in order to meet the problems of caring for an ageing population. By engaging in these roles local authorities can hope to make a modest contribution to the long-term solution of problems of skills, mobility and efficiency in the newly emerging technological age, whilst also concentrating on effective and productive short-term palliatives. In the present context of central-local relations in Britain the emphasis has to be on the modesty of this contribution. The strong contribution that local authorities could make to rejuvenation of traditional industrial regions depends on initiatives by central government: (1) reforms of capital markets to encourage new financing mechanisms; (2) national infrastructure programmes to support environmental improvements at the local level; and (3) a new education and training strategy to mobilise the output of microelectronics engineers on a major scale and thereby to breathe life into science parks, innovation centres and enterprise agencies.

CONCLUSION

The costs of failing to have a 'competitive' regional policy are not always fully appreciated. All too often the costs are seen in purely domestic terms: the South gains, the North loses. In the absence of an active industrial policy to ensure the competitiveness of the North another risk is rapidly emerging: that overcrowding and rising residential costs in the South will push firms to locate elsewhere in Western Europe rather than in the rest of Britain. Regional policy requires a European dimension additional to a consciousness of, and use of, EC policy instruments. It must be 'competitive' as a package in EC-wide terms.

The new emphasis on the indigenous development approach to economic rejuvenation begs the basic question: do local authorities have the legal powers, financial resources, staff expertise and political will (including strucural capacity for political leadership) to master the 'state-of-the-art' in technology and innovation policy instruments? The case studies in this volume suggest that the answer for Britain is no. By contrast, the chapters on France and West Germany indicate just how important the regional tier is as an animateur of local economic strategy. The implication of the indigenous development approach for the organisation of policy is a combination of regionalism with a decentralised approach. In this way it is possible to unleash the abundant resources of decency and entrepreneurship at the local level. Above all, however, this type of policy strategy and structure requires more open-minded and imaginative attitudes, less trapped in outdated political assumptions and doctrines.

NOTES

1. See eg. K. Dyson and S. Wilks (eds.), Industrial Crisis (Basil Blackwell, Oxford, 1983).

2. On West Germany, see K. Dyson, 'State, Banks and Industry in West Germany' in A. Cox (ed), State, Finance and Industry (Wheatsheaf, Brighton, 1986).

3. A. Ovenden, Competitiveness in UK Manufacturing Industry (BIM, London, 1987). Also The Making of Managers: A Report on Management Education (NEDO Books, London, 1987).

4. H. Ergas, Does Technology Policy Matter? (Centre for European Policy Studies, Brussels, 1986).

5. The Making of Managers, ibid; A. Daly et al, 'Productivity, Machinery and Skills in a Sample of British and German Manufacturing Plants', National Institute Economic Review, February 1985.

6. Ovenden, op.cit; S. Prais and K. Wagner, 'Schooling Standards in England and Germany: Some Summary Comparisons Bearing On Economic Performance', National Institute Economic Review, May 1985.

7. J. Goddard and M. Coombes, 'The North-South Divide: A Local Perspective', Institute of Economic Affairs conference, London, May 1987.

8. See, for instance, Economic Trends, August 1984 and August 1985; Advisory Council forApplied Research and Development (Acard), Exploitable Areas of Science (HMSO, London, 1986); and Select Committee on Science and Technology, Civil Research and Development, Vol.1 (HMSO, London, 1987).

9. P. Burns and J. Dewhurst (eds.), Small Business in Europe (Macmillan, London, 1986).

10. K. Auletta, The Underclass (Random House, New York, 1982)

11. Social Trends, 17 (Central Statistical Office, HMSO, London, 1987).

12. J. Rentow, The Rich Get Richer (Allen and Unwin, London, 1987).

13. Eg. A. Toffler, The Third Wave (W. Morrow, New York, 1980); W. Dizard, The Coming Information Age (Longman, London, 1982); and D. Bell, The Coming of Post-Industrial Society (Basic Books, New York, 1973).

14. A. Rajan, Services - The Second Industrial Revolution? (Institute of Manpower Studies report, Butterworth, London, 1987).

15. S. Cohen and J. Zysman, Manufacturing Matters: The Myth of Post-Industrial Society (Basic Books, New York, 1987).

16. Ibid.

17. D. Storey and S. Johnson, Small and Medium-Sized Enterprise and Employment Creation in the EEC Countries (report to the European Commission, CURDS, University of Newcastle, 1987).

18. D. Storey et al, The Performance of Small Firms (Croom Helm, Beckenham, 1987).

19. Storey and Johnson, op.cit.

20. W. Leontief, The Impacts of Automation on Employment

1963-2000 (Oxford University Press, London, 1987).
21. A. Rajan and R. Pearson (eds.), UK Occupation and Employment Trends to 1990 (Butterworth, London, 1986).

INDEX

For Product Safety Concerns and Information please contact our EU representative GPSR@taylorandfrancis.com Taylor & Francis Verlag GmbH, Kaufingerstraße 24, 80331 München, Germany

Batch number: 10725802

Printed by Printforce, the Netherlands